CANADIAN BABY NAMES

Carla MacKay

BLUE
BIKE
BOOKS

The Publisher: Blue Bike Books Ltd.
Website: www.bluebikebooks.com

Library and Archives Canada Cataloguing in Publication

MacKay, Carla, 1982–
    Canadian baby names / by Carla MacKay.

Includes bibliographical references.
ISBN 978-1-897278-55-0

    1. Names, Personal—Canada—Dictionaries. I. Title.

CS2377.M233 2009   929.4'40971   C2009-900192-6

Project Director: Nicholle Carrière
Project Editor: Pat Price
Cover Image: Photos.com
Illustrations: Roger Garcia

We acknowledge the support of the Alberta Foundation for the Arts for
our publishing program.

We acknowledge the financial support of the Government of Canada
through the Book Publishing Industry Development Program (BPIDP)
for our publishing activities.

PC: 1

CONTENTS

INTRODUCTION

When I began writing this book, I knew one thing for certain: including the stories of friends and family would give the book a special touch. I knew they had to have some interesting stories about how they were named—stories that would be much more intriguing than mine. I got my name—Carla Erin—because my mom liked it. That's it— no funny stories, no being named for anyone, no nothing. I remember asking my mom why she and my dad named me Carla, and she said she guessed I could say I was named for my great-grandfather, whose name was Carl. She *guessed* I could do that.

Don't get me wrong, I love my name, and I'm proud of it. Really, no other name would suit me better. Why? Because once people know you by a particular name, no other name seems right. Your name truly becomes part of your identity. I always feel a stab of annoyance and (sometimes) downright haughtiness if someone spells my first name "Karla," instead of "Carla," or my last name as "McKay," instead of "MacKay." Karla McKay is an entirely different person—someone I don't know and wouldn't recognize.

I see my mom in the same light. Although she was named Pamela Jill, her parents never called her Pamela, always Jill. But bills and letters that arrived in the mail for her were addressed to Pamela Jill, and the name always looked strange to me—my mom is just not a Pamela! She's a Jill, through and through.

My storytellers often didn't follow the trends of baby naming today—invented names no one has ever heard of or spell-ings of common names tweaked into unusual variations, for example—but their stories (which go back almost 30 years, in some cases) are interesting, reassuring, inspiring and funny. I hope they make you smile and reveal the humour behind the whole business of baby naming.

As millions of parents around the world (celebrities included) have discovered, there is an almost overwhelming number of things to consider when naming a baby. In this book, I think you'll find plenty of inspiration, ideas and guidance for what can be a daunting task—finding the perfect name for your baby.

Celebrities and
Baby Names

Names of the Rich and Famous

D o you sometimes wish you were a celebrity? Even if you do, I'm betting you're glad you're not the *newborn child* of a celebrity. Although you might grumble about your well-worn, "ordinary" name of Jessica or Paul, there's no telling what your name might have been if you were the offspring of a Hollywood star. When it comes to naming their children, celebrities from the A list to the D list have come up with names that often seem more suited to science fiction or were the hilarious-but-best-forgotten suggestions of the child's young siblings-to-be: "Let's welcome into this world Dump Truck!"

Although even celebrity children aren't generally saddled with names as unfortunate as Dump Truck, some come dangerously close. Consider Nicholas Cage's son, whose moniker, Kal-el, is the birth name of Superman; Bob Geldof's three daughters, blessed with the names Fifi Trixibelle, Peaches Honeyblossom and Little Pixie—choices for which there is no logical explanation; or Jason Lee's little boy, who was given the charmingly unassuming name of Pilot Inspektor. The odd names celebrities choose for their children often become subjects of ridicule among "normal" people—not to mention the tabloids—so why would a loving parent do such a thing to an innocent child?

According to a suite101.com article from 2007—when the likes of Geri Halliwell's daughter, Bluebell Madonna, and Richard Gere's son, Homer James Jigme, were born—unusual baby names have become the latest accessory for the rich and famous. Attaching the word "accessory" to a child might seem ludicrous, but so does attaching it to a dog, as per the fairly recent and now passé yet annoyingly persistent designer doggy trend among minor and major celebrities alike.

In the same article, psychologist Kent Evans suggests that celebrities give their children such out-of-the-ordinary names because they are seeking self-reinforcement. Um, don't Mommy and Daddy know children aren't supposed to reflect their parents' insecurities? Apparently not, because Evans also puts forward the idea that odd names are a reflection of the celebrity parents' quest for originality and their need to be considered creative.

Not all celebrities go for creativity, however. Some just stick with what they know, which, as you'll see from the following examples, can be taken to the extreme. For George Foreman, for example, finesse isn't an issue—but a psychologist would probably have a field day with Foreman's choices for his children's names: George Edward Junior, George Edward III, George Edward IV, George Edward V, George Edward VI, Freeda George and Georgetta. Similarly, Michael Jackson named his children Prince Michael, Prince Michael II and Paris Michael Katherine. Jack, Jackie, Jacqueline, Jack II and Jackie II, anyone?

The following is a sample of the displays of—ahem—originality, creativity and methods of self-reinforcement that some celebrities have come up with in their quest for unusual baby names. The owners of these unfortunate names range in age from toddler to adult.

- Alabama Gypsy Rose, daughter of Drea De Matteo and Shooter Jennings
- Apple and Moses, daughter and son of Gwyneth Paltrow and Chris Martin
- Audio Science, son of Shannyn Sossamon
- Banjo, son of Rachel Griffiths
- Camera, daughter of Arthur Ashe
- Dusti Raine and Keelee Breeze, daughters of Vanilla Ice
- Dweezil, Ahmet Emuukha Rodan, Moon Unit and Diva Muffin, son, son, daughter and daughter of Frank Zappa
- Elijah Bob Patricius Guggi Q. Hewson, son of Bono
- Ever Gabo, daughter of Milla Jovovich
- Free, son of Barbara Hershey

- Heavenly Hiraani Tiger Lily, daughter of the late Michael Hutchence
- Jermajesty, son of Jermaine Jackson
- Maddox Chivan, Zahara Marley, Pax Thien and Shiloh Nouvel, son, daughter, son and daughter of Brad Pitt and Angelina Jolie (they also have a set of twins, with the comparatively normal names of Vivienne Marcheline and Knox Leon)
- Moxie CrimeFighter, daughter of Penn Jillette
- Princess Tiaamii, daughter of British model Jordan and pop-singer husband Peter Andre
- Ptolemy John, son of Gretchen Mol
- Rocket Valentin, Racer Maximilliano, Rebel Antonio, Rogue and Rhiannon, son, son, son, son and daughter of Robert Rodriguez
- Rumer Glenn, Scout Larue and Tallulah Belle, daughters of Bruce Willis and Demi Moore
- Sage Moonblood, daughter of Sylvester Stallone
- Seven Sirius and Puma, son and daughter of Erykah Badu
- Speck Wildhorse, son of John Mellencamp
- Suri, daughter of Tom Cruise and Katie Holmes
- Tu Morrow, daughter of Rob Morrow
- Zuma Nesta Rock, son of Gwen Stefani and Gavin Rossdale

Not all celebrities are into this style of baby naming. Some have come up with names that range from the traditional to the lovely. It's comforting to know that some celebrities have common sense. Really, I think non-celebrities like us have more respect for stars who can stay relatively sane in what must be, at times, a very insane celluloid bubble.

Minnie Driver, for example, who gave birth to her son in September 2008, admitted that her surname proved a bit of a challenge when choosing a ridicule-free first name for her son, Henry. Charlie Sheen has also been quoted as saying, "I just think parents don't think 20 years ahead when they name their kid: 'This is my son Shalamar.' It becomes a curse for the child. It's terrible." He and his wife, Brooke Mueller, plan to name their twins something "traditional."

Imitation is the Sincerest Form of Flattery

When it comes to celebrity trends, baby names are no exception, and the masses have time and time again followed the celebrity lead by bestowing famous babies' names—traditional or not—on their own children. The result is that many previously popular names, such as good ol' Edna, Gertrude and Beatrice and sturdy and stoic Harold and Richard, are on the way out. According to statistician Dr. Geoff Ellis, the most popular names of 1907 failed to make the 100-most-popular-names lists in the years between 2003 and 2008.

Baby-name trends based on the names that celebrities give their children, however, have been on the rise. With the gossip-magazine baby-bump watches, alerts and rumours and entire pages devoted to celebrity baby trends (such as *US Weekly*'s "Baby Love" spread) comes a whole new meaning to the phrase "bringing home baby." It's difficult for the mere mortal to avoid celebrity-baby saturation, and baby-name ideas inevitably seep into the brains of parents-to-be because of it—perhaps more than we realize.

Can you name the celebrity parents associated with the names Jayden, Ava and Kingston? Chances are you can, and if you can't, well, let me jog your celebrity-gossip cranial recesses (or represses). Jayden is Britney Spears' second son with ex Kevin Federline, Ava is Reese Witherspoon's daughter with ex Ryan Philippe, and Kingston is the first son of Gwen Stefani and Gavin Rossdale. Each of these names has shot up the baby-name charts since their respective debuts. Jayden has become so popular, in fact, that it is no longer used exclusively as a boy's name and has made the leap into the unisex market. One of the most popular male-or-female names in North America, its variants—Jayden, Jaden, Jadyn, Jaiden and Jaidyn—allow for a bit of differentiation on the class attendance list, but, alas, they all sound the same. So if you like this name, be prepared to have your child spend his or her elementary school years explaining, "No, that's Jadyn with a *y* between the *d* and *n*, not the *J* and *y*, like Jayden (the boy) over there and Jayden (the girl) across the room."

As much as Toronto likes to think it's the centre of the universe, New York City eclipses it, hands-down, so if that city's health department states that Jayden is the second most popular boys name in the city and the number one boy's name among black and Hispanic parents, it must be true. The name broke into New York's top 10 in 2007, a year after Spears' son was born; as of 2008, it was still riding high in New York and everywhere else. Not only is the name itself a trend, the fact that Jayden (typically) ends with *en* gives it additional cachet. The name joins a plethora of Haydens and Braydens out there, all part of another popular trend: names that end in *en*.

Ava has also skyrocketed. Always the sophisticate, Fred Astaire named his daughter Ava in 1942, and the name has slowly gained popularity among celebrities and non-celebrities alike. The daughters of Aidan Quinn, Gil Bellows, Peri Gilpin and Heather Locklear all bear this elegant namesake, one of the top five most popular girls names in Canada.

Already on the list of parents who have given their children strange names, Gwen Stefani earns another mention here with her trendsetting choice of Kingston for her first son. In 2006, the year of his birth, the name Kingston failed to make the top 500 baby names in Canada. Jump ahead a year, and Kingston was on a steady climb, with BC placing it at 209th.

Another notable baby name that became a craze following the birth of a celebrity baby was Cody, the name of Kathy Lee Gifford's son. The co-host of *Live With Regis and Kathy Lee* chose a name that wasn't even in the top 50 most popular boys names in the 1980s. But the name broke into the top 25 in 1991 (a year after Gifford's son was born) and stayed there for 11 years. Showing true fad quality, the name soon crossed over into unisex territory, breaking into the top 1000 girls names in 1990 and 1991.

Big Names for Little Babies

Some of today's parents are looking beyond celebrities and their babies for inspiration, to the characters they play on the small and large screen. Thanks to *The Matrix* film trilogy, for instance, Trinity has become one of the most popular names for girls. Not even in the top 500 in the 1990s, Trinity, which had been climbing by leaps and bounds since 1999, made the list of top 50 girls names in 2004 (one year after the release of the final *Matrix* film). Also making the scene in the 1990s was the name Dylan, which owes its popularity to the introduction of brooding Dylan McKay's character in the hit series *Beverly Hills, 90210.*

Soap operas have also long been an inspiration for parents seeking names for their new arrivals. In the 1980s, Ashley—the name of a popular character on *The Young and the Restless*—zoomed up the charts. Also in the '80s, the name Kayla, then barely a blip on the popularity radar, suddenly popped up in homes everywhere, when the character Kayla Brady was introduced on *Days of Our Lives.*

Before Ashley from Edmonton, Alberta, was born, her mother found herself spending a lot of time on the couch in the last weeks of her pregnancy. *The Young and the Restless* was a daily draw, and the character of Ashley Abbott—beautiful, smart, successful and married to Victor—was enjoying quite a lovely life. The name suddenly became a lot more appealing to Ashley's mother. When Ashley's father, who was away overseas when Ashley was born, asked her mother how their little was Nicole doing, the reply was, "Ashley is just fine." *The Young and the Restless* was obviously popular with mothers-to-be at the time; Ashley told me that she knows three other girls her age (23) named for this same character. The soap was also responsible for Ashley's brother's name, Bradley. However, in a case of life *not* imitating art, Ashley did not marry Bradley, which is what eventually happened on the soap.

 **THE NAME GAME** A soap opera also inspired Monica's mother. Monica, from Toronto, Ontario, is named for a character on *General Hospital.* Although Monica, the character, is still on the show today, real-life Monica's mother doesn't watch anymore, preferring to keep her eyes on her own Monica.

Soap operas aren't the only TV shows to influence naming trends; sitcoms and dramas have also had a serious impact. One of the biggest hits on ABC, the Emmy-winning *Grey's Anatomy*, has plenty of fans—not just for the show itself, but for the names of the show's characters. Revealing just how ardent the show's following is, babycenter.com points out that *Grey's Anatomy*, whether by coincidence or conscious choice, has plenty of parents naming their babies after some of Seattle Grace's lovelorn doctors.

Addison. Addison, the name of Kate Walsh's character, Dr. Addison Montgomery, barely registered on the lists in the '80s—in fact, it wasn't popular at all, failing to make even the list of top 1000 girls names. Since the debut of the show in 2005, Addison has climbed into the top 50 in Canada.

Isobel. The lovely Isobel "Izzie" Stevens, portrayed by Katherine Heigl, can be proud that more than her red-carpet fashion sense has influenced the masses. The popularity of the more common variations of the name, Isabelle and Isabella, given frequently to young ladies in 1910, had plummeted in the 1950s, '60s and '70s. But, from 2005 to 2007, the names became more popular than ever before. In 2008, one variation or another of the name was in the top 20 in Ontario, Alberta, BC and New Brunswick.

Bailey. Dr. Miranda Bailey, Chandra Wilson's character, has had a positive influence on more than just her interns. Bailey's popularity, which began its rise in 2006, is growing quickly as a choice for girls among Canada's West Coast parents.

Callie. Once given to girls in the 1880s, Callie nosedived after the turn of the 19th century and didn't begin climbing again until the 1960s. The name spiked in 2006, one year after *Grey's Anatomy* first aired. Inspired by Dr. Callie Torres, played by Sara Ramirez, the name is currently climbing toward the top 100. Callie is Greek for "most beautiful," so it's no wonder the name is being chosen for all those pretty little baby girls out there!

Chad, from Kingston, Ontario, has celebrity influence written all over him. He is named for Elvis' character in *Blue Hawaii*.

Baby-naming connections to celebrities and the characters they play can be made over and over again, regardless of the year. Admit it, it's easy to fall into the trap of admiring a character in one of your favourite TV shows or movies and slowly realizing that you—in a forced-to-admit-it kind of way—think of the character as a real person. This connection can influence your name choice, because who doesn't want to choose the name of a "person" one admires? The downside, though, to choosing a current TV or silver-screen namesake for your most precious is that hundreds of other children are bound to be running around with the same name.

Here are a few more examples of baby names that have spiked in popularity because of a hearty celebrity influence:

Emma. This is one of the top five girls names in every province except Québec, where it is number 17. Courtney Cox's

Friends character, Monica, wanted it, but Jennifer Aniston's Rachel got it for her daughter. Ranked as the third most frequently given name in the 1880s, it was the second most given choice in 2002—the year Rachel gave birth. Its popularity has only risen since then, whether or not *Friends* fans remember the connection. I know an Emma who was born just over a year ago, and I'm sure you know one, too.

When Linda, from Kitchener, Ontario, was considering what to name her daughter, she knew to avoid anything with a negative connotation—as a teacher, she'd had plenty of opportunities to hear how kids could sully a child's name. Emma came to mind as a good choice, not because of *Friends*, but because of a few other influences. Linda had taught a well-mannered, adorable girl with the name, and Emma was also the name of Linda's great-grandmother, who was dearly loved. A compromise was struck between Linda and her husband (who preferred the name Kate), and Emma-Kate was born.

Mariah. No guessing required as to where this name comes from. Used in the 1880s through to the early 1900s, the name completely died out until its huge spike in 1991, just one year after songbird Mariah Carey released her debut album. The name became securely locked into the top 150 girls names in North America right up until 2007, in contrast to the 1980s, when it wasn't even in the top 500.

Angelina. A name that probably makes many cringe at the mere thought of giving it to a child (Camp Jolie or Camp Aniston?), Angelina experienced a rise in popularity in 2005, the year *Mr. & Mrs. Smith* was released. The film, as we now know, was the breeding ground for Jolie's relationship with Brad Pitt, who was married at the time to Jennifer Aniston, who was, of course, part of the Emma entry, and so the connections go round and round…but I digress. Angelina hit its top spot of 43 in 2005, only to fall slowly but steadily in popularity in the years since.

Sienna and **Sadie.** These names are paired, not only because of their rise in popularity in the mid-2000s, but because of their connection. Currently near the number 50 spot in BC, Sadie hasn't seen such a surge since the 1880s, when it was number 70 overall in North America. And, although Sienna didn't exist on the charts until the 1980s, it has climbed steadily since, rising high in popularity since 2006. The two celebrities connected to these names are Sadie Frost and Sienna Miller. Frost is the ex-wife of Jude Law, and Miller was his fiancée in 2004 and 2005, until he cheated on her with his children's nanny, Daisy Wright. Just for information's sake, Daisy took a slight dip in popularity in the mid-2000s but still remains in the top 500.

Aidan. Finally, a boy's name that is making waves in the baby-naming world! Much like Emma, Aidan is a name you probably also know well. I do. I would also love to know the celebrity character's namesake, Aidan Shaw, played by John Corbett, from the wildly popular *Sex and the City*. As the everyman who was caring, attentive and ultimately perfect (though imperfect for Carrie), Aidan made every woman like this name. Although the show no longer airs except in reruns, the name's popularity remains high—Aidan is the top boys name in Nova Scotia and is in the top 20 in Alberta, BC, Ontario, Saskatchewan and the Yukon.

Brody. Inspired, unfortunately, by one of my Top 10 People Who Really Shouldn't Be Celebrities, Brody Jenner, this name is definitely on the rise. Jenner became quasi-famous in the celebrity tabloids when he began dating Kristin Cavallari of *Laguna Beach*, then became even more quasi-famous with *The Hills* and his own show, *Bromance*. Coincidence or not, the name Brody made its biggest leaps from 2005 to 2007, years during which Jenner's profile also grew.

Jagger. We all think of one person when we hear this name: Rolling Stones band member Mick Jagger. No stranger to the touring scene, Jagger is still rocking it—and celebrity parents are choosing Mick's last name as a first name for their new-born boys and girls. Rascal Flatts guitarist Joe Don Rooney, former *Punky Brewster* star Soleil Moon Frye, Fuel singer Brett Scallions and tennis player Lindsay Davenport have all named their children Jagger. Not to be outdone by the celebrities, non-celebrities have also embraced the name—Jagger broke into the top 1000 boys names in 2003, then dropped completely off the charts until 2007, the year of the aforementioned births, when it re-entered the top 1000.

Frye inspired another celebrity trend: using boys names— more specifically, three boys names—for girls. Frye's daughter's full name is Jagger Joseph Blue, and the daughter of former *Law & Order* star Elisabeth Rohm was recently bestowed with Easton August Anthony. Rohm said the name Easton came to her in a dream and was the name her child would answer to when called, not the name Rohm had originally chosen, which was Grace. Jagger, however, was actually voted the worst girl's name by survey of about 5000 on babynames.com. Ouch.

Not knowing how their daughter's life would transpire, how her name would be treated, and what the trends of the future would be, Raffaela's parents gave her a beautiful name—a beautiful name that ended up being thrown by the wayside in favour of Ralph. Known by everyone as Ralph, she is now a playwright in Toronto, Ontario, and has written a play titled *A Girl Named Ralph*.

Political Inspiration

Famous politicos have also inspired new parents around the globe. More than half of the babies born near the end of 2008 at the New Nyanza Provincial Hospital in Kisumu, Kenya, were named either Barack or Michelle, obviously in reference to newly instated U.S. president Barack Obama and his wife, Michelle. And in a bizarre twist, as reported in 2008 in the *Victoria News Daily*, an Italian right-wing party in Italy has offered 1500 euros ($2390) to parents who name their babies for World War II fascist dictator Benito Mussolini or his wife, Rachele. The reasoning behind the MSI-Fiamma Tricolore party's offer is that the names are under threat of extinction. The party, a descendant of Mussolini's fascist party, wants to pay tribute to the fascist party's roots. The cash is being doled out to babies born in 2009 in five villages with particularly low birth rates.

Slip Sliding Away

As is their way, trends come and go, and celebrities, whose names once influenced people, often fall from grace. In Britney Spears' case, it was the princess of pop who fell, along with her name, which slid from the top 300 in the late 1990s, when she made her debut with the single "...Baby One More Time," right out of the top 500 in 2008. Turning from the squeaky-clean girl-next-door to an umbrella-wielding, shaved-head maniac apparently doesn't do great things for your popularity, or your name.

Having—or not having, if you believe Bill Clinton—sex with the president of the United States doesn't do much for your name, either. Monica, already on a steady decline through the 1990s, saw a dramatic drop in popularity after January 1998, when Monica Lewinsky's affair with Clinton was exposed.

Despite the ubiquitous presence of Ashleys in Hollywood—Ashlee Simpson, Ashley Olsen and Ashley Tisdale, from *High School Musical*—and the name's popularity in the 1980s, Ashley is slowly slipping down the charts. Lisa, a former number one name in the 1960s, has also taken a dive, declining most notably after the debut of *The Simpsons*. Although Lisa might be the smartest Simpson, evidently parents don't want their daughters to be associated with a goofy-looking cartoon character. Go figure!

As for the boys, the name Clay, which had been declining since the 1990s, went swiftly down the charts after Clay Aiken appeared on *American Idol* in Season 2. Ruben, however, as in Season 2 winner Ruben Studdard, saw a small spike in activity in 2005. And, although parents might be more inclined to name a child for Heath Ledger since his death and award-winning portrayal of the Joker in *The Dark Knight*, a year after the release of *Brokeback Mountain* in 2005, the name dropped almost 120 spots on baby-name popularity lists.

Identity Crisis

Some celebrities aren't happy with their names, opting to legally change their birth name to their more-popular and well-known nicknames or aliases. Destiny Hope Cyrus, famously known as Miley Cyrus, had her parents file the appropriate papers in 2008, requesting that her name be legally changed to Miley Cyrus. Cincinnati Bengals wide receiver Chad Johnson also changed his legal name in 2008—to Chad Ocho Cinco. Why? To reflect his oft-used nickname of Ocho Cinco, the Spanish translation of his Bengals jersey number of 85, of course. A bit strange, yes, but he's a celebrity, so maybe it's just par for the course, er, field.

Privileged Children

Here are some of the most notable celebrity babies born in 2008, whose names might (or might not) serve as inspiration (or shock and horror):

- Atticus, son of Casey Affleck
- Bronx Mowgli, son of Ashlee Simpson
- Callum Lyon, son of Kyle MacLachlan
- Clementine Jane, daughter of Ethan Hawke
- Ella Alexander, daughter of Alex Rodriguez
- Finley and Harper, twin daughters of Lisa Marie Presley
- Gia Zavala, daughter of Matt Damon
- Gisele Eme, daughter of Jeri Ryan
- Hania Riley, daughter of Vin Diesel
- Harlow Winter Kate, daughter of Nicole Ritchie
- Honor Marie, daughter of Jessica Alba
- Ignatius Martin, son of Cate Blanchett
- Kieran Lindsay, son of Julianna Margulies
- Levi, son of Matthew McConaughey
- Lily Aerin, daughter of Fred Savage
- Maddie Briann, daughter of Jamie Lynn Spears
- Max Liron, son of Christina Aguilera
- Max and Emme, twin son and daughter of Jennifer Lopez
- Nahla Ariela, daughter of Halle Berry
- Orion Christopher, son of Chris Noth
- Peanut Kai, son of Ingo Rademacher
- Sage Florence, daughter of Toni Collette
- Shaya Braven, son of Brooke Burke
- Stella Doreen, daughter of Tori Spelling
- Sunday Rose, daughter of Nicole Kidman
- Sunny Madeline, daughter of Adam Sandler
- Trig Paxson Van, son of Sarah Palin

Us and Baby Names

The Good, the Bad and the Out There!

When it comes to baby-naming trends that celebrities haven't influenced (or, maybe they have and we just don't realize it yet), the ways today's parents have found to mix it up are sometimes mind-boggling. Although we consider "our" baby names and "celebrity" baby names to be two distinct categories and often think of celebrity baby names as strange and indulgent, a quick look in the local newspaper provides proof that non-celebrity baby names can be just as offbeat. Here is a sampling of names found in the Sudbury, Ontario, newspaper *The Sudbury Star*:

Abbygail
Atlantis Rain
Avery Paiden
Beckham
Dayle Addie
Elizabeth Gael
Gwen Olivia Willow
Jakub
Julea
Kailyn Glenda
Kasidee Rianna Briar-Rose
Keynan
Kiera
Kohyn
Lanaya Jay
Leighton
Mackennah (and the variation McKenna)
Madisyn Caly
Milly Ann
Nova
Nyah Linda
Paityn
Shay-Lynn Connie Danielle
Tyce

There is no denying that these are interesting names, given to children by parents who are just like us, so who's to say that celebrities are the crazy ones? It's much easier to call celebrities out as insane, because you aren't going to tell your best friend you think the name she's chosen for her first-born is ridiculous.

That said, we want our children to stand out so much that hundreds of babies each year are named Unique. Hundreds! Overuse, however, is usually one of the first indicators that a name's popularity will soon plummet and then fade into obscurity. As a result, certain names become symbolic of a particular period, often making them unattractive to parents in the future.

Sometimes, however, the cat does indeed come back.

Something Old, Something New

According to babynamewizard.com, one of the biggest trends of 2008 among new parents was the use of what the website calls "antique revivals." What's old is new again. From what I can tell, however, the trend only applies to modern-sounding old names—names that sound flowery, delicate and definitely "of a certain era" for girls and that are sturdy and strong for boys—but also hip and current without really meaning to be. Take Ava, for instance. Extremely popular in Canada, the name is old-fashioned— but it's old-fashioned in a way that's somehow chic. Ida, however, is part of a dying breed. A quick scan of the obituaries in PEI's newspaper, *The Guardian*, turns up names such as Florence Edith, Irene Mary, Lloyd Thayer and Bertha—names you aren't likely to find on a 2009 kindergarten attendance list. So, although turn-of-the-20th-century names that are poetic and romantic for girls and upstanding for boys are the bee's knees, so to speak, names that make people think *old* just don't make the cut in the fair-weather world of baby-name trends.

Spell it Out

Parents who are really stuck on Ida but want a modern variation that won't embarrass their eventual tween around her friends Atlantis, Nova and Dayle have another choice: creative spelling—the way of the future! Parents beware, however— you might find yourself reading about your child's frustrations in a future baby-name book.

Caroline. How would you pronounce this name? Probably CaroLINE, right? Well, not so for Caroline of Toronto, Ontario. Her parents decided that Caroline should be pronounced CaroLYN but not spelled that way. Says Caroline: "It left me with a lifetime of either a misspelled name or a mispronounced name."

Here's another example of how to spell innovatively: my name, Carla, could be spelled Kahrla, Cahrla, Carlah, Karlah or Carela (pronounced with a silent *e*). You can see how things might get out of control when parents get "creative." In keeping up with the Joneses, I also incorporated the use of the silent killer—the letter *h*—which is useless phonetically but all-encompassing in its placement because it is part of its very own trend. How about Unickhe (as in Unique) for your baby girl. Anyone?

Following are two examples of popular names whose spellings range from lovely to gnarled, to say the least:

MacKenzie: Mackenzie, Mckenzie, Mackenzi, Mackenzee, Mackinzie, Mackensie, Mackinzy, Mackinsey, Mackenzy, Mackenzey, Machenzie, Mackynzi, Mackinze, Mackenziee, Mackanzie, Macinzee, Machkenzie, Macenzie, Mckinzie, Mckenzee, Mckenzi, Mckynzie, Mckinzee, Mckenzye, Mckenzy, Mckenzey, Mckenze, McKenzie, Makenzie, Makenzi, Makenzy,

Makensie, Makynzie, Makynze, Makynzye, Makynzi, Makinzy, Makinzie, Makinzi, Makenzee, Makinze, Makinsy, Mykenzie

Caden: Cadin, Cayden, Caiden, Caeden, Caidan, Cadyn, Caydan, Caydn, Caidyn, Cadan, Cadon, Cadaan, Caedon, Caedan, Kaidan, Kaiden, Kayden, Kaidyn, Kaidynn, Kaidon, Kaidin, Kaden, Kaeden, Kadin, Kaedyn, Kaedan, Kadyn, Kaedon, Kaedin, Kadan, Kadon

As you can see, creative spelling runs smoothly into the trend of replacing vowels for vowels (*e* for *i*, for example) and consonants for consonants (*c* for *k*).

If the vowel/consonant change doesn't appeal to you, consider the up-and-coming trend of spelling names by inserting apostrophes into them. When I thought about this one, the only name I could come up with was D'Arcy, but other examples are Chlo'E, Brook'Lyn and Cam'Ron. If extraneous apostrophes are your thing, this might be the inspiration you've been looking for.

Making It Up as You Go Along

It's not hard to see why the pool of names parents can pick from today is nearly infinite—parents can make up any name they want. In the 1950s, according to Lauren Wattenberg, author of *The Baby Name Wizard*, the top 10 names for boys and girls accounted for a quarter of all baby names—today's top 10 names account for less than a tenth of all the names out there. Because of the rise (and popularity) of making up baby names, none of the top 10 girls names from the 1950s made the top-10 list from 2006. Case in point—do you know anyone with the previously mentioned names from the *Sudbury Star*? Do you know any children named Mary or Jane or Richard? If so, do you know more than one or two children with these names? If you do, you must run in some unickhe circles!

 Kristy, from Toronto, Ontario, told me her brother's name is Dalin—which she admitted is a completely made-up name. Her father wanted Dallas, but her mother wasn't having it. Dalin was agreed on. Coincidentally, Dalin contains all the letters of Kristy's mother's name: Linda.

 Joanne, from Edmonton, Alberta, has a cousin named Mara—another fabricated name. Mara's parents, Maria and Ralph, used the first two letters of their names as inspiration for the person who eventually became Mara.

Girls Versus Boys

The majority of names from the *Sudbury Star* list presumably belong to girls (it can be hard to tell nowadays)—which brings me to an observation: the number of girl-name choices as compared to those for boys. In fact, in the last century, the pool of names for boys has been smaller than that for girls. This might be because parents prefer traditional names for boys, but it might also be because there are no apparent limits to pretty-sounding girls names. Beauty is in the eye of the beholder, as revealed by the staggering number of girls names you can find—and make up!

Going Backwards

Speaking of girls names, does the name Nevaeh sound familiar? It might if you read it backwards: Heaven. This name, which has been on the rise since 2006, wasn't even on the charts a year earlier. As we've seen, once an idea, such as spelling a name backwards, is released into the baby-naming world, there's no telling how far it will go. If you can believe it, Semaj—James spelled backwards—was in the top 1000 boys names in 2008. James, however, is still one of those traditional names that parents love—it's the only name to have stayed in the top 10 from 1890 to 1990. Although it was still in the top 20 in 2008, the name has been slowly slipping down the charts. Does that mean, in 50 years, that Semaj will take its place?

Using My Religion

Taking a cue from the bestselling book of all time, biblical names remain one of the top naming trends year after year. The immensely popular Jacob and its variations have been at the top of boys names lists throughout Canada for years. Abigail and its various incarnations have also been enormously popular. If this trend is for you, try searching the family Bible for inspiration. Your child's name will come from a source that is not only special to you but that is an heirloom near and dear to your family's history, filled with the names of past generations.

Here is an interesting story from Sahrah, of Toronto, Ontario, that melds religion and royalty:

My dad is really religious, and my mum was in love with British royalty, so they both agreed to name me Sara, for different reasons. One was to name me for Abraham's wife and the other was to name me for Sarah Ferguson. However, my name changed to Sahrah because of the way my family pronounced Sara with their Korean accents. On my first day of school, I was introduced to my new kindergarten teacher as 'Sah-rah' and since then, my name was always spelled Sahrah."

Say What You Mean

Another way to be inventive is to choose a name with meaning. You pick a word that means something to you, and, just like magic, you have a name for your baby. In a *New York Times* article from 2003, these types of names were predicted to become popular, and, lo and behold, now they are. The article went on to state that parents really took note of "meaning" names when Christie Brinkley named her daughter Sailor, because Brinkley and her then-husband liked to sail.

Places that have meaning for parents are also influencing recent naming trends, and the trend promises to continue to be big in 2009. Brooklyn, Milan, Houston, Aspen, Geneva and Savannah are all popular names—the parents of 2008 must have gone on a lot of great vacations!

Kendra, of North Bay, Ontario, was given a name full of meaning for her father. It was his dream to travel to Alaska and see the wilderness, but the trip wasn't in the budget for a young man with one daughter and another on the way. Kendra's mother bought her husband a biography about a woman named Kendra who travelled extensively until landing her dream job as a teacher in Alaska. Inspired by the book's heroine and by the death of his best friend, Ken, in a car accident, Kendra's father felt no other name in the world was more suited to his daughter.

Baby Names Around the World

But who says you have to actually visit a place to use it as a name for your child? You can find inspiration just by opening an atlas. Names with an international flavour were all the rage in 2008 into 2009—particularly Celtic or Italian ones. Celtic names at the top of the lists include Cameron (Cam'Ron?),

Aidan, Brynn and Kennedy. You can also expand your horizons with truly one-of-a-kind Gaelic names that are deeply rooted in cultural traditions dating back hundreds of years. True, there might be some pronunciation issues (Aodhan, for example), but if very masculine and feminine names with a twist are what you're looking for, your search is over.

The romanticism of the Italians has also engendered a host of unequivocally male and female names. In vogue are girls names ending in *-la*, *-ella* and *–ia*, having the sound "ah" at the end. Some of the most popular names in Italy between 2004 and 2008 were:

Girls: Guilia, Alessia, Alice, Chiara and Gaia
Boys: Andrea, Lorenzo, Simone, Paolo and Marco

As the world grows more globally conscious, Arabic, Greek, Russian and Swahili influences on our most popular names have also increased. From suite101.com's pregnancy and childbirth section, here is a sampling of the top boys names from around the world:

Australia: Jack, Lachlan, Thomas, Ethan, William
Belarus: Artem, Vladislav, Nikita, Aleksej, Ivan
Belgium: Milan, Wout, Senne, Seppe, Thomas
Brazil: Gabriel, Gustavo, Giulherme, Mateus, Vitor
Chile: Benjamin, Mathias, Vincente, Martin, Sebastian
Croatia: Luka, Ivan, Marko, Filip, Karlo
Czech Republic: Jan, Jakub, Tomáš, Adam, Ondrej
Estonia: Markus, Rasmus, Kevin, Kaspar, Daniel
Finland: Juhani, Johannes, Mikael, Matias, Olavi
France: Enzo, Mathis, Lucas, Hugo, Mathéo
Germany: Maximillian, Leon, Lukas, Fynn
Hungary: Bence, Máté, Balázs, Dávid, Dániel
Ireland: Jack, James, Matthew, Daniel, Ryan
Israel: Uri, Ro'I, Amit, Yosef, Moshe
Japan: Yuuki, Haruto, Souta, Yuuto, Haruki
Lithuania: Lukas, Mantas, Tomas, Deividas, Rokas

Mexico: Alejandro, Juan Carlos, Miguel Angel, Eduardo, Fernando
Netherlands: Dan, Sem, Thomas, Tim, Lucas
Norway: Markus, Mathias, Jonas, Kristian, Tobias
Philippines: Michael, Ronald, Ryan, Joseph, Joel
Poland: Marcin, Adam, Marek, Piotr, Tomasz
Romania: Alexandru, Radu, Vlad, Ion, Marin
Russia: Alexandr, Andrey, Daniil, Dmitry, Ivan
Scotland: Lewis, Jack, Ryan, James, Callum
Slovakia: Peter, Jan, Michal, Jozef, Martin, Miro
Spain: Alejandro, Daniel, Pablo, David, Javier
Sweden: Lucas, Oscar, William, Elias, Filip
Tunisia: Mehdi, Youssef, Aziz, Karim, Slim
Turkey: Arda, Yusuf, Mehmet, Mustafa, Emirhan
Ukraine: Olexandr, Vadim, Gleb, Taras, Maksim
United Kingdom: Jack, Thomas, Joshua, Oliver, Harry

And the top names for girls, internationally:

Australia: Ella, Emily, Olivia, Chloe, Sophie
Belarus: Darja, Anastasija, Maria, Polina, Anna
Belgium: Lotte, Julie, Emma, Amber, Fleur
Brazil: Julia, Givanna, Maria Eduarda, Isabela, Gabriela
Chile: Constanza, Catalina, Valentina, Javiera, Martina
Croatia: Lana, Lucija, Petra, Ana, Emma
Czech Republic: Tereza, Eliška, Adéla, Natálie, Anna
Estonia: Laura, Maria, Anna, Sandra, Lisette
Finland: Maria, Emilia, Sofia, Aino, Olivia
France: Emma, Lea, Manon, Clara, Chloe
Germany: Marie, Sophie, Maria, Anna, Leonie
Hungary: Anna, Viktoria, Reka, Vivien, Zsofia
Ireland: Emma, Sarah, Katie, Amy, Aoife
Israel: Noa, Roni, Yael, Adi, Sarah
Japan: Hina, Yui, Miu, Haruka, Sakura
Lithuania: Gabriele, Gabija, Viktorija, Karolina, Greta
Mexico: Gabriela, Maria Carmen, Adriana, Alejandra, Maria Guadalupe

Netherlands: Sanne, Emma, Anna, Iris, Anouk
Norway: Thea, Emma, Julie, Ida, Nora
Philippines: Maricel, Michelle, Jennifer, Janice, Mary Grace
Romania: Maria, Ioana, Ana-Maria, Cristina, Andreea
Russia: Alexandra, Alina, Anastasia, Ekaterina, Anna
Scotland: Sophie, Emma, Erin, Katie, Lucy
Slovakia: Katarina, Zuzana, Janka, Lucia, Hana
Spain: Lucia, Maria, Paula, Laura, Marta
Sweden: Emma, Maja, Agnes, Julia, Alva
Turkey: Elif, Zeynep, Irem, Busra, Merve
Ukraine: Valeriya, Sofiya, Victoriya, Anastasiya, Anna
United Kingdom: Olivia, Grace, Jessica, Ruby, Emily

Some names with an international flavour are popular on both sides of the Atlantic. Olivia, Sophia and Emma, three of the most used girls names in the early 21st century, not only have a distinguishable presence in the international list, they're pretty popular in Canada, too.

Name that Tradition

Canadian parents don't usually involve tradition when bestowing names on their children, beyond announcing them to family and friends through emails and Facebook. Around the world, however, ceremony and tradition play an important part in baby naming. Here are some of the baby-naming traditions followed by other countries and cultures:

Italy: Italian children are traditionally named after their grandparents, choosing from the father's side of the family first. As a rule, the first-born son is named after his paternal grandfather and the second after his maternal grandfather. The first daughter is given her paternal grandmother's name, and the second daughter receives her maternal grandmother's name.

Japan: In Japan, a baby is traditionally honoured with a naming ceremony seven days after birth. The baby is given a first and last name but no middle name.

Czech Republic and **Slovakia:** Czech and Slovak parents traditionally give their children names from the Roman Catholic calendar of saints. Each saint corresponds to a particular day of the year, which means that all those with the same name celebrate a second birthday on that day—their "name day."

China: When naming a baby in China, some parents still follow the traditional "Red Egg and Ginger" ceremony. The baby, which is not named until this ceremony takes place, is given a temporary "milk" name while still in the womb—usually something undesirable, such as Dirt—to keep evil spirits away. In the Red Egg and Ginger ceremony, held after the first month of life, the egg (considered to be a delicacy in ancient China) represents fertility and is dyed red for good luck. During the ceremonial feast, the baby's head is shaved and he or she is presented with gifts. In the modern adaptation, Chinese parents hand out coloured eggs as party favours at their baby-naming celebration.

However, no matter how creative Chinese parents try to be, for the most part, their child will share his or her last name with many others: in China, 85 percent of the population shares only 100 surnames. Ninety-three million Wangs and 92 million Lis can make for some confusing classrooms. The name pool in China has grown even smaller with the ban on names containing Western characters and on the use of double surnames (such as Wang-Li or Li-Wang).

Morocco: Moroccan parents don't have to worry about the pressures of coming up with a unique name for their baby—they're required to choose from a mostly Arabic name list. They can, however, pay a fee for the opportunity to use a name that is not on the list. Moroccans living outside of Morocco still must consult the approved list, because babies with unauthorized names can have difficulty entering the country later on in their lives!

Sierra Leone: In Sierra Leone, a baby is traditionally named only after its umbilical cord has fallen off, because it is believed that, until that point, the child has no identity of its own. During the naming ceremony, the baby's head is shaved and the paternal aunt offers the infant a chewed kola nut and pepper from her own mouth to wish the child a long and brave life.

Nigeria: A Nigerian baby born in the Yoruba tribe is given an *orukui* name—a name that describes the circumstances surrounding its birth. For example, Abegunde is a boy's name meaning "born during a holiday." Yoruba children are also given a second name, or *oriki*, at a later time. This name describes the family's hopes for their child's future. An example is Titilayo, which means "eternal happiness."

Kenya: Similar in some ways to the traditions of the Yoruba tribe, the custom in Swahili-speaking Kenyan tribes dictates that babies have their birth name—the *jina la utotoni*—chosen by an elderly relative; this name is usually a reflection of the baby's looks. An example is the name Biubwa, which means soft, smooth and baby-like. After a baby is given its birth name, he or she is given an adult name—the *jina la ukab-wani*—up to 40 days later. This name is chosen by the baby's parents or paternal grandparents.

Maasai: In Africa, the Maasai name their babies only after they are a year old. The Maasai believe this gives the family enough time to determine a name that reflects their baby's personality.

Hindu: In keeping with the seemingly ubiquitous tradition of withholding a baby's name until a certain number days after its birth, Hindus traditionally wait 12 days after a baby's birth before bestowing the child with a name. The naming ceremony, called the *Namkaran* (which can be spelled differently and varies slightly from region to region), involves a *havan*, or sacred fire. While sitting around the fire, the baby's father holds the child in his lap and whispers the baby's name into its ears. The father then declares the name to everyone in attendance.

Buddhist: Buddhists follow a similar tradition but call theirs the *Namkaram*, which takes place either within the first three months of the baby's life or when it is thought the baby can hear. The mother writes the baby's name on a banana leaf then covers the leaf with handfuls of uncooked rice. After laying the baby on the banana leaf, she whispers the baby's name three times in its ear. All of the baby's relatives and guests then do the same.

Jewish: A Jewish boy is given his Hebrew name at a ceremony called a bris, which usually takes place eight days after his birth. At this ceremony, he is also circumcised by a *mohel* (a Jewish man or woman specially trained in ritual circumcision). A Jewish girl is given a ceremony in her honour 8 to 15 days after her birth. The ceremony includes a public reading of the Torah. During the reading, a special blessing is said that involves a prayer for the mother's health, the announcement of the baby's name and a prayer that the child may grow into a wise and understanding person of goodness.

Parents, take note: there's much to be learned from these international parents, who might think leafing through a baby-name book is quite a curious practice.

Last Name First

The Celtic-name trend overlaps with another—the use of last names as first names, such as Cameron and Kennedy. Other popular last-names-as-first-names are Addison (whose popularity we already know about) and Emerson. Emerson is the middle name of Courtney Thorne-Smith's son, born in 2008, and Teri Hatcher, whose public profile has grown since the debut of *Desperate Housewives*, named her daughter Emerson in 1997. It is truly impossible to escape celebrity.

As for boys names, showing up on birth certificates around the country are last-names-as-first-names reflecting occupations—for example, Mason, Cooper, Hunter and Carver.

In fact, almost 25 percent of the 100 most popular boys names in 2008 were also last names.

 Brenda, from Espanola, Ontario, chose last names as first names for both of her boys, Turner and Carter. She had only last names on her baby-name list when Turner, her first, was born, and the idea stuck—when her second son was born, he was named Carter. Born in the 1990s, Turner and Carter were ahead of the curve!

Going Green

Another influence on naming trends is the "green movement." Cloth grocery bags, recycling, electric cars…babies? River, Forest, Ocean and Meadow are some examples of names that can help you do your part.

Double Vision

Let's not leave out the miracle that is a set of twins. Because naming the twins River and Stream is just a bit too precious, parents are trying out new ideas. For instance, cracking a name in half and giving one piece to each sibling: Ellie and Nora, Alex and Xander—you get the idea. Also popular with multiples and siblings is alliteration, a trend that never really went away. Fashionable right now are Jacob and Joshua, Matthew and Michael, Daniel and David, Isaac and Isaiah and Ella and Emma.

Making Connections

Unisex names are yet another trend you can follow. Better still, start your own trend and give a name like Craig to your daughter. If you are actually naming your *son* Craig, however, you're in line with the current craze of giving boys names that start with *c*. Included in the top 100 names for boys in 2008 were Caden, Caleb, Connor, Carter, Chase, Cole, Colton, Carson and Cooper, which, in another *Grey's Anatomy* connection, is the name of one of Addison's colleagues in her spinoff show, *Private Practice*.

Not only is it hard to escape the celebrity influence, it's also difficult to avoid the news, and, unfortunately, some parents are just too eager to keep their fingers on the pulse of society. Let's take a brief foray into nicknames and news, so you can see what a name gone wrong looks like.

Nickname No-Nos

As is bound to happen with almost any name, at some point in your child's life, someone will make up a nickname for it. But what if your child's name is already a nickname? Parents these days are spurning names like Jason and Benjamin and going straight to Jace and Ben. But some are taking things a step further. In 2008, the UK newspaper *The Guardian* published an article on the rise in the number of "text-speak baby names." Examples included An, Conna and Lora as technologically friendly substitutes for Anne, Connor and Laura. Now, is texting responsible for these names, or are parents just trying to get creative? According to John Dunford, the general secretary of the Association of School and College Leaders, "some of it is genuine misspelling, some is parents looking for a unique way to spell a name and some is just carelessness." Yikes! No one wants to be accused of being careless about naming their child, so all you über-texters out there, beware.

Tales from the Dark Side

Unfortunately, despite labouring over a choice that avoids the trends and gnarly spelling, you might still choose a name that your child winds up hating. Those who pine for something else often change it later in life, but some push it to the extreme. Take George Garratt, for example, previous owner of this nice, upstanding name—new owner of Captain Fantastic Faster Than Superman Spiderman Batman Wolverine Hulk And The Flash Combined. In 2008, this 19-year-old Briton spent $20 to ditch his name and acquire a new one through a British online service. The proud owner of what is believed to be the longest name in the world, he is giving Rhoshandiatellyneshiaunneveshenk Koyaanisquatsiuth Williams—the woman thought to have the longest name in the U.S.—a run for her money.

Other bizarre tales from the world of baby naming include two from New Zealand, one in which a nine-year-old girl was made a ward of the court so she could change her name, which was Talula Does The Hula From Hawaii. New Zealand law does not allow parents to pick names that cause offence to a reasonable person or that contain more than 100 characters. Unfortunately, some names—such as Number 16 Bus Shelter, Violence and the aforementioned Talula—slip through the cracks. On the plus side, Fish and Chips (twins), Yeah Detroit, Fat Boy, Keenan Got Lucy and Sex Fruit were denied existence in government records.

To prevent this kind of ridiculousness, many countries have laws against names such as Captain Fantastic's. In 2007, the Venezuelan government put forth a bill barring parents from naming their children anything unusual or that is unrecognizable as one gender or the other. The government also issued a list of 100 acceptable names from which parents can choose. To prevent Venezuelan babies from being saddled with a moniker that's hard to pronounce, causes ridicule or casts doubt on the baby's gender, it was requested that the names Hengelberth, Maolenin, Githanjaly and Yurbiladyberth be banned from ever appearing on Venezuelan birth certificates again.

The Mexican state of Chihuahua also has rules on what parents can name their children. Names we might consider pretty tame in Canada (taking current trends into account), such as Lluvia (meaning rain) and Azul (blue) have been deemed improper.

And, if a baby is given a Western first name, that baby must be given a Spanish middle name to compensate for it.

Across the pond, Denmark also has a list—much longer than Venezuela's—with 7000 mostly Western European and English approved names. Likewise, Portugal has a 39-page list of permitted names—as well as a 40-plus-page list of banned names, such as Maradona and Mona Lisa. In Germany, first names must be gender specific, must not be a trademark and must not endanger a child's well-being. Forbidden on Germany's lists, for obvious reasons, are Hitler and Osama.

Unfortunately for the people at the DMV, these laws are largely designed to protect *newborns* from their parents' flights of fancy. Captain Fantastic's name is in the clear because Captain (as he's called, for short) is, technically, an adult.

Terrified yet? Or feeling inspired and full of ideas? Baby naming can be a minefield through which you must carefully tread. To help you out, the next chapter offers tips on choosing a name for your baby and a few more stories from Canadians on baby names.

10 Tips Plus One for Naming Your Baby

Do's and Don'ts of Baby Naming

Although most parents don't care what others think and will name their child whatever they want, in-laws be damned, as we've seen in the previous two chapters, there are many ways for a parent to go wrong when naming a little one.

For those who want to avoid saddling their child with a malapropos moniker, here are 10 tips, plus one more, to help you out.

1. Avoid giving your child a name that results in unfortunate initials. Derek Ulysses Martin is D.U.M.; Francesca Alice Thompson is F.A.T.; Danica Olivia Gordon is a D.O.G. You get the idea.

2. Say your first and last name picks together, out loud. I remember my dad telling me a story when I was young about a girl named Ima Hogg. This was a made-up story to make me laugh, but oblivious parents can easily make this mistake. Even if you love the first name you've chosen and think it fits beautifully with your child's last name, don't do it if it creates a crude sentence like poor Ima Hogg's! No child wants to serve as the impromptu inspiration for a series of Bart-Simpson-calling-Moe's jokes.

   It's important that a last name suits the first; after all, this is the name you and your child will hear and see forever—on birth certificates, permission forms, birthday party invitations, honour rolls, team rosters, diplomas, paycheques and office doors. Speaking the name aloud—first, middle and last, and then just first and last—is the best way to decide what works.

 When Sheri from Waterloo, Ontario, was yet to be born, her father was wise enough to do the enunciation test—with positive results. Sheri's mother was all for Dawn Sheri as her new daughter's first and middle

names, but Sheri's dad was adamantly against Dawn Sheri because he thought it sounded too much like Don Cherry. And with that excellent point, Sheri Dawn was born.

3. Avoid choosing a name that conjures up negative associations. Most parents realize this on their own—any mother-to-be can supply, without hesitation, at least a few names that she absolutely hates and would never consider giving her child. You can even ask your own mother, as an interesting experiment; it's a great way to hear stories about your friends and family that you might not have heard before. Parents certainly don't want to be reminded daily of that jerk from down the street who threw a rock at their head when they were nine years old or that idiot one of them used to date before they met their soul mate. Bottom line: don't be pressured by someone else into choosing a name you truly don't like!

 Erin, from Toronto, Ontario, was given her name because her mother's family hails from the Emerald Isle and because it means "from Ireland" in Gaelic. In keeping with tradition, Erin was given her middle name, Elizabeth, in honour of one of her grandmothers. But, perhaps the real reason for Erin being named Erin? She was supposed to be named Heather until her parents babysat a brat with that name.

4. Avoid giving your child an unpronounceable name. Spelling and pronunciation go hand in hand when considering baby names. Think of the frustration your child will experience every time his new teacher (and just about every other person unfamiliar with his name) stutters and stumbles over that garbled moniker on the class list. Consider this: the average person says his or her name

a million times in a lifetime. It must be possible to be creative without saddling your child with the double whammy of an unpronounceable and hard-to-spell name.

5. Consider the trends of the times when choosing a name. And when I say consider the trends, I mean beware of them. Certain names can be reflective of particular eras, as we've seen with names such as Gertrude and Wilmer, which are dying a rapid death, and with all of the 21st-century-born Sophias, Emmas, Olivias, Addisons, Carsons and Cadens running around. Choose a name that is reflective of you and how you see your child, not the namesake of half the kids on the block. Try to pick a name that will grow with your child and that is unique and meaningful to you.

6. Likewise, avoid naming your child for big-time, one-name celebrities. No one wants their child's name to be scoffed at as an example of "what were they thinking?" Elvis, Cher, Madonna, Beyonce, Rihanna. Admit it, you think of the celebrity right away—and you won't be the only one. If you must give your child a celebrity name, go for the names of their children, not the celebrities themselves.

7. Be sure to check out all the meanings of names you like. Different countries and cultures give varying meanings to the same name. For instance, did you know that Andy in Greek means womanly? Everyone looks up or finds out the meaning of his or her name eventually—what if your child discovers that her name means "mud"? Or "sacred pig"? Or worse, "mistake"? Enough said.

THE NAME GAME

Melanie's son, Evan, was two, when she discovered that she was pregnant with her second child. As a two-year-old boy is wont to do, he played with cars and trucks constantly, and when Melanie, of Espanola, Ontario, asked him what the new baby should be named, Evan responded with Car and Truck—with an emphasis on the "and." Although she wondered if her little son was having premonitions about twins, Melanie quickly found out that she was pregnant with only one baby, a boy. She and her husband couldn't agree on a name throughout the pregnancy, though they did toss around the names Lincoln, Adrian and Tanner. When their second son was born, Melanie again asked Evan what his new brother should be named. Evan responded, having apparently been listening to his parents more than they realized, with Lincoln. And, with that, Lincoln was brought forward as a frontrunner, but not until Melanie's husband did extensive research on any association with Lincoln he could find. Once he was satisfied that the name was free of any negative meaning, Lincoln Tanner was officially named.

8. Balance the lengths of the first and last names. Pair a long last name with a short first name or a short last name with a long first name. You'll know when you've found the right combination. And, once you find the right combination for the name of one gender of baby, pick one that's appropriate for the opposite sex. You never know. Lastly, even though it can cause battles of epic proportions, be sure that you and your spouse agree on the name!

Terri, from Hamilton, Ontario, has two boys—Michael and Daniel. When pregnant with Michael, Terri's husband was convinced the two of them were going to have a girl—and had Terri so convinced that they already had a name picked out, Sarah Marie. One day, Terri's husband came home with a pink shirt emblazoned with the name "Sarah" in blue letters. The shirt also sported a blue arrow pointing down to Terri's growing belly. She didn't wear the shirt much, because she didn't want to jinx anything. When their "girl" was born, of course, it wasn't a girl at all but a bouncing baby boy—for whom they had no name. Terri quickly decided she wanted their son's middle name to be her maiden name, Allan, but as for the first name, Terri and her husband were at a loss. They tried Jeffrey on the first day, but it didn't seem to fit, so the second day they tried Steven. That wasn't right, either. On the third day, they tried Michael and found a name that was just right.

As for Michael's older brother, Daniel, Terri says it was her favourite name of all time and thinks it might have had some-thing to do with her love for the Elton John song "Daniel," which was popular during her teenage years. Daniel's middle name, George, is also his father's, grandfather's and great-grandfather's name.

Although Melissa, of Hamilton, Ontario, was only a child when her younger brother was born, she has never forgotten the story of how he got his name. Melissa comes from a family with three children, and, though her mother was in charge of naming the first and second children, her father was given the duty of naming the third. He came up with Wade, a name that Melissa's mother tried out for a few days but then changed to Brandon. Although Brandon is the name on his birth certificate, hospital records still have his name on file as Wade.

9. Avoid choosing first names that end with a vowel or consonant that is the same as your baby's last name. These can sound nursery-rhyme-ish and gimmicky. They can also be mouthfuls to say. For example:

Miriam McGee, Ella Ecker, Gary Gilbert. It doesn't take much to imagine these names in a Dr. Seuss–type story.

10. Possible nicknames should also be considered in your thought process. My mom hated the idea of anyone making up nicknames or shortened versions of my or my brother's name, so she picked Carla and Darcy. Nevertheless, "Car" was attached to me semi-regularly, and my brother was sometimes called "Darce." So, although my mom didn't completely succeed, she did a pretty good job with her choices, because neither of those nicknames stuck. When you choose a name, go through all the nicknames and rhyming words you can associate with it—and really think about it, no holds barred, because kids can come up with some pretty nasty insults. As you will see from the following stories, parents can find it truly challenging to find a nickname-free name.

 Sometimes children impose their own nicknames on themselves, much to their parents' chagrin. Susie, from Toronto, Ontario, discarded her mother's much-preferred Susanne in favour of Susie in kindergarten. Susie is still the way most people in Susie's life—except for her mom, of course—refer to her!

 In another case of a self-declared nickname, Alex, from Ottawa, Ontario, was originally named Sandy by his mother, who absolutely loved the name as it was. Soon after high school, Sandy decided enough was enough and opted to go by Alex instead, a short form of Alexander, which is the long form, of course, of Sandy. His

mother's beloved name has been left in the dust; after years of solid determination, Alex is now known by his preferred moniker.

Joanne, from Edmonton, Alberta, is known by this name by almost everyone in her life, but her real name is actually Giovanna. Joanne or Joanna are the names she has always answered to—simply because that's what everyone called her. She said that she once looked up Giovanna in an "exotic" baby-names book and discovered that the short form of her name was Jean. When she read that, she was happy that Joanne was the name that stuck.

11. Finally, if you haven't already told people what you're going to name your baby—don't. You will be part of the smug 71 percent of parents-to-be who stay mum on the subject. Think about it. Do you really want everyone you know weighing in on your choice? Screeches of "Whaaaaaaat?!" from your family? Awkward nods from friends? Not worth it! At least when your baby is born, people will be less inclined to put down your chosen name, because now this little person is "real" and just so cute! How can you not love little Zebulon Elvis Xavier?

Shelley, a classmate from my hometown of Espanola, Ontario, told me her mother originally wanted to name her Carly because Shelley's father's name is Carl. However, Shelley's paternal grandmother, of Ukrainian heritage, didn't think Carly was a proper Ukrainian name. So, even though Shelley is an Anglo-Saxon name, everyone approved and a new Shelley was born.

At the end of the day, no one can tell you how and what to name your baby, but consider the advice given in these chapters. I hope you're feeling inspired. But if you are still struggling, I will leave you with one last story from a real Canadian and some baby names worksheets (see page 334) to help you sort through your name choices and your partner's choices. And don't worry—the worksheets provide space to veto, if necessary.

If you're still wondering how other expectant Canadian parents choose names, here is an example from Sandra, of Montague, Prince Edward Island, who has four children:

When naming her first child, Mia, Sandra's foremost thought was the literal meaning of the name. Mia, which means "mine" in Italian, convinced her that she made the right choice for her first daughter. With Mia, Sandra also started the tradition of giving her children middle names with personal meaning, and Mia's is Karen, Sandra's sister's name.

Sandra's close second choice for Mia was Lily, so when Sandra knew she was going to have another girl, there was no question that her next daughter would have this "gentle and sweet" name. Lily's middle name is Therese, for her paternal grandmother.

Looking for inspiration for a boy's name during her third pregnancy, Sandra flipped through an old book about soldiers who had died or been declared missing in action. She stopped when she came to the name Benjamin MacNeill, thinking it was a good, solid boy's name—and, as a plus, there weren't many children around with the name at the time. And so, when her son was born, Ben he was. Ben's middle name is John, for his father.

Last but not least, Sandra's third daughter and fourth child, Kimberly, was named for Sandra's close friend, Kim, who died of cancer around the time Lily was born. Sandra knew that if she had another daughter, Kim's name would live on with her. Kimberly's middle name, fittingly, is Sandra.

How to Use the Baby Names Lists

The following baby names lists should give you plenty of options to choose from for your baby. Just remember to research all the meanings associated with your chosen name. A name, or a variation of it, can have very different meanings in different countries and cultures.

For names with variations—If a name has variations listed, the definition for that name and its variants accompanies the first listing only. In some cases, a name's meaning is culturally consistent with its variants; in others, it is not. I wish you luck in discovering a name with the right sense of meaning—literally—that reflects the ideal choice for you and your baby.

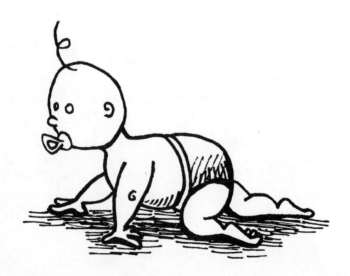

Baby Names Lists

Top 10 Names
by Province

~ Alberta ~

Rank	Girls	Boys
1	Sarah/Sara	Ethan
2	Ava	Joshua
3	Emma	Jacob
4	Emily	Logan
5	Hannah	Aidan/Aiden
6	Madison	Matthew
7	Abigail	Noah
8	Kaitlyn/Katelyn	Nathan
9	Olivia	Liam
10	Grace	Carter

~ British Columbia ~

Rank	Girls	Boys
1	Emma	Ethan
2	Emily	Aidan/Aiden
3	Ava	Jacob
4	Sara/Sarah	Matthew
5	Sofia/Sophia	Joshua
6	Olivia	Nathan
7	Hannah	Liam
8	Ella	Benjamin
9	Isabella	Ryan
10	Madison	Logan

~~~ Manitoba ~~~

Rank	Girls	Boys
1	Emily	Ethan
2	Emma	Matthew
3	Madison	Joshua
4	Hannah	Noah
5	Sarah	Logan
6	Abigail	Dylan
7	Jessica	Alexander
8	Hailey/Haley	Tyler
9	Paige	Nathan
10	Olivia	Ryan

~~~ New Brunswick ~~~

Rank	Girls	Boys
1	Emma	Jacob
2	Olivia	Alexandre/Alexander
3	Emilie/Emily	Ethan
4	Madison	Samuel
5	Sarah/Sara	Noah
6	Chloe	Mathieu/Matthew
7	Abigail	Logan
8	Hannah	Benjamin
9	Hailey/Haley	Caleb/Kaleb
10	Isabel/Isabelle	Nicholas

—∾— Newfoundland —∾—

Rank	Girls	Boys
1	Sarah/Sara	Ethan
2	Emma	Nathan
3	Madison	Jacob
4	Chloe	Noah
5	Hailey/Haley	Ryan
6	Jenna	Joshua
7	Emily	Matthew
8	Riley	Logan
9	Abigail	Alexander
10	Brooklyn	Evan

—∾— Nova Scotia —∾—

Rank	Girls	Boys
1	Emma	Aiden/Aiden
2	Madison	Ryan
3	Ava	Ethan
4	Olivia	Jacob
5	Sarah/Sara	Noah
6	Hannah	Liam
7	Emily	Owen
8	Abigail	Alexander
9	Ella	Matthew
10	Chloe	Jack

–ᴚ– Ontario –ᴚ–

Rank	Girls	Boys
1	Emma	Matthew
2	Emily	Ethan
3	Sarah/Sara	Joshua
4	Olivia	Jacob
5	Madison	Ryan
6	Hannah	Nicholas
7	Julia	Michael
8	Jessica	Alexander
9	Lauren	Daniel
10	Abigail	Benjamin

–ᴚ– Prince Edward Island –ᴚ–

Rank	Girls	Boys
1	Emma	Connor
2	Emily	William
3	Madison	Ethan
4	Ella	Landon
5	Anna	Alexander
6	Ava	Cameron
7	Hannah	Carson
8	Chloe	Carter
9	Maggie	Evan
10	Taylor	Nathan

~~ Quebec ~~

Rank	Girls	Boys
1	Lea	William
2	Oceane/Oceanne	Samuel
3	Sarah/Sara	Matis/Mathis/Mathys
4	Jade	Zachary/Zackary
5	Megan/Megane	Alexis
6	Rosalie	Jeremie/Jeremy
7	Florence	Nathan
8	Laurie	Thomas
9	Anabelle/Annabelle	Antoine
10	Emy/Emmy	Gabriel

~~ Saskatchewan ~~

Rank	Girls	Boys
1	Ava	Ethan
2	Madison	Noah
3	Emma	Owen
4	Emily	Carter
5	Brooklyn	Logan
6	Hannah	Joshua
7	Hailey/Haley	Jacob
8	Chloe	Aiden
9	Olivia	Austin
10	Paige	Nathan

～ Yukon ～

Rank	Girls	Boys
1	Emily	Logan
2	Hannah	Ethan
3	Emma	Andrew
4	Madison	Daniel
5	Olivia	James
6	Alyssa	Joshua
7	Sarah	Tristan
8	Brooke	Cameron
9	Jessica	Jacob
10	Morgan	Adam

Top 25 Names in Canada & the U.S.

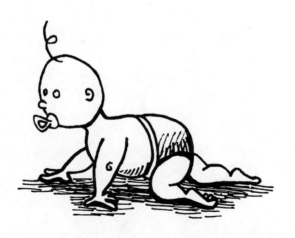

⚬⚬⚬ Top Boys Names ⚬⚬⚬

Rank	Boys Names in Canada
1	Matthew
2	Jacob
3	Ethan
4	Alexander
5	Nathan
6	William
7	Nicolas
8	Joshua
9	Zack
10	Samuel
11	Ryan
12	Noah
13	Benjamin
14	Michael
15	Justin
16	Aidan
17	Tomas
18	Liam
19	Lucas
20	Daniel
21	Owen
22	Logan
23	Dillan
24	Anthony
25	Adam

~~ Top Boys Names ~~

Rank	Boys Names in the U.S.
1	Jacob
2	Michael
3	Ethan
4	Joshua
5	Daniel
6	Christopher
7	Anthony
8	William
9	Matthew
10	Andrew
11	Alexander
12	David
13	Joseph
14	Noah
15	James
16	Ryan
17	Logan
18	Jayden
19	John
20	Nicholas
21	Tyler
22	Christian
23	Jonathan
24	Nathan
25	Samuel

~ Top Girls Names ~

Rank	Girls Names in Canada
1	Emma
2	Emily
3	Sarah
4	Olivia
5	Madison
6	Hannah
7	Megan
8	Abigail
9	Chloe
10	Hailee/Haley
11	Jessica
12	Julia
13	Grace
14	Sophia
15	Isabella
16	Maya
17	Lauren
18	Elisabeth
19	Victoria
20	Rachel
21	Samantha
22	Kaitlin
23	Ava
24	Alissa
25	Lea

⚬ Top Girls Names ⚬

Rank	Girls Names in the U.S.
1	Emily
2	Isabella
3	Emma
4	Ava
5	Madison
6	Sophia
7	Olivia
8	Abigail
9	Hannah
10	Elizabeth
11	Addison
12	Samantha
13	Ashley
14	Alyssa
15	Mia
16	Chloe
17	Natalie
18	Sarah
19	Alexis
20	Grace
21	Ella
22	Brianna
23	Hailey
24	Taylor
25	Anna

Top 10 Names by Decade

~~ 1900 ~~

Rank	Girls	Boys
1	Mary	John
2	Helen	William
3	Margaret	James
4	Anna	George
5	Ruth	Joseph
6	Elizabeth	Charles
7	Dorothy	Robert
8	Marie	Frank
9	Mildred	Edward
10	Alice	Henry

~~ 1910 ~~

Rank	Girls	Boys
1	Mary	John
2	Helen	William
3	Dorothy	James
4	Margaret	Robert
5	Ruth	Joseph
6	Mildred	George
7	Anna	Charles
8	Elizabeth	Edward
9	Frances	Frank
10	Marie	Walter

1920

Rank	Girls	Boys
1	Mary	Robert
2	Dorothy	John
3	Helen	James
4	Betty	William
5	Margaret	Charles
6	Ruth	George
7	Virginia	Joseph
8	Doris	Richard
9	Mildred	Edward
10	Elizabeth	Donald

1930

Rank	Girls	Boys
1	Mary	Robert
2	Betty	James
3	Barbara	John
4	Shirley	William
5	Patricia	Richard
6	Dorothy	Charles
7	Joan	Donald
8	Margaret	George
9	Nancy	Thomas
10	Helen	Joseph

-⚬- 1940 -⚬-

Rank	Girls	Boys
1	Mary	James
2	Linda	Robert
3	Barbara	John
4	Patricia	Willam
5	Carol	Richard
6	Sandra	David
7	Nancy	Charles
8	Judith	Thomas
9	Sharon	Michael
10	Susan	Ronald

-⚬- 1950 -⚬-

Rank	Girls	Boys
1	Mary	Michael
2	Linda	James
3	Patricia	Robert
4	Susan	John
5	Deborah	David
6	Barbara	William
7	Debra	Richard
8	Karen	Thomas
9	Nancy	Mark
10	Donna	Charles

～ 1960 ～

Rank	Girls	Boys
1	Lisa	Michael
2	Mary	David
3	Karen	John
4	Susan	James
5	Kimberly	Robert
6	Patricia	Mark
7	Linda	William
8	Donna	Richard
9	Michelle	Thomas
10	Cynthia	Jeffrey

～ 1970 ～

Rank	Girls	Boys
1	Jennifer	Michael
2	Amy	Christopher
3	Melissa	Jason
4	Michelle	David
5	Kimberly	James
6	Lisa	John
7	Angela	Robert
8	Heather	Brian
9	Stephanie	William
10	Jessica	Matthew

—ᴡ— 1980 —ᴡ—

Rank	Girls	Boys
1	Jessica	Michael
2	Jennifer	Christopher
3	Amanda	Matthew
4	Ashley	Joshua
5	Sarah	David
6	Stephanie	Daniel
7	Melissa	James
8	Nicole	Robert
9	Elizabeth	John
10	Heather	Joseph

—ᴡ— 1990 —ᴡ—

Rank	Girls	Boys
1	Ashley	Michael
2	Jessica	Christopher
3	Emily	Matthew
4	Sarah	Joshua
5	Samantha	Jacob
6	Brittany	Andrew
7	Amanda	Daniel
8	Elizabeth	Nicholas
9	Taylor	Tyler
10	Megan	Joseph

Fun Baby Names

-∽- Palindromes -∽-

Rank	Name	Gender
1	Anna	Girl
2	Hannah	Girl
3	Ava	Girl
4	Elle	Girl
5	Ada	Girl
6	Reidier	Boy
7	Otto	Boy
8	Bob	Boy
9	Eve	Girl
10	Aja	Girl

-∽- Fictional Literature -∽-

Rank	Boy's Name	Book
1	Jay Gatsby	*The Great Gatsby,* 1925
2	Holden Caulfield	*The Catcher in the Rye,* 1951
3	Humbert Humbert	*Lolita,* 1955
4	Leopold Bloom	*Ulysses,* 1922
5	Sherlock Holmes	*Hound of the Baskervilles,* 1902
6	Gregor Samsa	*The Metamorphosis,* 1915
7	Ignatius Reilly	*A Confederacy of Dunces,* 1980
8	George Smiley	*Tinker, Tailor, Soldier, Spy,* 1974
9	Scout Finch	*To Kill a Mockingbird,* 1960
10	Philip Marlowe	*The Big Sleep,* 1939

~ Fictional Literature ~

Rank	Girl's Name	Book
1	Molly Boom	*Ulysses,* 1922
2	Lily Bart	*The House of Mirth,* 1905
3	Holly Golightly	*Breakfast at Tiffany's,* 1958
4	Lolita	*Lolita,* 1955
5	Clarissa Dalloway	*Mrs. Dalloway,* 1925
6	Scarlett O'Hara	*Gone With the Wind,* 1936
7	Hazel Motes	*Wise Blood,* 1952
8	Jean Brodie	*The Prime of Miss Jean Brodie,* 1961
9	Sula Peace	*Sula,* 1973
10	Phoebe Caulfield	*The Catcher in the Rye,* 1951

~ Herbs & Spices ~

Rank	Name	Gender
1	Vera (Aloe)	Girl
2	Angelica	Girl
3	Rosemary	Girl
4	Ginger	Girl
5	Ambrosia	Girl
6	Sage	Girl or Boy
7	Basil	Boy
8	Herb	Boy
9	Juniper	Girl
10	Lavender	Girl

~~ Hockey Draft Picks ~~

Year	Name	Team
2008	Steve Stamkos	Tampa Bay Lightning
2007	Patrick Kane	Chicago Blackhawks
2006	Erik Johnson	St. Louis Blues
2005	Sidney Crosby	Pittsburgh Penguins
2004	Alexander Ovechkin	Washington Capitals
2003	Marc-Andre Fleury	Pittsburgh Penguins
2002	Rick Nash	Columbus Blue Jackets
2001	Ilya Kovalchuk	Atlanta Thrashers
2000	Rick DiPietro	New York Islanders
1999	Patrik Stefan	Atlanta Thrashers

~~ Miss Canada ~~

Year	Name	Region of Representation
1992	Nicole Dunsdon	BC Interior
1991	Leslie McLaren	Edmonton, AB
1990	Robin Lee Ouzunoff	Niagara Region, ON
1989	Juliette Powell	Laurentians Region, PQ
1988	Melinda Gillies	London, ON
1987	Tina May Simpson	Niagara Region, ON
1986	Rene Newhouse	BC Interior
1985	Karen Elizabeth Tilley	Calgary, AB
1984	Cynthia Kereluk	Edmonton, AB
1983	Jodi Yvonne Rutledge	Manitoba

-᠅- Girl Songs -᠅-

Rank	Name	Song and Artist
1	Mary	Proud Mary (Creedence Clearwater Revival)
2	Barbara	Barbara Ann (The Beach Boys)
3	Amanda	Amanda (Boston)
4	Donna	Oh Donna (Richie Valens)
5	Laura	Think of Laura (Christopher Cross)
6	Sara	Sara (Fleetwood Mac)
7	Jane	Jane (Jefferson Starship)
8	Paula	Hey Paula (Paul and Paula)
9	Sherrie	Oh Sherrie (Steve Perry)
10	Maggie	Maggie May (Rod Stewart)

-᠅- Boy Songs -᠅-

Rank	Name	Song and Artist
1	Daniel	Daniel (Elton John)
2	Brian	Brian Wilson (Barenaked Ladies)
3	Joe	Hey Joe (Jimi Hendrix)
4	Jeremy	Jeremy (Pearl Jam)
5	Tom	Tom's Diner (Suzanne Vega)
6	Bennie	Bennie and the Jets (Elton John)
7	Buddy	Buddy Holly (Weezer)
8	Louie	Louie Louie (The Kingsmen)
9	Mickey	Hey Mickey (Toni Basil)
10	Jude	Hey Jude (The Beatles)

GIRLS NAMES

A

Name	Origin	Definition
Aaliyah	*Hebrew*	High exalted
Aayesha	*Arabic*	The prophet Muhammad's wife
Aba	*African*	Bright
Abagail, Abbe, Abbey, Abigail, Abihail	*Latin*	A father's joy
Abaigael, Abaigeal, Abegayle, Abhy, Abichail	*Hebrew*	Bringer of joy
Abarrane	*Hebrew*	Father of many
Abba	*African*	Clever
Abella	*French*	Breath
Abena, Abina	*African*	Female born on a Tuesday
Abey	*Native American*	Leaf
Abha	*Indian*	Lustrous beauty
Abhaya	*Indian*	Fearless
Abia	*Arabic*	The Lord is my father
Abiona	*African*	Born on a journey
Abira	*Hebrew*	Strong
Abra	*Hebrew*	Lesson
Abril	*Spanish*	April, spring
Acacia, Acantha, Acatia, Acazia	*Greek*	Thorny
Acelin	*Teutonic*	Noble
Achal, Achala	*Indian*	Steady

Name	Origin	Definition
Achan	*African*	Female child in the first pair of twins
Achazia	*Hebrew*	The Lord holds
Achen	*African*	A twin
Achlys	*Greek*	Mist, darknesss
Ada, Adah	*Teutonic*	Happy
Adailia, Adaleee	*Hebrew*	Noble kind
Adaira, Adairia	*Scottish*	From the oak-tree ford
Adalene, Adalyn, Adelynn, Adilene	*French*	Good humour
Adali, Adalia, Adalicia, Adalie, Adaliz	*German*	Noble
Adamina	*Hebrew*	Daughter of the Earth
Adana	*Spanish*	Created by God
Adanna	*African*	Father's daughter
Adara	*Latin*	Beauty
Addi, Addie	*Hebrew*	Created by God
Addisyn	*Hebrew*	Joyful, kind
Adela	*Teutonic*	Good humour
Adelaide, Adele	*French*	Adorned
Adelia, Adelina, Adelisa, Adelise	*French*	Noble
Adena, Adenna, Adinah, Adinna	*Hebrew*	Delicate, sensual
Adette	*German*	Noble, sweet
Adia	*English*	Wealthy
Adine	*Hebrew*	Tender

Name	Origin	Definition
Adira	*Arabic*	Strong
Adiva	*Arabic*	Pleasant
Adolpha	*German*	Noble hero
Adona, Adonna, Adonne	*Hebrew*	A lady
Adoncia	*Spanish*	Sweet
Adonia	*Spanish*	Beautiful
Adora	*French*	Beloved one
Adrea, Adreena, Adri, Adria, Adriana, Adrianne	*Latin*	Dark one
Ady	*Hebrew*	Noble kind
Aedre	*Anglo-Saxon*	Stream
Aefre	*Anglo-Saxon*	Forever
Aeldra	*English*	Noble
Aelfwine, Aethelwyne	*English*	Friend of the elves
Aerlene, Aeryn	*Anglo-Saxon*	Elfin
Afrodite	*Greek*	Goddess of love
Afton	*English*	River name
Agacia, Agdta	*Spanish*	Kind
Agape	*Greek*	Love of the next
Agata, Agate, Agatha, Agathe, Aggie, Aggy	*Irish*	Good, kind
Aghna	*Irish*	Pure, innocent
Agnes	*Spanish*	Chaste
Ahava, Ahuda, Ahuva	*Hebrew*	Dearly loved
Ai, Aiko	*Japanese*	Love
Aida, Aidia	*French*	Help

Name	Origin	Definition
Aiesha, Aisha	*Arabic*	Woman
Aife	*Celtic*	Great warrior woman
Aila	*Scottish*	From the strong fortress
Aileen, Aileene	*Irish*	Giver of life
Ailey, Aili, Ailia	*Irish*	Light
Ailisa, Ailise	*Irish*	Noble
Allison	*Irish*	Honest
Ailsa, Ailsie	*Hebrew*	Devoted to God
Ailse	*German*	Sweet
Aimee, Aimelin	*Latin*	Beloved
Aina, Aine	*African*	Joy
Aingeal	*Irish*	Angel
Ainslee, Ainsley, Ainsly	*Scottish*	My meadow
Airleas	*Irish*	Oath
Airlia	*Greek*	Ethereal
Aislin, Aisling	*Irish*	Vision
Aissa	*African*	Grateful
Aithne	*Celtic*	Fire
Aiya	*Hebrew*	Bird
Aja	*African*	High priestess of Mecca
Ajala	*Indian*	The Earth
Ajana	*Native American*	Eternal bloom
Akako	*Japanese*	Red
Akala	*Australian Aboriginal*	A parrot
Akhila	*Indian*	Complete

Name	Origin	Definition
Akiha, Akiva	*Hebrew*	Protected
Akilah	*Arabic*	Wise
Akilina	*Latin*	Eagle
Akina	*Japanese*	Spring flower
Akira	*Scottish*	Anchor
Akua	*African*	Female born on a Wednesday
Alaina, Alana, Alani, Alanna, Alannah, Alayna	*Irish*	Dear child
Alala	*Greek*	War goddess
Alandra	*Spanish*	Protector of mankind
Alarica, Alarice	*German*	Rules all
Alastrina, Alastrine, Alastriona	*Celtic*	Protector of mankind
Alavda	*French*	Fun
Alberta, Alberteen, Albertyne	*English*	Noble
Alcina	*Greek*	Strong-minded
Alda	*Spanish*	Long-lived
Aldea	*Teutonic*	Rich
Aldene	*Spanish*	Wise
Aldis, Aldys	*English*	From the old house
Aldora	*English*	Noble
Alea, Aleah, Aleaseya, Aleeya, Alia, Aliya, Aliyah	*Hebrew*	Exalted
Aleda	*English*	Ancient
Aleece	*Spanish*	Of the nobility

Name	Origin	Definition
Aleen, Aleena, Alena, Alene, Allena, Allene	*Celtic*	Good-looking
Aleeza	*Hebrew*	Joyous
Alegria	*Spanish*	Merry
Alejandra	*Spanish*	Protector of mankind
Aleka, Aleksey, Alesandra, Alex, Alexa, Alexavia, Alexis	*Greek*	Protector of mankind
Alessa, Alison, Alissa	*German*	Noble, truth
Aleta	*English*	Winged
Alethea	*Greek*	Truthful one
Aletta, Alette, Alidia, Allida, Allidia	*Latin*	Small, winged one
Algoma	*Native American*	Valley of flowers
Alhertine	*French*	Bright
Alice, Alicia, Alisha, Alyce, Alyssa, Alika, Aliki	*German*	Noble, truth
Alima	*Arabic*	Learned
Alina	*Irish*	Beautiful
Alisa, Alise	*Spanish*	Noble, truth
Alita	*English*	Winged
Aliz	*Hungarian*	Kind
Aliza, Alizah	*Hebrew*	Joyous
Alkira	*Australian Aboriginal*	The sky
Allaire, Alleffra	*French*	Cheerful
Allaryce	*English*	Noble ruler
Allegra, Allston	*Latin*	Brisk, cheerful

Name	Origin	Definition
Alley	*Greek*	Protector of mankind
Alli, Allie, Ally	*Gaelic*	Beautiful
Allison, Allyson, Alseia	*French*	Noble, truth
Allora	*Australian Aboriginal*	The place of the swamp
Allura, Alura, Alurea	*English*	Divine counsellor
Allyce	*Spanish*	Of the nobility
Allyn, Alyn	*Irish*	Beautiful
Almaye, Almira	*Arabic*	Princess
Alodie	*Anglo-Saxon*	Rich, wealthy
Aloise, Aloysia	*Spanish*	Famous in battle
Alpina	*Scottish*	Blond
Alsatia	*French*	From Alsace
Altaira	*Arabic*	Bird
Altha, Althia	*English*	Healer
Alva, Alvara, Alavarie	*German*	Army of elves
Alvera	*Spanish*	Speaker of truth
Alvy	*Irish*	Olive
Amada	*Spanish*	Beloved
Amadis	*Latin*	Love of God
Amal	*Arabic*	Clean, pure
Amalia	*Spanish*	Industrious, striving
Amanda, Amandine	*English*	Precious thing
Amani	*African*	Peace
Amara	*German*	Paradise
Amarande	*German*	Eternal, immortal
Amaris	*English*	Child of the Moon
Amaris, Amarisa	*Hebrew*	Given by God

Name	Origin	Definition
Amata	*French*	Beloved
Amber, Amberlee, Amberly, Amberlyn, Ambria, Ambra, Ambre	*English*	Precious jewel
Amedee	*French*	Loves God
Ameena, Ameenah, Amina	*Arabic*	Trustworthy
Ameerah, Amira, Amirah	*Arabic*	Princess
Ameilie, Amela	*Latin*	Beloved
Amelia	*Latin*	Industrious
Ames	*Latin*	Loves
Amethyst	*Greek*	Precious stone
Ami, Amia, Amie, Amy	*French*	Dearly loved
Amita	*Indian*	Limitless
Amity	*English*	Friend
Amora, Amory	*Spanish*	Love
An	*Chinese*	Peace
Ana, Analee, Analena, Anamarie	*Spanish*	Grace
Anabel, Anabelle, Anabeth	*Latin*	Lovable
Anais	*Hebrew*	Grace
Anastasia, Anastice	*Greek*	Resurrection
Anaya	*African*	Look up to God
Anca	*Hebrew*	Gracious
Ancelin	*French*	Handmaiden
Andeana	*Spanish*	Leaving

Name	Origin	Definition
Andee, Andena, Andera, Andie, Andrea, Andree	*English*	Courageous
Andra	*Greek*	Protector of mankind
Andraya	*Latin*	Trusted by God
Andreana	*Latin*	Womanly
Andromeda	*Greek*	Ruler of men
Ane	*Hebrew*	Prayer
Aneisha, Anessa, Anisha	*English*	Grace
Anemone	*Greek*	Breath
Aneta, Anetta, Aneya, Anita, Anitia	*Hebrew*	Grace
Ange, Angel, Angela, Angelica, Angelina, Angelique	*French*	Angel
Anica, Anika	*Spanish*	Grace
Anja	*Hebrew*	Gracious
Anjanette, Anjanique, Anjeanette	*English*	Gift of God's favour
Anju	*Indian*	One who lives in the heart
Anka	*Hebrew*	Night star, shining
Anna, Annabel, Annabella, Annalee, Annaliese, Anne	*Latin*	Grace
Annora, Annorah	*Hebrew*	Honour
Anoush	*Arabic*	Sweet
Anthea	*Greek*	Lady of flowers

Name	Origin	Definition
Antoinetta, Antoinette, Antonia	*Latin*	Flourishing, flower
Anushka, Anya	*Hebrew*	Gracious
Aphria	*Celtic*	Agreeable
Aphrodesia, Aphrodite	*Greek*	Goddess of love
Apollina, Apolline	*French*	Gift from Apollo
April, Aprille, Apryl	*English*	Blooming, open
Aquene	*Native American*	Peace
Aquilina	*Spanish*	Sharp-eyed
Ara	*Arabic*	Opinionated
Arabel, Arabella, Arabella	*German*	Beautiful eagle
Araxie	*Arabic*	River said to inspire poetic expression
Arcadia	*Spanish*	Adventurous
Arda, Ardelia, Ardyne, Ardys	*English*	Warm
Ardath	*Hebrew*	Flowering field
Arden, Ardena, Ardene	*English*	Lofty, eager
Ardith	*Anglo-Saxon*	Good war
Ardra	*Celtic*	Noble
Arella	*Hebrew*	Golden
Aretha	*Greek*	Nymph
Aria, Ariah	*English*	Beautiful melody
Ariadne, Ariana, Arianne, Arie	*Latin*	Melody
Arial, Ariel, Ariela, Aryel	*Hebrew*	Lioness of God
Ariette	*English*	Melody

Name	Origin	Definition
Arlyne, Arleen, Arlena, Arlene	*Irish*	Oath
Arla, Arlana, Arleana, Arleena, Arline	*English*	Strong woman
Arleigh, Arleine, Arlen, Arlyn	*German*	Pledge, vow
Arliss	*Irish*	Place name
Armina	*Latin*	Of a high degree
Aroha	*Maori*	Love
Artemis	*African*	Moon
Asa	*Hebrew*	Healer
Asha	*Arabic*	Lively
Ashe	*English*	Ash tree
Ashleah, Ashlee, Ashleigh, Ashley	*English*	Meadow of ash trees
Ashling	*English*	Vision
Ashten, Ashton, Ashtyn	*English*	Town of ash trees
Asia	*Arabic*	Woman
Aspasia	*Greek*	Welcome
Aspen	*English*	Place name
Asta, Astera, Astra, Astred, Astyr	*Greek*	Star
Atalia, Atalie, Athalia	*Hebrew*	God is great
Atara	*Hebrew*	Crowned
Atena, Athena, Athene	*Greek*	Goddess of wisdom
Atia	*Arabic*	Ancient
Atifa	*Arabic*	Affection
Aubine	*French*	Blond

Name	Origin	Definition
Aubree, Aubrey, Aubriana, Aubrie, Aubry	*French*	Rules with elf wisdom
Auda, Aude	*French*	Wealthy
Audelia, Audene, Audra, Audrey, Audriana, Audrina	*English*	Nobility, strength
Aurea, Aurelia, Aurelie	*Latin*	Gold
Aurora	*Latin*	Dawn
Austine	*French*	Exalted
Autumn	*English*	Autumn
Ava	*German*	Life
Avaline	*Celtic*	Lively
Avasa	*Indian*	Independent
Avena	*English*	Oats
Avera	*Hebrew*	Transgresses
Averil, Averyl, Avril	*English*	Born in April
Avery	*Anglo-Saxon*	Ruler of the elves
Avia	*Hebrew*	Spring time
Avianna	*English*	Grace
Avice	*French*	War-like
Avis	*English*	Refuge in battle
Aya	*Hebrew*	Bird
Ayala	*Hebrew*	Doe
Ayda	*Arabic*	Benefit
Ayeisha, Ayesha, Ayisha	*Arabic*	Woman, life
Ayla	*Hebrew*	Oak tree
Ayo	*African*	Joyful
Azalea, Azelia, Azhara	*Arabic*	Flower

Name	Origin	Definition
Azinza	*African*	Mermaid
Azrael	*Latin*	Free of material things
Azura, Azure, Azurine	*French*	Sky blue
Azy	*Arabic*	Precious

B

Name	Origin	Definition
Babette, Babs	*French*	Foreign, exotic
Bahati	*African*	Luck
Bahira	*Arabic*	Sparkling
Baibre	*Irish*	Strange
Bailee, Bailey, Bayley	*French*	Able
Baka	*Indian*	Crane
Bala	*Indian*	Young girl
Balinda	*African*	Patience, endurance
Bambi	*Italian*	Child
Banan, Baraka	*Arabic*	White
Bandhura	*Indian*	Pretty
Bar, Bari	*French*	Marksman
Bara	*Hebrew*	To choose
Barbarella, Barb, Barbara, Barbie	*Latin*	Strange, mysterious
Barika	*African*	Bloom
Barina	*Australian Aboriginal*	The summit
Basha	*Hebrew*	Daughter of God
Bashira	*Arabic*	Joyful

Name	Origin	Definition
Basia	*Hebrew*	Brave
Basya	*Hebrew*	Daughter of the oath
Bathilda, Bathilde	*German*	Heroine
Baxley	*English*	Baker
Bea, Beah, Beatirsa, Beatrice, Beatrix	*Latin*	Bringer of joy
Beate	*Latin*	Divinely blessed
Bebe	*French*	Baby
Becca, Becha, Becka, Becky, Bekki	*Hebrew*	Captivating
Bedelia	*French*	Strength
Bel, Bella, Belva	*French*	Beautiful
Belicia	*Spanish*	Devoted to God
Belinda, Belle, Belynda, Blinda	*Italian*	Beautiful woman
Bellanca	*Greek*	Stronghold
Bemadette, Berdine, Bernadette	*German*	Has the courage of a bear
Bena	*Native American*	Pheasant
Benita	*Spanish*	Blessed
Berdina	*German*	Glorious
Berenice, Bernice, Bernicia, Berry	*French*	One who brings victory
Berit, Berta, Bertha, Berthe	*Celtic*	Glorious
Beryl	*English*	Dazzling jewel
Bess, Betsy, Bette, Betty	*English*	God's oath
Beta	*Czech*	Devoted to God

Name	Origin	Definition
Beth	*English*	Lively
Betha	*Celtic*	Life
Bethanee, Bethany	*Hebrew*	House of God
Bettine	*French*	Devoted to God
Bev, Beverely	*English*	Meadow of beavers
Bevin	*Irish*	Lady with a sweet song
Bharati	*Indian*	Universal monarch
Bhavana	*Indian*	Sentiment
Bhavya	*Indian*	Grand, splendid
Bianca, Biancha	*English*	White
Bidelia, Bidina	*Irish*	Protective
Biene	*Latin*	Sabine woman
Billie, Billy	*Teutonic*	Resolute protector
Bina	*Indian*	Intelligent
Binda	*Australian Aboriginal*	Deep water
Birdie, Birdine	*Celtic*	Little bird
Birgit	*Celtic*	Strength
Birte	*Celtic*	Splendid
Blair, Blaire	*Scottish*	From the plain
Blanca, Blanche	*Italian*	White
Blanchefleur, Blancheflor	*French*	White flower
Blenda	*Teutonic*	Dazzling
Bliss, Blyss, Blysse	*Anglo-Saxon*	Happy
Blithe, Blythe	*English*	Joyful
Blossom	*English*	Lovely
Bluinse	*Irish*	White

Name	Origin	Definition
Bly	*Native American*	Tall
Blyana	*Irish*	Strong
Boadicea, Bodiccea, Bodicea	*Anglo-Saxon*	Victory
Bobbi, Bobbie	*English*	Bright
Bohdana	*Russian*	From God
Boni, Bonita, Bonnibelle, Bonnie, Bonny	*Scottish*	Sweet and good
Borgny	*Norwegian*	New
Bracha, Brachah	*Hebrew*	A blessing
Brandee, Brandelyn, Brandi, Brandy, Brandyn	*English*	Brandy
Brann	*Dutch*	Raven
Branwen, Branwyn	*Celtic*	Daughter of Llyr
Brea, Breanne, Bria, Briana, Brianne, Briannon, Brienne	*Irish*	Strong
Breck	*Irish*	Freckled
Bree	*Celtic*	Hill
Breen	*Irish*	Sadness
Breena	*Irish*	Fairy palace
Brenda, Brendolyn	*German*	Beacon on the hill
Brenna	*Celtic*	Dark-haired
Bret, Brett, Bretta, Brettany	*French*	From England
Bric, Brigg	*Celtic*	Swift

Name	Origin	Definition
Bridget, Bridgett, Bridgette, Brigetta, Bridhid	*Irish*	Resolute
Brie	*Celtic*	Resolute
Brier	*French*	Heather
Brigida, Brigidia	*Spanish*	Strong
Brina	*Irish*	Protector
Brione, Brioni, Briony, Bryony	*English*	Flowering vine
Brisa, Brisha, Brisia, Brissa, Briza	*Spanish*	Achilles' lover
Brit, Brita, Britany, Brite, Britney, Britt, Brittany, Brittyn	*Celtic*	From England
Brona	*Irish*	Sorrow
Bronwyn	*Welsh*	Fair breast
Brook, Brooke, Brooklyn	*English*	Lives by the stream
Brucie	*French*	Forest sprite
Bruna, Brune	*German*	Dark-haired
Brunhild, Brunhilde	*German*	Dark, noble
Bryana, Bryann	*Celtic*	Strong
Bryce	*Celtic*	Swift
Bryn, Brynn	*Welsh*	Coat
Buena	*Spanish*	Good
Buffy	*Hebrew*	God's oath
Bunny	*Greek*	One who brings victory
Burilda	*Australian Aboriginal*	Black swan

Name	Origin	Definition
Byrdene	*English*	Little bird
Bysen	*Anglo-Saxon*	Unique

⸺ C ⸺

Name	Origin	Definition
Caddie	*Greek*	Pure, innocent
Cadee, Cadence, Cadencia, Cady	*Irish*	Rhythmic flow of sounds
Caffara	*Irish*	Helmet
Cahira	*Irish*	Warrior
Cailin	*Irish*	Child
Caine	*Gaelic*	Warrior
Cait, Caitie, Caitlan, Caitlyn, Caitrin	*Irish*	Pure
Cala	*Arabic*	Castle
Calandra, Calandria	*Greek*	Fun
Calanthe	*French*	Beautiful flower
Cale	*Hebrew*	Brave
Caledonia	*Latin*	From Scotland
Caley	*Gaelic*	Slender
Calida	*Latin*	Warm, loving
Calinda, Calli, Calynda	*English*	Fun, beautiful woman
Calista, Call, Callee, Callia	*Greek*	Most beautiful
Calla	*German*	Chatter
Calliope	*Greek*	Beautiful voice
Caltha	*Latin*	Yellow flower

Name	Origin	Definition
Calvin, Calvyn	*Latin*	Bald
Calypso	*Greek*	Conceal
Cam, Camm	*English*	Crooked
Cambria	*English*	Wales
Camelia, Camella, Carmellia	*Latin*	Flower name
Cameron, Camyron	*Scottish*	Bent nose
Camila, Camilla	*French*	Attendant
Camile, Camillei, Cammi	*French*	Noble
Camira	*Australian Aboriginal*	Of the wind
Candace, Candi, Candice, Candis, Candys	*Greek*	Glowing, glittering
Candida	*Spanish*	Pure
Candra	*Latin*	Luminescent
Cane	*Gaelic*	Warrior
Capri	*Anglo-Saxon*	The goat
Caprice	*Italian*	Fanciful, unpredictable
Cara	*Celtic*	Beloved, dear
Caraid	*Irish*	Friend
Caralyn, Carilyn, Caro, Caroline, Carolyn	*English*	Strong
Caren, Carin, Caron, Caryn	*Greek*	Pure, innocent
Caressa, Caresse, Carressa	*French*	Tender touch
Carey	*Celtic*	Honest one

Name	Origin	Definition
Cari	*Greek*	Flows like water
Carina	*Italian*	Beloved
Carine	*French*	Friend
Carissa	*Greek*	Love, grace
Carla, Carletta, Carlita, Carlotta	*English*	Strong woman
Carleigh	*German*	Freeholder
Carlen	*Teutonic*	Woman
Carling	*English*	Hill where old women or witches gather
Carly	*German*	Melody, song
Carmela, Carmelina, Carmeline, Carmella	*Hebrew*	Golden
Carmelita, Carmelle, Carmen, Carmita	*Spanish*	Fruit garden
Carmya	*English*	Song
Carnation	*French*	Flesh-coloured
Carol, Carola, Carolina	*French*	Joy, song of happiness
Carree, Carrie	*English*	Joyful
Carrington	*Celtic*	Beautiful
Casandra, Cascadia, Cassandra, Cassie	*Spanish*	Protector of mankind
Casee, Casey, Caycee	*Irish*	Brave, watchful
Casidhe	*Irish*	Clever
Cassidy	*Irish*	Curly-haired
Casta	*Spanish*	Pure

Name	Origin	Definition
Cat, Catalina, Cate, Catelyn, Caterina, Catherine, Cathie, Cathleen, Catriona	*Greek*	Pure, innocent
Cavery	*Indian*	Name of a river
Cay, Caylah, Cayleigh	*Gaelic*	Party
Cearo	*Anglo-Saxon*	Sorrow
Cece, Cecilia, Cecile, Cecily, Celia, Celie	*Latin*	Blind
Cedra, Cedrina	*English*	Battle leader
Ceire	*Irish*	Saint
Celena, Celene	*Greek*	Moon
Celesse, Celeste, Celestia, Celestine	*French*	Heavenly
Cerdwin	*Celtic*	The mother goddess
Cerelia	*English*	Mistress, lady
Ceri, Ceria	*Spanish*	Proud
Cesara	*Spanish*	Long-haired
Chaitra	*Indian*	Aries sign
Chalina	*Spanish*	Rose
Chana	*Hebrew*	Graceful
Chandra	*Indian*	Moon
Chandrika	*Indian*	Moonlight
Chanel, Chanelle	*French*	Canal
Chantae, Chantal, Chantel, Chantrell	*French*	Singer
Charee, Cher, Chereen, Cherese, Cheri, Cherice	*French*	Beloved, darling
Charisma	*Greek*	Grace

Name	Origin	Definition
Charity	*Latin*	Goodwill, love
Charla, Charlee, Charlene, Charlotta, Charlotte	*English*	Strong
Charmain, Charmaine	*French*	Petite, feminine
Charo	*Spanish*	Beautiful
Charon	*Hebrew*	Princess
Chastity	*Latin*	Purity
Chatzie	*French*	Petite, feminine
Chava, Chaya	*Hebrew*	Life
Chavive	*Hebrew*	Dearly loved
Chelsee, Chelsey, Chelsy	*English*	Place name
Cherise, Cherish, Cheryl	*English*	Beloved, dear
Chesna	*Slavic*	Peaceful
Cheyanne, Cheyenne	*French*	Algonquian tribe
Chiara	*Irish*	Bright, shining
Chimalis	*Native American*	Bluebird
Chinara	*African*	May God receive
Chloe, Cloe	*Greek*	Blooming
Chloris	*German*	Pale
Cho	*Japanese*	Butterfly
Chris, Chrissa, Chrissy, Christa, Christabel, Christal, Christina	*Irish*	Follower of Christ
Chrisanne, Chrysann	*Spanish*	Shining, clear
Chriselda	*German*	Strong

Name	Origin	Definition
Ciaira	*Latin*	Famous
Ciara, Cierra	*Irish*	Saint's name
Cibil	*English*	Prophetess
Cidney, Cydnee, Cydney	*English*	From the city of St. Denis
Ciel	*Dutch*	Scholar
Cilla	*Latin*	From ancient times
Cimberleigh	*English*	From the royal meadow
Cinda, Cindel, Cindi, Cindy	*English*	Moon
Cinnia, Cinnie	*Celtic*	Beautiful
Cinzia	*Greek*	Moon
Cipriana	*Spanish*	From Cyprus
Cira, Ciri	*Spanish*	Lordly, proud
Circe	*Greek*	Seductive
Cirilla	*English*	Mistress, lady
Cissy	*Latin*	Blind
Claefer	*English*	Clover
Clair, Claire, Clara, Clare, Claressa, Claribel, Clarice, Clarissa, Clarisse	*French*	Bright, shining
Clarimonde	*German*	Brilliant protectress
Clarinda	*French*	Beautiful
Claudelle, Claudette, Claudia, Claudine	*English*	Lame
Clea, Cleo, Clio	*Greek*	Praise
Cleantha	*English*	Glory

Name	Origin	Definition
Clementina, Clementine	*French*	Mercy
Cleonie	*Irish*	Daughter of a river god
Cleva	*English*	From the cliff
Cliantha	*Greek*	Flower of glory
Cloris	*German*	Pale
Clothilde, Clotilde, Clover	*English*	Clover
Coco	*Spanish*	Help
Codi, Cody	*Irish*	Helpful
Coira	*Scottish*	Seething pool
Colby	*English*	Dark-skinned
Coleen, Colene, Colleen	*Irish*	Girl
Colette	*Greek*	People's victory
Columbia	*English*	Dove
Comfort	*French*	Strength
Comyna	*Irish*	Shrewd
Concepcion	*Spanish*	Fertile one
Connie, Constance, Constancia	*English*	Faithful
Consuela	*Spanish*	Consolation
Cora, Coralee, Coralie	*Scottish*	Maiden
Coral, Coraline	*English*	Coral
Cordelia, Cordy	*Latin*	Heart, a sea jewel
Coreen	*Irish*	The end of the hills
Coretta, Coriann, Corianne, Corisa	*Irish*	From the round hill
Corette	*French*	Little maiden

Name	Origin	Definition
Corey	*Irish*	From the court
Corin	*Greek*	Spear-bearer
Corina, Corinna, Corinne	*Greek*	Maiden
Cornelia	*Latin*	Horn
Cortney, Court, Courtney	*English*	From the court
Cosette	*French*	People's victory
Courtlyn	*French*	Courteous
Crescent	*French*	One who creates
Cressida	*Greek*	Gold
Crissa, Crissie, Cristie, Cristin	*Irish*	Follower of Christ
Csilla	*Hebrew*	Defender, guard
Cuyler	*Celtic*	Chapel
Cwen, Cwene	*English*	Queen
Cybele, Cybil, Cybill	*Latin*	Asiatic goddess
Cyla	*Latin*	From ancient times
Cym, Cyne	*English*	Ruler
Cymberly, Cynburleigh, Cyneburhleah	*English*	From the royal meadow
Cyna	*Gaelic*	Wise
Cynthia	*Greek*	Moon, Greek god
Cyprien	*French*	Cypriot
Cyrene	*Greek*	Name of a mytho-logical nymph
Cyrilla	*Greek*	Mistress, lady
Cytheria	*Latin*	Venus
Cyzarine	*Russian*	Royalty

D

Name	Origin	Definition
Dabria	*Latin*	Name of an angel
Dacey	*Gaelic*	Southerner
Dacia	*Latin*	From Dacia
Dae	*Korean*	Greatness
Dael, Dale, Dallen	*English*	Lives in the valley
Daelyn, Dalene	*English*	Small valley
Daena, Daina, Dana, Dayna	*English*	From Denmark
Daganya	*Hebrew*	Ceremonial grain
Dagna	*German*	A splendid day
Dagny	*Norwegian*	Brightness, new day
Dahlia, Dalia, Daliah, Daliyah, Dalis	*Hebrew*	To draw water
Dai	*Japanese*	Great
Daisey, Daisi, Daisie, Daisy	*English*	Flower name
Dakota	*Native American*	Friend
Dalena, Dalenna	*English*	Woman from Magdala
Dalila	*Spanish*	Desired
Dallas, Dallis	*Scottish*	The valley meadows
Daly	*English*	Adviser
Damalis, Damara	*Greek*	Gentle
Damia, Damiana, Damiane	*French*	Untamed
Damini	*Indian*	Lightning

Name	Origin	Definition
Damita	*Spanish*	Noble
Danae, Danele, Danelle, Danette, Dania	*Hebrew*	God is my judge
Danica	*Slavic*	Morning star
Daniella, Danielle, Danita	*Hebrew*	God is my judge
Danise	*English*	God will judge
Danna, Dannah, Dannia, Dany, Danya	*English*	God will judge
Daphna, Daphne, Daphnis	*Hebrew*	Victory
Dara, Darra	*Hebrew*	Small great one
Daracha	*Scottish*	From the oak
Darah	*Hebrew*	Wise
Daralis	*English*	Beloved
Darby	*Gaelic*	Without envy
Darcey, Darci, Darcia, Darcy, D'arcy	*Irish*	Dark
Dareen, Darice, Darissa	*Hebrew*	Wise
Daria	*Spanish*	Queen
Darika	*Indian*	Maiden
Darine	*Persian*	Queen
Darla, Darleane, Darleen, Darleena, Darlene	*Anglo-Saxon*	Darling
Darolyn	*English*	Dearly loved
Darri	*Australian Aboriginal*	A track
Dasha	*Greek*	Gift of God

Name	Origin	Definition
Davan, Daveen	*Hebrew*	Beloved one
Daveney	*French*	Place name
Davi, Davinia	*Hebrew*	Cherished
Davia, Davianna, Davida, Davina, Davita	*English*	Beloved one
Dawn, Dawna, Dawne, Dawnika	*English*	Dawn
Daya	*Indian*	Kindness, mercy
Dayla	*Hebrew*	Branch, bough
Deana, Deane, Deanne, Deena, Dena, Dene	*English*	Presiding official
Deanda, Deandra, Deandria, Deeana	*English*	Divine protector
Deb, Debbie, Debora, Debra	*Hebrew*	To speak kind words
Dechtire	*Celtic*	Mythical nursemaid
Dedre	*Irish*	Sorrowful
Dee, Deedee, Deedra, Deidra, Deirdra, Dierdre	*English*	Young girl, broken-hearted
Deepali	*Indian*	Collection of lamps
Deepika	*Indian*	Little light
Deepti	*Indian*	Glow, shine
Deiene, Deina	*Spanish*	Religious holiday
Deja, Dejah	*French*	Before
Delaine	*Gaelic*	From the elder-tree grove
Delaney	*Gaelic*	From the River Slaney

Name	Origin	Definition
Delbin, Delfina, Delphia	*Greek*	Dolphin
Delcine	*Spanish*	Sweet
Delia	*Celtic*	Sea jewel
Delice, Delicia, Delight, Delisa, Deliza	*English*	Gives pleasure
Delila, Delilah	*Hebrew*	Amorous, desired
Della	*Teutonic*	Bright, noble
Delmar, Delmara	*Spanish*	Of the sea
Delmy	*German*	Noble protector
Delora, Delores, Dolores	*English*	Lady of sorrows
Delphine	*French*	Thirteenth-century French saint
Demi	*English*	Mythological goddess of corn and harvest
Denby	*Swedish*	Home of the Danes
Deneise, Denice, Deniece, Denise	*Greek*	Of Dionysus
Denia, Denica, Denni	*English*	Divine valley
Denna	*Hebrew*	Judgment
Deona, Deondra, Deonna, Deone	*English*	Divine
Dereka, Derica, Dericka, Derrica	*English*	Gifted ruler
Derora	*Hebrew*	Free
Derry	*Irish*	Oak grove
Desarae	*French*	Desired one
Desdemona	*Greek*	Ill-fated, misery

Name	Origin	Definition
Desi, Desideria, Desirae, Desiree	*Latin*	So long hoped for
Desta	*African*	Happiness
Destanee, Destina, Destini, Destiny, Desyre	*French*	Mythological Greek god of fate
Desty	*Latin*	Modest
Deva	*Celtic*	Divine
Devan, Devin, Devon, Devyn, Devynn	*French*	Divine
Devaney, Devony	*Irish*	Dark-haired
Devera	*Spanish*	Task
Devery	*Hebrew*	Place name
Devi	*Hebrew*	Fighter of wrong
Devondra	*French*	Divine
Devora, Devorah, Devra	*Hebrew*	To speak kind words
Dhara	*Indian*	Constant flow
Dhatri	*Indian*	Earth
Di, Diahann, Diana, Diandra, Diane, Diannah	*French*	Divine
Dia	*Spanish*	Day
Diamanda, Diamond	*English*	Of high value, brilliant
Dianthe	*Greek*	Divine flower
Diella	*Latin*	Worships God
Diera	*Anglo-Saxon*	From Diera
Digna	*Spanish*	Worthy
Dillian	*Latin*	Worshipped one

Name	Origin	Definition
Dinah	Hebrew	Judgment
Diondra, Dione, Dionne	English	From the sacred spring
Dior	French	Golden
Dita	Spanish	Joyous
Divia, Divya	Indian	Divinely brilliant
Dixie	English	Powerful ruler
Dolce	Spanish	Sweet
Dolley, Dollie, Dolly	Greek	Gift of God
Domenica, Domenique, Dominique	Spanish	Of the Lord
Domina, Donna	Italian	A lady
Donata	Italian	Gift from God
Dora	Greek	Lady of sorrows
Dorcey	English	Dark
Doreen	French	Moody
Dori, Dory	Greek	Of the sea
Doria	Greek	Place name
Dorie	Greek	Place name
Doro, Dortha, Dot, Dottie	English	Gift of God
Dorota, Doroteia	Spanish	God's gift
Dorothy	Greek	Talented one
Dorsey	English	Tribe near the sea
Dreama	Greek	Joyous song
Dreena, Drina	Spanish	Protector of mankind
Drew	Greek	Wise
Drisana	Indian	Daughter of the Sun
Dru	French	Sturdy

Name	Origin	Definition
Dubhain	*Irish*	Dark
Duena	*Spanish*	Chaperon
Dulce, Dulcea, Dulcie, Dulcina	*Spanish*	Sweet
Dustee, Dusti, Dusty	*English*	Valiant fighter
Dyan, Dyana	*Latin*	Divine
Dymphna	*Gaelic*	Suitable one
Dyna	*Greek*	Powerful
Dyre	*Scandinavian*	Dear heart
Dysis	*Greek*	Sunset

⟶ E ⟵

Name	Origin	Definition
Eada, Edina	*English*	Wealthy
Eadlin	*Anglo-Saxon*	Princess
Eadwine	*English*	Wealthy friend
Eara, Earie	*Scottish*	From the East
Earlena, Earlene, Earlina	*English*	Noble woman
Earna	*English*	Eagle
Earnestine	*German*	Earnest
Earric	*English*	Powerful
Eartha	*German*	Worldly
Earwine, Earwyn, Erwyna	*English*	Friend of the sea
Easter, Eastre	*Anglo-Saxon*	Born at Easter
Eathelyn, Edlen, Edlin	*English*	Noble waterfall
Eavan	*Irish*	Fair

Name	Origin	Definition
Ebere	*African*	Mercy
Ebonie, Ebony	*English*	Dark beauty
Echo	*Greek*	A nymph
Eda, Edda	*English*	Rich
Edana	*Celtic*	Passionate
Edee	*English*	Spoils of war
Edeen, Edine	*Scottish*	From Edinburgh
Edelina, Edeline, Ediline	*English*	Gracious
Eden, Edenia, Edie	*Hebrew*	Delightful, pleasure
Edita, Edith, Editha, Edithe, Edyth, Edythe	*Anglo-Saxon*	Joyous
Edlyn, Edlynn, Edlynne	*Anglo-Saxon*	Princess
Edna	*Hebrew*	Fire
Edra, Edrea	*Hebrew*	Powerful
Edria	*Hebrew*	Mighty
Edris, Edrys	*Anglo-Saxon*	Wealthy ruler
Edwina, Edwinna, Edwynna	*German*	Rich in friendship
Eerin	*Australian Aboriginal*	A small, gray owl
Effie	*English*	Pretty in face
Eglantina, Eglantine	*French*	Wild rose
Eila, Eileen, Eileene, Eilena	*Irish*	Giver of life
Eilen	*Celtic*	Lively
Eilis	*Celtic*	God's oath
Eily	*Irish*	Light
Eirene	*Greek*	Peace

Name	Origin	Definition
Eirica	*Scottish*	Ruler
Eistir	*Irish*	Star
Eithne	*Irish*	Graceful
Ekaterina	*Greek*	Pure, innocent
Elaina, Elaine, Elayna, Elayne, Eleanor, Eleanora	*French*	Shining light
Elanora	*Australian Aboriginal*	A home by the sea
Elberte, Elbertine	*English*	Noble, glorious
Electra	*Greek*	Bright
Elena	*Russian*	Light
Eleora	*Hebrew*	God is light
Eleta	*French*	Chosen
Elethea, Elethia	*English*	Healer
Elfie	*English*	Good elf
Elia, Eliana, Eliane	*Hebrew*	Jehovah is God
Elicia	*French*	Devoted to God
Elida	*English*	Winged
Elie, Elin	*Greek*	Light
Elina	*Spanish*	Intelligent
Elinore	*French*	Light
Eliora	*Hebrew*	God is light
Elisa, Elisabet, Elizabeth, Elisavet, Elise, Elisha	*Spanish*	Devoted to God
Eliska	*Czech*	Truthful
Elita	*French*	Chosen
Elka, Elke	*Hebrew*	Oath to God

Name	Origin	Definition
Ella, Ellie	*English*	Beautiful fairy woman
Elle	*Hebrew*	Woman, girl
Ellee, Ellesse, Ellia, Elly	*English*	Shining light
Elleen, Ellene, Elynn	*Irish*	Most beautiful woman
Ellen, Ellyn	*English*	Courage
Ellette	*Anglo-Saxon*	Little elf
Ellice, Ellison, Ellyce, Elyce	*English*	Jehovah is God
Ellin	*Hebrew*	To move
Elodie	*Greek*	White blossom
Eloisa, Eloise	*German*	Warrior maiden
Elora	*Hebrew*	Crown of victory
Elouise	*French*	Intelligent
Elpeth, Elsbeth, Elsie, Elsje, Elspeth	*German*	God's oath
Elsa	*German*	God is bountiful
Else	*Hebrew*	Noble
Elsha	*Celtic*	Noble
Elswyth	*Anglo-Saxon*	Elf from the willow trees
Elthia	*English*	Healer
Elva, Elvia, Elvinia, Elvyne, Elvie	*Irish*	Elf
Elvera	*Spanish*	Close
Elwine, Elwyna	*Anglo-Saxon*	Friend of the elves
Elyn	*Hebrew*	Mercy
Elyse	*Spanish*	Devoted to God

Name	Origin	Definition
Elysia	*Hebrew*	Sweetly blissful
Elyta	*English*	Winged
Em, Emaline, Emelia, Emelie, Emelyn	*Latin*	Hardworking, eager
Ema	*German*	Serious
Emalia	*Latin*	Flirt
Emanuela, Emmanuella	*Hebrew*	Faith
Ember	*English*	Precious jewel
Emele	*Latin*	Beloved
Emerald, Emeraude, Esma, Esmaralda	*Spanish*	A bright green gem
Emery, Emory	*Latin*	Loving
Emesta, Emestine	*Spanish*	Serious
Emilia, Emelie	*Latin*	Flattering
Emily, Emma, Emmaline, Emmalyn, Emmy	*French*	Hardworking
Emlyn	*Welsh*	Place name
Emmie	*German*	Universal
Endora	*Hebrew*	Fountain
Engracia	*Spanish*	Graceful
Enid, Enyd	*English*	Quiet womam
Enola	*Native American*	Solitary
Enrica, Enriqua, Erica, Ericka, Erika, Eryka	*English*	Ever-powerful
Eny	*Irish*	Ardent
Enye	*Yiddish*	Grace
Eolande	*Greek*	Modest

Name	Origin	Definition
Eostre	*Anglo-Saxon*	Goddess of the dawn
Eranthe	*Greek*	Spring flower
Erea	*Celtic*	From Ireland
Erela, Erelah	*Hebrew*	Angel
Erendira, Erendiria	*Spanish*	Name of a princess
Erie	*Celtic*	From Ireland
Erin, Erina, Eryn, Erynn	*Irish*	From Ireland
Erith, Eritha	*Hebrew*	Flower
Erleen, Erlene, Erlina	*English*	Noble woman
Erling	*Scandinavian*	Descendant
Erskina	*Scottish*	From the top of the cliff
Eshe	*African*	Life
Esi	*African*	Born on Sunday
Esme, Esmee, Esmie	*Spanish*	Esteemed
Espen	*Scandinavian*	Bear god
Esperanza	*French*	Hope
Essie, Esta, Estee, Estel, Estella, Estelle, Esther	*Latin*	Star
Estephanie	*Spanish*	Crown, wreath
Etain	*Celtic*	Sparkling
Etania	*Native American*	Wealthy
Etel, Ethel	*Hebrew*	Noble
Etenia	*Native American*	Rich
Ethna	*Irish*	Graceful

Name	Origin	Definition
Ethne	*Celtic*	Fire
Etney	*Irish*	Little fire
Etsu	*Japanese*	Delight
Etta	*English*	Adorned
Etty	*English*	Rules her household
Eudocia	*Greek*	Esteemed
Eugenia, Eugenie	*French*	Born lucky
Euphrosyne	*Greek*	Joy
Eustacia	*Latin*	Tranquil
Ev, Eva, Evacsa, Eve, Evelyn, Evette, Evy	*Hebrew*	Life
Evadne	*Greek*	A water nymph
Evaline, Evalyn	*English*	Giver of life
Evangeline	*Greek*	Like an angel
Evanthe	*Greek*	Flower
Evia, Eviana	*Hebrew*	Living one
Evina	*Scottish*	Right-handed
Evon, Evonna, Evonne, Evony	*French*	Archer
Eyota	*Native American*	Great

 **F**

Name	Origin	Definition
Fabienne, Fabya	*French*	Bean grower
Fae, Fay, Faye, Fe, Fealty	*French*	Faithful
Fafelina, Fafelyna, Fafylena, Farfalla, Farfa	*Italian*	Butterfly

Name	Origin	Definition
Faiga	*German*	Bird
Faina	*Anglo-Saxon*	Joyous
Fainche	*Irish*	Free
Fairuza	*Arabic*	Turquoise
Faith, Faithe, Faythe	*English*	Faithful
Fala	*Native American*	Crow
Falana	*Greek*	Adoring
Faline, Fallon, Fallyn, Falon	*Irish*	In charge
Fana	*African*	Light
Fanchone	*French*	Free
Fanette	*French*	Crown of victory
Fanni, Fannia, Fannie, Fanny	*English*	Free
Fanta	*African*	Beautiful day
Fantina, Fantine	*French*	Child-like
Fara	*English*	Traveller
Farah, Farra	*English*	Beautiful
Faren, Farin, Farron, Farryn, Ferran	*English*	Adventurous
Farran	*Irish*	Baker
Farrin	*English*	The land
Fascienne	*Latin*	Black
Fatima, Fatma	*Arabic*	Captivating
Faun, Fauna, Faunia, Fawn	*French*	Young deer
Fausta, Faustina	*Spanish*	Lucky
Favel, Flavia	*Latin*	Blond, golden

Name	Origin	Definition
Favor	*French*	Approval
Fayette	*French*	Little fairy
Fayina	*Russian*	Free
Fayme	*French*	Famed
Fayre	*English*	Beautiful
Fearn, Fearne, Fern, Ferne	*English*	Leafy plant
Federica	*German*	Peaceful ruler
Fedora, Feodora	*Greek*	Gift of God
Felcia	*Polish*	Lucky
Felda	*German*	From the field
Felecia, Felice, Felicia, Felicienne, Felicity	*French*	Happy
Felipa, Felipe	*Greek*	Loves horses
Felisse, Felyce	*Latin*	Happy
Femi	*African*	Love me
Fenella, Finola, Fionnula, Fionnghuala	*Scottish*	Of the white shoulders
Fernly	*English*	Leafy plant
Feronia	*Latin*	Goddess of springs and woods
Fey	*French*	Fairy
Fia	*Italian*	Flame
Fianna	*Celtic*	Legendary tale
Fifi	*French*	God will multiply
Fifna, Fifne	*Hebrew*	He shall add
Finn	*Greek*	Oracle
Fiona, Fione, Fionn	*Irish*	Fair
Firtha	*Scottish*	Arm of the sea

Name	Origin	Definition
Flair	*English*	Style
Flanna	*Irish*	Red-haired
Fleta, Flyta	*English*	Swift
Fleur, Flora, Florence, Florencia, Floria, Floris, Flory	*French*	Blooming, flourishing
Fleurette	*French*	Little flower
Fontanne	*French*	Fountain
France, Francene, Frances, Francesca, Francia, Francine, Franki	*French*	Free
Freda, Freddi, Fredericka, Frieda, Friede	*German*	Peaceful ruler
Freia, Freja, Freya	*Norwegian*	Godess of love and seduction
Fuscienne	*Latin*	Black

～ G ～

Name	Origin	Definition
Gabbryela, Gabby, Gabriela, Gabrielle 	*Hebrew*	God is my strength
Gaea	*Greek*	Merry
Gaetana, Gaetane	*French*	From Gaete
Gaia	*Greek*	Goddess of the Earth
Gail, Gaila, Gale, Gayle, Gaylene	*English*	Joyful
Gaines	*English*	Increase in wealth

Name	Origin	Definition
Gaira, Garia	*Scottish*	Short
Galatee	*French*	White
Galea, Galena	*English*	Festive party
Galen	*English*	Calm
Galena	*Spanish*	Small, intelligent one
Galia	*Hebrew*	God is my strength
Galiana, Galiena	*German*	Haughty
Galice	*Hebrew*	Fountain
Galila, Gallia	*Hebrew*	God shall redeem
Galina	*Russian*	Most beautiful woman
Galla	*French*	From Gaul
Galya, Gavra, Gavrila	*Hebrew*	God is my strength
Gana	*Hebrew*	Garden
Garabina, Garabine, Garbina	*Spanish*	Purification
Gardenia	*English*	Flower
Garland	*French*	Crowned in victory
Gauri	*Indian*	Yellow
Gavenia, Gavina	*Scottish*	White hawk
Gelsey, Gelsy	*Persian*	Flower
Gemma	*French*	Jewel
Geneva, Geneve, Genevieve, Genivee	*French*	Of the race of women
Genna	*English*	White wave
Georgeanne, Georgette, Georgia, Georgie, Georgine, Giorgia	*Greek*	Farmer

Name	Origin	Definition
Geraldene, Geraldine, Geri	*Teutonic*	Rules by the spear
Germaine, Germana	*French*	From Germany
Geva	*Hebrew*	Hill
Gezana, Gezane	*Spanish*	Incarnation
Ghera	*Australian Aboriginal*	A gum leaf
Giacinta	*Italian*	Hyacinth flower
Gianina, Gianna	*Italian*	God is gracious
Gidget	*Celtic*	Resolute
Gila, Gilah, Gilana, Gilia	*Hebrew*	Eternal joy
Gilda	*Celtic*	Golden
Gillian	*Latin*	Youthful
Gina	*Latin*	Queenly
Ginessa	*Celtic*	White
Ginger	*Latin*	Liveliness
Ginia, Ginnette, Ginny	*Latin*	Chaste
Gioa	*English*	Joyful
Giovanna	*Hebrew*	God is gracious
Gipsy, Gypsy	*English*	Wandering tribe
Gisela, Gisella, Giselle	*German*	Pledge, oath
Gitana	*Spanish*	Gypsy
Giustina	*Latin*	Just, true
Giza	*Hebrew*	Cut stone
Glenna	*Irish*	From the valley
Gloria	*Latin*	Glory
Gloriana, Gloriane	*English*	Glorious grace

Name	Origin	Definition
Glynis, Glynn	Welsh	Little valley
Glynna	Irish	Of the glen
Godiva	English	Gift from God
Golda, Goldie	English	Flower
Gordania	Scottish	Heroic
Gosceline	Latin	Happy
Grace, Gracia, Graciana, Gracie, Graziana	English	Grace
Graeae	Greek	Grey one
Grainne, Grania	Irish	Charming
Grear	Scottish	Watchful
Greta, Gretchen, Grete	Latin	Child of light
Gretel	Latin	Pearl
Gricelda, Griselda, Griselde	German	Grey-haired
Guadalupe	Spanish	Named for the Virgin Mary
Guendolen, Guennola, Gwendolin, Gwendoloena, Gwenn	English	White
Guida	German	Guide
Guilaine	German	Pleasant oath
Guillelmine	Teutonic	Fierce protector
Guinevere	Celtic	White lady
Gurice	Hebrew	Cub
Gurley	Australian Aboriginal	A native willow
Gweneth, Gwenith, Gwenneth, Gwynne	Celtic	Blessed

Name	Origin	Definition
Gyda	*Scandinavian*	Gods
Gylda, Glydan	*English*	Gilded
Gymea	*Australian Aboriginal*	Little bird
Gytha	*English*	A gift, an offering

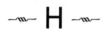 **H**

Name	Origin	Definition
Habika	*African*	Sweetheart
Hadara	*Hebrew*	Adorned with beauty
Hadasa	*Hebrew*	Flowering myrtle
Hadiya, Hadiyah	*African*	Gift
Hadley	*English*	Heath-covered meadow
Hadu, Hedda	*German*	Vigorous battle maiden
Hadya	*Arabic*	Well-behaved
Haesel	*English*	Nut
Haidee	*Greek*	Modest
Haifa	*Arabic*	Slender
Hailey, Haleigh	*Scandinavian*	Field of hay
Hala	*Indian*	Strong, beautiful
Halag	*German*	Pious, righteous
Halah	*Arabic*	Nimble
Haldis	*Norse*	Reliable
Hale	*English*	Hero
Haleah, Haleigha	*Hawaiian*	House of the rising sun

Name	Origin	Definition
Halette	*French*	Little Hal
Haley	*Scandinavian*	Hero
Halfrid, Halfrida, Halifrid	*German*	Peaceful heroine
Halfrith	*English*	Peaceful home
Hali	*Hebrew*	Sea
Halima, Halimah	*African*	Gentle, kind
Halle	*Scandinavian*	Heroine
Halley	*English*	From the manor-house meadow
Hallie	*Greek*	Thinking of the sea
Hamia	*Anglo-Saxon*	Syrian goddess
Hamsa	*Indian*	Swan
Hana	*Japanese*	Flower, blossom
Hanan	*Arabic*	Mercy
Hanna, Hannah	*Hebrew*	God is merciful
Hannalee, Hannele	*Hebrew*	Grace
Hanriette, Harriet, Harriette, Hattie, Henriette	*French*	Rules the home
Hanya	*Australian Aboriginal*	Stone
Harika	*Arabic*	Wonderful
Harimanne	*German*	Warrior maiden
Harlie	*English*	From the hare's meadow
Harmonie, Harmony	*English*	Unity
Harva, Harvina	*English*	Army warrior
Hasana	*African*	First born of twins

Name	Origin	Definition
Hasina	*African*	Good
Hasna	*Arabic*	Beautiful
Hatria	*Latin*	Dark one
Hava	*Hebrew*	Life
Haya	*Japanese*	Life
Hayden, Haylee, Hayleigh, Hayley	*English*	From the hay meadow
Hayfa	*Arabic*	Slender
Hazel	*English*	Hazelnut tree
Hea, Hei	*Korean*	Grace
Heather	*English*	Flowering evergreen plant
Hedia, Hedya	*Hebrew*	Voice of the Lord
Hedva	*Hebrew*	Joyous
Hedvige	*French*	Fighter
Hedy	*German*	Strife
Heida, Heide, Heidi	*German*	Noble
Helaine, Helen, Helena, Helene	*French*	Most beautiful woman
Helki	*Native American*	To touch
Helma	*Teutonic*	Fierce protector
Heloise	*French*	Renowned warrior
Helsa	*Hebrew*	Devoted to God
Henka	*Teutonic*	Ruler of an estate
Hepsiba, Hepzibeth	*Hebrew*	She is my delight
Herta, Hertha	*German*	Of the Earth
Hesper, Hester	*Greek*	Evening star
Hida	*German*	Warrior

Name	Origin	Definition
Hika	*Polynesian*	A daughter
Hilaire, Hilary, Hillary	*French*	Joy, cheer
Hild, Hilda, Hilde	*English*	Noble
Hildegarde	*German*	Warfare
Hildemara	*German*	Glorious
Hildireth	*German*	Battle counsellor
Hildred	*Anglo-Saxon*	Mild
Hinda	*Indian*	Female deer
Hisa	*Japanese*	Long-lasting
Hisolda	*Irish*	The fair
Hita	*Indian*	Lovable
Hlynn	*English*	Waterfall
Hoku	*Polynesian*	Star
Hola	*African*	Saviour
Holde	*German*	Beloved
Hollee, Holli, Hollie, Holly, Hollye	*English*	Plant with red berries
Honbria, Honbrie	*English*	Sweet
Honey	*English*	Honey, sweet
Honor, Honora, Honore, Honoria	*Irish*	Honor
Hope	*English*	Hope
Hosanna	*Hebrew*	Prayer
Hoshiko	*Japanese*	Star
Hue	*Vietnamese*	Lily
Huette, Hugiherahta	*French*	Intelligent
Hugiet	*English*	Little Hugh
Hulda, Hulde	*German*	Beloved

Name	Origin	Definition
Huyana	*Native American*	Rainfall
Hyacinth	*Greek*	Hyacinth flower
Hylda	*German*	Warfare
Hypatia	*Greek*	Highest

Name	Origin	Definition
Ianthe	*Greek*	Violet-coloured flower
Ibernia, Ierne	*Irish*	From Ireland
Ice, Isis	*African*	Supreme goddess
Ida	*English*	Prosperous
Idalie	*German*	Active
Idelle	*Celtic*	Bountiful
Idetta, Idette	*German*	Hard-working
Idla	*English*	Battle
Idoia, Idurre	*Spanish*	Reference to the Virgin Mary
Idola	*Greek*	Idolized
Idonia	*German*	Industrious
Ielena	*Russian*	Shining light
Ignacia	*Spanish*	Fire
Ila	*Indian*	From the island
Ilana, Ilani	*Hebrew*	Sunshine
Ilane	*Irish*	Island
Ilaria	*Latin*	One who is merry
Ilde	*English*	Battle

Name	Origin	Definition
Ileanna, Iliana	*Spanish*	Shining light
Ilena, Ilene	*English*	Giver of life
Ili	*African*	Blessed
Ilia	*Hebrew*	God is Lord
Ilisa	*African*	Blessed
Ilona, Ily	*Hungarian*	Beautiful
Ilsa	*German*	Devoted to God
Ilse	*English*	God's oath
Ilyse	*German*	Noble
Imala	*Native American*	Discipline
Iman, Imani	*African*	Faith
Imelda	*Spanish*	Powerful fighter
Imogene	*Latin*	Image
Inas	*Polynesian*	The wife of the Moon
Inda, Indee, India, Indiana	*English*	Country of India
Indrina	*Indian*	Deep
Induma	*Indian*	Moon
Ines, Inez	*Spanish*	Pure, chaste
Inga	*Swedish*	Hero's daughter
Inge	*Swedish*	Island
Inghean, Inghinn	*Scottish*	Daughter
Ingrid	*Teutonic*	Hero's daughter
Inis	*Irish*	From the river island
Inocenta	*Spanish*	Innocent
Iolande, Iolanthe, Iona	*Greek*	Violet flower
Ionanna	*Hebrew*	Grace
Ione	*Celtic*	From the king's island

Name	Origin	Definition
Irene	*Spanish*	Peace
Iria, Iris	*Greek*	Rainbow
Irmgard, Irmigard, Irmine	*German*	War goddess
Irvette	*English*	Friend of the sea
Isabeau, Isabel, Isabela, Isabelle, Isabael, Isibeal, Izzy	*French*	My God is bountiful
Isadora	*Greek*	Gift of the Moon
Isane	*German*	Strong-willed
Isaura	*Greek*	Soft air
Isha	*Hebrew*	Protector
Ishana	*Indian*	Rich
Isleen, Islene	*Irish*	Vision
Isleta	*Spanish*	Little island
Isold, Isolda, Isole	*Celtic*	Ruler of ice
Issa	*African*	Grateful
Istas	*Native American*	Snow
Iva	*Japanese*	God's gracious gift
Ivalyn, Ivey, Ivie, Ivy, Ivyanne	*English*	A plant, ivy
Ivana	*Hebrew*	Gift from God
Ivette, Ivonne	*Spanish*	Archer
Ivory	*English*	White, pure
Iyana	*Hebrew*	Sunshine
Izar, Izarra, Izarre	*Spanish*	Star
Izett	*Irish*	The fair
Izza	*African*	Grateful

—∿— **J** —∿—

Name	Origin	Definition
Jacalyn	*French*	Supplanter
Jacee, Jacelyn, Jacey, Jaci, Jacinda	*English*	Beautiful
Jacinthe	*French*	Hyacinth flower
Jacki, Jackie, Jackleen, Jacky, Jaclyn	*English*	Supplanter
Jacobienne, Jacqueline	*Hebrew*	Supplanter
Jacquenette	*French*	Little Jacques
Jada	*Arabic*	Wise
Jade, Jadira, Jady, Jaida	*Spanish*	Jewel
Jadee, Jaeda	*Arabic*	Goodness
Jae	*English*	Healer
Jael	*Hebrew*	To ascend
Jaena, Jeanette, Jaylynn	*English*	Blue jay
Jaffa	*Hebrew*	Beautiful
Jaha	*African*	Dignity
Jaime, Jaimelynn	*Scottish*	Supplanter
Jaimie	*French*	Love
Jala	*Arabic*	Charity
Jamari	*French*	Warrior
Jamila, Jamilia, Jamille	*Arabic*	Beautiful
Jan, Jana, Janae, Jane, Janene, Janet	*Hebrew*	Gracious
Janais, Janaye	*English*	God has answered
Janetta, Janette, Janie, Janina, Janis	*Scottish*	Gift from God
Janna	*Hebrew*	Flourishing

Name	Origin	Definition
Jardena	*Hebrew*	To descend
Jarra	*Australian Aboriginal*	Eucalyptus tree
Jaslynn, Jasmeen, Jasmin, Jasmine, Jasmyne	*English*	Gift from God
Jaxine	*English*	Hyacinth, purple
Jaya	*Indian*	Victory
Jaydra	*Arabic*	Goodness
Jaynie	*English*	God is gracious
Jazlyn, Jazmina, Jazzalyn, Jazzmyn	*English*	Gift from God
Jean, Jeane, Jeanelle, Jeanette, Jeanie, Jeanne,	*French*	God is gracious
Jemima	*Hebrew*	Little dove
Jemina	*Hebrew*	Listened to
Jemma	*English*	Jewel
Jen, Jenni, Jennie, Jenny, Jennyver	*English*	God is gracious
Jenda	*Hebrew*	Gift from God
Jenilynn, Jenina, Jenise	*English*	God is gracious
Jennarae, Jennasee, Jenneva	*English*	White wave
Jennay	*English*	God has answered
Jennifer	*Celtic*	Fair
Jeno	*Greek*	Heaven
Jenralyn, Jeralyn	*English*	Waterfall
Jensi, Jensine, Jensyn	*Hebrew*	God is gracious
Jeovana, Jeovanna	*English*	Gift from God

Name	Origin	Definition
Jera, Jerica	*Teutonic*	Spear maiden
Jeri	*Teutonic*	Rules by the spear
Jerusha	*Hebrew*	Married
Jess	*Persian*	God's grace
Jessamina	*French*	Jasmine
Jessamine, Jessamyn	*Persian*	Gift from God
Jesse	*Hebrew*	Wealthy
Jessica, Jessykah	*Hebrew*	Rich
Jewel, Jewell, Jule	*French*	Jewel
Jiba	*Australian Aboriginal*	The Moon
Jihan	*Arabic*	Universe
Jill, Jillian, Jyl	*English*	Girl, youthful
Jillayne, Jilene, Jillianna	*English*	Jove's child
Jilly	*English*	Youthful
Jin	*Japanese*	Treasure
Jinny	*English*	God is gracious
Jinx	*Latin*	A charm
Jirka	*Greek*	To work the earth
Jirra	*Australian Aboriginal*	Kangaroo
Jiselle	*English*	Pledge, vow
Jo, Jolanda	*Greek*	Modest
Joakima	*Hebrew*	The Lord will judge
Joan, Joana, Joanie, Joanna, Joanne	*English*	God is gracious
Joaquina, Joaquine	*Spanish*	God shall establish
Jocelin, Jocelina, Jocelyn, Jocelyne	*Hebrew*	Supplanter

Name	Origin	Definition
Jodee, Jodi, Jodie, Jody	*English*	God will multiply
Joella, Joella	*French*	Jehovah is God
Johnnie	*English*	God is merciful
Johyna	*Hebrew*	Persecuted
Joi, Joia, Joie	*French*	Rejoicing
Joka	*Hebrew*	Gift from God
Jola	*Hebrew*	Jehovah is God
Jolanka	*German*	County
Jolee, Joleen, Joleigh, Jolena, Joli, Jolie,	*French*	Cheerful, pretty
Jonette, Joni	*English*	God is merciful
Jora	*Hebrew*	Autumn rain
Jordan, Jordana, Jordane, Jordann, Jordyn, Jori	*Hebrew*	To descend
Jorja	*English*	Farmer
Josalind, Josalyn, Josalynn	*English*	Playful, happy
Josefa, Josefina, Josepha, Josephine, Josie	*Spanish*	God will multiply
Jovana, Jovanna, Jovina	*Spanish*	Roman mythological god Jupiter
Joy, Joya, Joyanna, Joyce, Joyelle	*English*	Rejoicing
Juana, Juanita	*Spanish*	Gift from God
Juba	*African*	Born on a Monday
Juci, Jucika, Jude, Judeana, Judeena	*Hebrew*	Praised
Judith, Juditha, Judy	*Hebrew*	Praise, admired

Name	Origin	Definition
Julee, Jules, Julia, Juliana, Julianne, Julie	*French*	Youthful
Juliet, Julieta, Juliette	*Latin*	Youthful, gentle
July	*English*	Born in July
June	*Latin*	Name of a month
Justeen, Justene, Justina, Justine, Justyne	*French*	Just, true
Jyoti	*Indian*	Light

⚘ K ⚘

Name	Origin	Definition
Kaatje	*Dutch*	Pure
Kacee, Kacey, Kaci, Kacia, Kacy, Kasey	*English*	Brave, watchful
Kadee, Kadi, Kadia, Kadie, Kadienne, Kady	*English*	Rhythmic flow of sounds
Kadischa, Kadisha	*Hebrew*	Holy
Kaede	*Japanese*	Maple leaf
Kaelah, Kaeleigh, Kaelene, Kaeley, Kaelin, Kaylee, Kayla, Kaylah	*English*	Keeper of the keys
Kaesha	*English*	Brave
Kaethe	*Greek*	Pure
Kahli, Kalli, Kallie	*English*	Fun
Kai	*Native American*	Sea
Kaia	*Greek*	Earth
Kaie	*Celtic*	Combat

Name	Origin	Definition
Kaine	*Gaelic*	Warrior
Kaitlan, Kaitlin, Kaitlyn	*Irish*	Pure, innocent
Kaiya	*Japanese*	Forgiveness
Kal, Kalista	*Greek*	Most beautiful
Kala	*Indian*	Fire
Kali	*Indian*	Energy
Kalika, Kalyca	*Greek*	Rosebud
Kalila, Kalilah	*Arabic*	Dearly loved
Kalinda	*Indian*	Sun
Kama	*Indian*	Love
Kambria	*English*	Wales
Kamelia, Kami	*English*	Flower name
Kameron, Kamren, Kamrin	*Scottish*	Bent nose
Kamila, Kamilla	*Arabic*	Perfect
Kamilia	*Slavic*	Sweet flower
Kamini	*Indian*	Woman
Kamlyn, Kammi	*English*	Flower name
Kamna	*Indian*	Desire
Kandice, Kandis, Kandy	*Greek*	Glowing, glittering
Kantha	*Indian*	Name of a god
Kapri, Kaprice	*English*	Caprice
Kara, Karan, Karen, Karena, Kari	*Latin*	Pure, innocent
Karida	*Arabic*	Virgin
Karima	*Arabic*	Generous
Karisma	*English*	Favour, gift
Karissa	*Greek*	Love, grace

Name	Origin	Definition
Karla, Karlee, Karlen	*German*	Strong woman
Karlotta	*French*	Petite, feminine
Karmel, Karmelita, Karmelle, Karmen, Karmina	*Latin*	Fruit garden
Karo, Karol, Karolina, Karolyne, Kerrolyn	*German*	Strong
Karra	*Latin*	Dear
Karston	*Irish*	Follower of Christ
Kary	*Arabic*	Flows like water
Karyan	*Arabic*	The dark one
Kasa	*Native American*	Fur robe dress
Kasamira, Kasmira	*Slavic*	Demands peace
Kasandra, Kassandra, Kassi	*Spanish*	Protector of mankind
Kasen, Kasia, Kassia	*Greek*	Pure
Kasinda	*African*	Born to a family with twins
Kassidy	*English*	Curly-haired
Kat, Kate, Katelyn, Katharina, Katherine, Kathe	*English*	Pure, innocent
Katja	*Greek*	Pure
Katyin	*Australian Aboriginal*	Water
Kavindra	*Indian*	Mighty poet
Kavita	*Indian*	Poem
Kay	*English*	Fire

Name	Origin	Definition
Kayle	*Australian Aboriginal*	A boomerang
Kazia	*Hebrew*	Plant with cinnamon-like bark
Keana, Keanna, Keiana, Kiahna, Kiana, Kiandra, Kiandria	*Irish*	Ancient
Keara	*Irish*	Saint's name
Keasha	*African*	Pretty
Keavy	*Irish*	Graceful
Kecia	*English*	Joyful
Keelan, Keeler, Keeley, Keely	*Gaelic*	Beautiful, graceful
Keelia, Keelin	*Celtic*	Slender, fair
Keera	*Latin*	Light, sun
Keesha, Keisha	*Hebrew*	Joyful
Kei	*Japanese*	Rapture, reverence
Keiko	*Japanese*	Adored
Keilah	*Irish*	Lively
Keira, Kera, Keri, Keriana, Keriann, Kerra, Kerri, Kiera	*Irish*	Dark-haired
Kel, Kelda, Kell	*Teutonic*	Clear mountain spring
Kelcey, Kelcie, Kelcy, Kellsey, Kelsee, Kelsey	*English*	Brave
Kellan	*Gaelic*	Warrior princess
Kelly	*Gaelic*	Lively
Kelson, Kelton	*Scandinavian*	Beautiful island
Kelula	*Hebrew*	Victorious

Name	Origin	Definition
Kelyn	*Hebrew*	Beautiful
Kemina	*Spanish*	Strong
Kendal, Kendalia, Kendaline, Kendall, Kendel, Kendra, Kenna	*English*	Ruler of the valley
Kendria	*English*	Royal protector
Kenisha	*English*	Royal obligation
Kennocha	*Celtic*	Lovely
Kenya	*African*	Artist
Kenzy	*Scottish*	The fair one
Keran, Keren	*Hebrew*	Horn
Kerwin	*Gaelic*	Small, dark-skinned
Kesara	*Spanish*	Youthful
Kesia	*African*	Favourite
Ketzia, Kezia	*Hebrew*	Cassia, cinnamon
Keva, Kevia	*English*	Beautiful child
Keyne	*Gaelic*	Warrior
Khalila	*Arabic*	Beloved
Khatiti	*African*	Tiny, little
Khristina	*English*	Follower of Christ
Khrystalline	*English*	Bright, shining
Kiah	*Australian Aboriginal*	From the beautiful place
Kiara	*Irish*	Dark
Kiauna	*Irish*	Ancient
Kiba	*Hebrew*	Protected
Kichi	*Japanese*	Fortunate
Kiele	*Hawaiian*	Gardenia
Kier, Kiersten	*Greek*	Christian

Name	Origin	Definition
Kiley	*Australian Aboriginal*	A boomerang
Kim, Kimball, Kimbell	*English*	Noble, brave
Kimberley, Kimberly, Kimbra, Kimmi, Kimmie	*English*	Royal fortress meadow
Kimi	*Native American*	Secret
Kindall, Kindell	*Celtic*	Ruler of the valley
Kindra	*English*	Royal protector
Kinnette	*Hebrew*	Harp
Kiona, Kionah, Kioni	*Irish*	Ancient
Kira	*Japanese*	Light, sun
Kiran	*Indian*	Ray
Kiri	*Polynesian*	The bark of a tree
Kirra	*Australian Aboriginal*	A leaf
Kirsten, Kirsti, Kirstie	*English*	Follower of Christ
Kisha	*African*	Pretty
Kishori	*Indian*	Young girl
Kiska	*Russian*	Pure
Kismet	*English*	Fate, destiny
Kissa	*African*	Born after twins
Kita	*Japanese*	North
Kitlyn	*English*	Pure, innocent
Kiva	*Hebrew*	Protected
Klaudia	*Latin*	Lame
Kolena, Kolina	*English*	Pure, innocent
Kolora	*Australian Aboriginal*	A freshwater lagoon

Name	Origin	Definition
Kora	*Australian Aboriginal*	A companion
Kordelia	*Celtic*	Heart, a sea jewel
Koren, Kori, Korrie	*Greek*	Maiden
Kris, Krissy, Krista, Kristeena, Kristen, Kristiane, Kristy	*Scandinavian*	Follower of Christ
Kristabelle, Kristal, Kristalena, Kristen, Krstal	*English*	Bright, shining
Kriti	*Indian*	A work of art
Ksena	*Hebrew*	Praise be to God
Kunjal	*Indian*	Nightingale
Kura	*Polynesian*	Treasure
Kusuma	*Indian*	Flower
Kusumita	*Indian*	Blossomed
Ky, Kyla, Kylee, Kylene	*English*	Honour
Kyaw	*Burmese*	Famous
Kyeema	*Australian Aboriginal*	Of the dawn
Kyi	*Burmese*	Clear
Kyine	*Burmese*	Smell sweet
Kyli	*Australian Aboriginal*	A boomerang
Kyn	*Vietnamese*	The golden one
Kyna	*Gaelic*	Wise
Kyndall	*English*	Royal valley
Kyne	*Gaelic*	Wise
Kyoko	*Japanese*	Mirror
Kywe	*Burmese*	Rich

 **L**

Name	Origin	Definition
Lace, Lacee, Lacey, Laci, Lacie, Lacy	*French*	Place name
Lael	*Hebrew*	Belonging to God
Laetitia, Laticia	*Irish*	Joy
Laila, Laili, Lailie, Layla	*Hebrew*	Dark as the night
Laina	*English*	Fair, beautiful
Laine	*French*	Light
Lair, Laire, Lara	*Scottish*	Mare
Lakeisha	*African*	Favourite one
Lala	*Slavic*	Tulip
Lalana	*Indian*	A girl
Lalasa	*Indian*	Love
Lali	*Spanish*	Darling girl
Lali, Lalia	*Indian*	Well-spoken
Lalita	*Indian*	Beauty
Lally	*French*	From the alder grove
Lamilla	*Australian Aboriginal*	Stone
Lana, Lanna	*Polynesian*	Fair, beautiful
Landa	*Greek*	Modest
Landra	*Spanish*	Counsellor
Lane, Layne	*English*	Narrow road
Laney	*Russian*	Light
Lani	*Spanish*	Sky, heaven
Laquisha, Lateisha	*English*	Joyful
Laraine	*English*	Sea bird

Name	Origin	Definition
Lareina	*English*	The queen
Laren, Laria	*Scottish*	Serves Lawrence
Larissa	*Russian*	Cheerful
Lark, Larke, Larkin	*English*	Lark
Laura, Laural, Lauralyn, Laurana, Laurentia	*Latin*	Honour, victory
Lauranne, Laure, Laureen, Lauren, Laurena, Laurie, Laurin	*Latin*	Honour, spirit
Lavali	*Indian*	Clove
Lavani	*Indian*	Grace
Lavin, Lavine, Lavinia	*Latin*	Purity
Layna	*English*	Narrow road
Lea, Leah, Leatrice, Lia	*Greek*	Woman
Leala, Lealia	*French*	Loyal
Leana, Leann, Leanna, Leeann, Lianne	*Scottish*	Youthful
Leandra	*Greek*	Lion woman
Leatrice	*Greek*	Woman
Lecia	*English*	Happy
Ledah	*Hebrew*	Birth
Lee, Leigh	*English*	Poet
Leela	*Indian*	Play, amusement
Leena	*Irish*	Wet meadow
Leia	*English*	Meadow
Leigha	*Hawaiian*	House of the rising sun
Leila, Leilahm, Lela	*Irish*	Born at night

Name	Origin	Definition
Lena, Lene	*English*	Child of light
Lenore, Leonne, Leonora	*Latin*	Alluring
Lenya, Leyna, Leyns	*German*	Little angel
Leola	*Latin*	Loyal, faithful
Leona, Leonda, Leone	*French*	Lion
Leopolda, Leopoldine	*German*	Bold leader
Leota	*German*	Of the people
Lera	*Spanish*	Reference to the Virgin Mary
Leslee, Leslie, Lesly	*Scottish*	Dweller in the grey castle
Leta	*Greek*	Joy
Letha, Lethia	*Greek*	Forgetful
Letice, Leticia, Letitia	*Latin*	Joy
Letya	*French*	Womanly
Lexa, Lexann, Lexie, Lexine	*Greek*	Protector of mankind
Ley	*English*	Meadow
Leya	*Spanish*	Loyalty
Liadan	*Irish*	Grey lady
Libby	*English*	God's oath
Liberty	*English*	Freedom
Licia	*English*	Noble, truth
Lida	*Latin*	Beautifully dressed
Lidia	*Greek*	Beauty
Lien	*Chinese*	Lotus
Liesbet, Liese, Liesheth	*Hebrew*	Devoted to God
Liesl	*English*	Beloved by God

Name	Origin	Definition
Lila, Lilah, Lilith, Lily	*Hebrew*	Delicate, desired
Lilia, Liliana, Lilias	*Latin*	Flower
Lilian, Liliane	*English*	Innocence, purity
Lilibet, Lilibeth, Lilybell	*English*	My God is bountiful
Lina	*Latin*	Delicate
Linda	*Italian*	Beautiful woman
Linden, Lindi, Lindy	*English*	Pretty
Lindiwe	*African*	Have waited
Lindsay, Lindsey, Linsey	*Celtic*	From the linden-tree island
Linetta, Linn, Linnette	*French*	Flaxen
Liora	*English*	Honour, victory
Lis, Lisa, Lisabet, Lisbeth, Lise	*Latin*	Devoted to God
Lissa, Lyssa	*English*	Bee, honey
Litsa	*Greek*	One who brings good news
Liv, Livia, Livvy	*French*	Kind one
Livana	*Greek*	White
Livania	*Greek*	Goddess
Liz, Liza, Lizzie	*English*	Devoted to God
Llaynie	*Irish*	Fair, beautiful
Lochana	*Indian*	Eye
Locke	*English*	Stronghold
Loella	*English*	Elfin
Logan	*Scottish*	Little hollow
Lois	*German*	Warrior maiden
Loki	*Scandinavian*	Trickster god
Lola, Loleta, Lolita	*Spanish*	Strong woman

Name	Origin	Definition
Lona	*English*	Beautiful
Loni	*English*	Solitary
Lonyn	*English*	Crown of victory
Lora, Lorah	*Latin*	Honour, victory
Loralei	*German*	Temptress
Lorenza, Loreta, Lorette, Lori, Loria	*Latin*	Honour, victory
Lorry	*Latin*	Honour, fame
Lotte, Lottie	*German*	Petite, feminine
Lotus	*Greek*	Lotus flower
Lotye	*French*	Tiny, womanly
Louella	*French*	Famous elf
Louisa, Louisane, Louise, Luana, Luane	*German*	Warrior maiden
Lourdes, Louredes	*Spanish*	Reference to the Virgin Mary
Love, Lovie	*English*	Affection
Lowana	*Australian Aboriginal*	A girl
Loyce	*German*	Warrior maiden
Lucena, Lucette, Luci, Lucia, Luciana, Lucila, Lucille, Lucy	*Spanish*	Illumination
Lucrece, Lucretia, Lucrezia	*French*	Riches
Luell, Luella, Luelle	*English*	Famous elf
Lulie	*German*	Warrior maiden
Lulu	*English*	Pearl, precious
Luna, Lune	*Latin*	Moon

Name	Origin	Definition
Lundy	*French*	By the Island
Lurleen, Lurlina	*German*	Temptress
Luvena, Luvina	*English*	Little beloved one
Luyu	*Native American*	Wild dove
Lwin	*Burmese*	Outstanding
Lydia, Lydie	*Greek*	Beauty
Lyla	*English*	Dark as the night
Lynda, Lyndall, Lyndee, Lyndsay	*English*	Beautiful
Lynessa, Lynley, Lynne	*English*	House, church
Lyonesse	*Celtic*	Little lion
Lyra, Lyric, Lyri	*French*	Of the lyre or song
Lyvia	*English*	Olive tree

—⚬— M —⚬—

Name	Origin	Definition
Maata	*Maori*	A lady
Mabel, Mabella, Mabry	*French*	Fair maid, lovely
Mabelle	*French*	Lovable
Macee, Macey, Maci, Macie, Macy	*French*	Gift of God
Macha	*Irish*	Plain
Mackenzie	*Scottish*	Fair, favoured one
Mada	*Irish*	From Mathilda

Name	Origin	Definition
Madailein, Madalen, Madalena, Madalyn, Madelaine, Madigan, Madlin	*Irish*	One who is elevated
Maddalen, Maddalena, Maddalene, Maddalyn	*German*	Magnificent
Maddie, Maddy	*English*	Battle maiden
Madeira	*Spanish*	Sweet wine
Madelhari	*German*	War counsellor
Madena, Madia, Madina	*Spanish*	Woman from Magdala
Madge, Maergrethe, Mag	*Latin*	Child of light
Madison	*English*	Gift of God
Madonna	*Italian*	A lady
Madora, Medea, Medora	*Latin*	Middle child
Madra, Madre	*English*	Mother
Mady, Maegth, Magd	*English*	Maiden
Mae, Maelee, Maelynn	*Anglo-Saxon*	May
Maertisa	*English*	Famous
Maeve	*Irish*	Mythical queen
Maeveen	*Celtic*	Nimble
Magan	*Teutonic*	Powerful
Magda, Magdalen, Magdalena, Magdaline	*German*	Woman from Magdala
Magee, Maggi, Maggie, Maggy	*Latin*	Pearl
Magena	*Hebrew*	The coming moon
Magna	*Latin*	Large

Name	Origin	Definition
Magnild, Magnilda, Magnilde	*German*	Strong battle maiden
Magnolia	*French*	Flower
Mahala	*Hebrew*	Tenderness
Mahala, Mahalah, Malahar, Mahalia, Mahela	*Arabic*	Woman
Mai	*Japanese*	Brightness
Maia, Maiya	*Latin*	May
Maialen, Maighdlin	*Hebrew*	From the tower
Maibelle	*French*	Fair maid
Maible	*Irish*	Lovable
Maida, Maidie, Maidy	*Anglo-Saxon*	Maiden
Maille	*Irish*	Pearl
Mair, Maira, Maire, Mairi	*Hebrew*	Bitter
Maisie, Maisy	*Scottish*	Child of light
Maite, Maitena	*English*	Dearly loved
Maitilda, Mathilde	*Irish*	Strong battle maiden
Majori	*French*	Pearl
Makeda	*African*	Beautiful armrest
Makena	*African*	The happy one
Mala	*Hebrew*	Necklace, garland
Malati	*Indian*	Jasmine
Malca, Malcah, Malka	*Hebrew*	Queen
Malena	*Greek*	Gentle one
Malha, Mali, Maliha	*Indian*	Strong, beautiful
Malia, Malita	*Spanish*	Bitter
Malika	*African*	Queen, princess

Name	Origin	Definition
Malin	*German*	Little warrior
Malina	*Hebrew*	Dark
Malinda, Malinde	*English*	Gentle one
Malini	*Hebrew*	Florist
Mallaidh	*Hebrew*	Bitter
Mallie	*Greek*	Gentle one
Mallorey, Mallorie, Mallory, Mally	*German*	Army counsellor
Malti	*Indian*	Small, fragrant flower
Malva, Melva	*Gaelic*	Slender, soft
Malvie, Malvina	*Gaelic*	Smooth snow
Manasi, Manini	*Indian*	A lady
Manda, Mandalyn, Mandi, Mandie, Mandy	*Spanish*	Love, precious
Mandara	*Indian*	Mythical tree
Manette, Manon, Maree	*French*	Bitter
Manhattan	*Scottish*	Whiskey
Manilla	*Australian Aboriginal*	A winding river
Manoela	*Spanish*	With God
Mansi	*Native American*	Plucked flower
Manuela	*Hebrew*	God is with us
Manya	*French*	Small
Maola, Maoli	*Irish*	Handmaiden
Mara	*German*	Immortal, steadfast
Marabel	*Spanish*	Extraordinary
Marala	*Indian*	Swan

Name	Origin	Definition
Maralyn	*English*	Waterfall
Marcail	*French*	Pearl
Marcela	*Spanish*	Warring
Marcelia, Marcey, Marci, Marcia, Marsi, Marsy	*Latin*	Martial
Marcelin, Marceline, Marcella, Marciana	*French*	God of war
Marel, Maretta, Marette	*Hebrew*	Bitter
Marella	*Irish*	A lady
Maren	*Hebrew*	Sea
Margaret, Margareta, Margaretha, Margarethe, Margo, Margot	*Latin*	Child of light
Margarida, Margarita, Margaux, Marge, Margery, Margherita, Margie	*Persian*	Pearl
Mari	*Hebrew*	Flower
Maria	*Spanish*	Bitter
Mariabella, Mariabelle, Maribelle	*Italian*	My beautiful Mary
Mariah, Marian, Mariane, Marie, Marielle, Mariette	*French*	Bitter
Maricelia, Maricelle	*Spanish*	God of war
Marigold	*English*	Flower
Marika	*Hebrew*	Quiet and careful

Name	Origin	Definition
Marilla	*Celtic*	Shining sea
Marina	*Latin*	Of the sea
Marinna	*Australian Aboriginal*	Song
Marion, Marisha	*French*	Bitter
Maris	*Hebrew*	I am the Sun
Marisa, Marise, Mariska, Marisol, Marla	*English*	Bitter
Marja	*Scandinavian*	Sadness from the sea
Marjani	*African*	Coral
Marjolaina	*French*	Flower
Marjorie, Marjory	*French*	Child of light
Marlana, Marlayna, Marlayne	*English*	Woman from Magdala
Marleigh, Marley	*English*	Marshy meadow
Marlin	*English*	Sea hill
Marlis, Marlo	*German*	Little hawk
Marna, Marne, Marni, Marny	*Hebrew*	Rejoice
Marquisa, Marquise	*French*	Royalty
Marta, Martha, Mathe	*Spanish*	A lady
Maru	*Polynesian*	Gentle
Marva, Marveille, Marvelle	*French*	Miracle
Mary, Marya, Maryann, Marylin	*English*	Bitter
Mathild, Mathilda, Mathilde	*German*	Mighty battle maiden
Mattie, Matty	*French*	A lady

Name	Origin	Definition
Maud, Maude	*French*	Strong battle maiden
Maura, Maureen, Maurin, Maurizia	*Gaelic*	Great, dark-haired
Mausi	*Native American*	Plucks flowers
Mava	*Hebrew*	Pleasant
Mave, Mavis	*Irish*	Joy
Maxie, Maxine	*English*	The greatest
Maya	*Indian*	Industrious
Maybelle, Maybelline	*French*	Fair maid
Mayda, Mayde	*Anglo-Saxon*	Maiden
Mayra, Mayrah	*Irish*	Spring, the wind
Meagan, Megan, Megann, Meghan	*Welsh*	Strong
Mearr	*Irish*	Bitter
Meda	*Native American*	Prophetess
Medha	*Indian*	Intelligence
Medina	*Arabic*	City of the prophet
Meeda	*Irish*	Thirsty
Meera	*Indian*	Merry
Meg	*Latin*	Strong
Megha	*Indian*	Clouds
Mehala	*Hebrew*	Tenderness
Mei	*Latin*	Great one
Meira	*Hebrew*	Light
Mel	*Greek*	Wisdom
Melaina, Melanie	*French*	Dark

Name	Origin	Definition
Melia	*Greek*	Nymph daugher of Oceanus
Melicent	*Greek*	Industrious
Melina, Melinda	*Latin*	Gentle one
Melisande	*German*	Strength, determination
Melissa, Melisse	*Greek*	Bee, honey
Melodie, Melody	*Greek*	Song
Melosia	*Spanish*	Sweet
Meranda	*Latin*	Extraordinary
Mercedes	*Spanish*	Mercy
Mercer	*French*	Merchant
Merci, Mercia, Mercina, Mercy	*French*	Compassion, pity
Meredith, Meri	*Welsh*	Protector of the sea
Meriel	*Latin*	Myrrh
Merla, Merlyn, Merryl	*French*	Blackbird
Merle	*Latin*	Sea
Merrily, Merry	*English*	Joyful
Merrisa	*Latin*	Of the sea
Merritt	*Latin*	Little famous one
Merriwell	*Latin*	Deserving
Meta	*Latin*	Ambitious
Mevin	*Gaelic*	Smooth snow
Mia	*Italian*	Mine
Micaela, Micheline, Michelle, Michelyn, Mikhaeli	*Hebrew*	Like God

Name	Origin	Definition
Michaela, Michaelina, Mikaela, Mikayla	*English*	Gift from God
Midge	*Latin*	Child of light
Midori	*Japanese*	Green
Mieze	*Hebrew*	Small
Mignon, Mignonette	*French*	Delicate
Mildraed, Mildred, Mildryd, Milli	*English*	Mild
Millicent	*German*	Industrious
Mimi	*Hebrew*	Resolute protector
Mina	*German*	Love
Minda, Mindy	*German*	Gentle one
Minerva	*Latin*	Power
Ming	*Chinese*	Smart, intelligent
Minka	*Teutonic*	Strong, resolute
Minna	*Scottish*	Love
Minnie	*Teutonic*	Fierce protector
Minta, Mintha	*Greek*	Mint
Minya	*Australian Aboriginal*	Small
Mira, Mirabel, Mirabelle, Miranda, Mirelle, Mirabella	*Spanish*	Extraordinary
Mireille	*French*	Miracle
Miriyan	*Australian Aboriginal*	Star
Mirrin	*Australian Aboriginal*	A cloud
Missie, Missy	*English*	Young girl

Name	Origin	Definition
Misty	*English*	Covered by mist
Mitzi	*German*	Bitter
Moana	*Maori*	Wide expanse of water or sea
Modeste	*Spanish*	Modest one
Moina, Moyna	*Irish*	Mild, tender
Moira	*Celtic*	Exceptional
Moireach	*Scottish*	A lady
Mollie, Molly	*Irish*	Bitter
Mona	*Gaelic*	Individual
Monica, Monique	*English*	Adviser
Montag, Montague	*French*	Steep mountain
Morcan	*Welsh*	Bright sea
Morella	*Spanish*	Little blueberry
Morena, Moria, Moriah	*French*	Great, dark-haired
Morgan, Morgana, Morgandy	*Celtic*	Lives by the sea
Morgayne	*Irish*	Bright sea
Morgen	*German*	Morning
Morrigan	*Celtic*	A war goddess
Morrin	*Irish*	Long-haired
Moya	*Hebrew*	Exceptional
Muirgheal	*Irish*	Knows the sea
Mya	*Burmese*	Emerald
Myesha	*Arabic*	Lively woman
Myfanwy	*Welsh*	Sweet lady
Myla	*English*	Merciful
Myna	*German*	Love
Myo	*Burmese*	Relative

Name	Origin	Definition
Myra	*Hebrew*	Quiet song
Myrilla	*Latin*	Extraordinary
Myrla	*French*	Blackbird
Myrna	*Arabic*	Tender
Myrtia, Myrtis	*Greek*	Flower
Mythily	*Indian*	Wifely, womanly

—∿— N —∿—

Name	Origin	Definition
Nadeen, Nadia	*French*	Hope
Nadie	*Native American*	Wise
Nadifa	*African*	Born between two seasons
Nadina, Nadine	*German*	The courage of a bear
Nadira, Nadra	*African*	Unusual
Nadja, Nadya	*German*	Hope
Naia	*Greek*	Flowing
Naiad, Naida, Naiia, Nayad	*Greek*	Water nymph
Naiara	*Spanish*	Reference to the Virgin Mary
Nailah	*African*	Success
Naimah	*Arabic*	To live an enjoyable life
Naina	*Indian*	Eyes
Nainsi, Nan, Nance, Nancey, Nanci, Nancy	*Irish*	Grace

Name	Origin	Definition
Nairna	*Scottish*	Dwells at the alder-tree river
Nairne	*Scottish*	From the narrow river glade
Nalani	*Hawaiian*	Calmness of the skies
Nalda	*Spanish*	Strong
Nalini	*Indian*	Lovely
Nama	*Australian Aboriginal*	Tea tree
Nanda	*Burmese*	Great achiever
Nanette, Nanine, Nanon	*French*	Grace
Naoma, Neomi	*Hebrew*	Pleasant
Naomi	*Japanese*	Beautiful
Nara	*Gaelic*	Joyous
Narcissa, Narcisse	*Greek*	Self-love
Narda	*Latin*	The annointed
Nareen, Nareena	*Celtic*	Contented
Narella, Narelle	*Greek*	Bright one
Narmada	*Indian*	Arouses tender feelings in others
Nashota	*Native American*	Twin
Nashwa	*African*	Wonderful feeling
Nastassia, Natala, Nataleigh, Natalia, Natalja, Nathalie	*Latin*	Born at Christmas
Nata	*Slavic*	Hope
Nataniella, Natanielle	*Hebrew*	Gift from God

Name	Origin	Definition
Natasa, Natasha, Natashia	*Latin*	Born at Christmas
Nathaira, Nathara	*Scottish*	Snake
Navit	*Hebrew*	Pleasant
Nawar	*Arabic*	Flower
Nayana	*Indian*	Eyes
Naysa	*Hebrew*	Miracle of God
Nazirah	*Arabic*	Equal, like
Ndila	*African*	Billy goat
Neala, Nealah, Neela, Neely, Neila	*Irish*	Champion
Nealie	*Celtic*	Ruler
Nearra	*English*	Nearest
Neci	*Latin*	Intense, fiery
Neda, Nedda, Neddy	*Slavic*	Born on Sunday
Nediva, Nedivah	*Hebrew*	Giving
Nedra	*English*	Guardian of prosperity
Neema	*African*	Born at a prosperous time
Neerja	*Indian*	Lotus flower
Neha	*Indian*	Love, rain
Nehama	*Hebrew*	Comfort
Nehanda	*African*	The beautiful one has arrived
Neiva, Neva, Nevada, Nieve	*Spanish*	Snowy
Nekana	*Spanish*	Sorrows
Nelda	*Irish*	By the alder tree

Name	Origin	Definition
Nelia, Nelina	*Spanish*	The bright one
Nell, Nella, Nelle, Nellie	*English*	Shining light
Nellwyn, Nelwin	*English*	Bright friend
Neola	*Greek*	Youthful
Neoma, Neona	*Greek*	New Moon
Neorah	*Hebrew*	Light
Nerea	*Spanish*	Mine
Nerida	*Slavic*	Flower
Neroli, Nerolia, Nerolie	*Italian*	Orange blossom
Nessa, Nessia	*Irish*	From the headland
Nessie, Nessy	*Greek*	Butterfly
Neta	*Hebrew*	Serious
Netra	*Indian*	Eyes
Netta	*Hebrew*	Plant
Nevea, Nevia	*Spanish*	Snow-clad
Neya	*Hebrew*	Grace
Neysa, Neza	*Greek*	Pure
Ngaire, Niree, Nyree	*Maori*	Flaxen
Nia	*African*	Purpose
Nica	*Latin*	True image
Nichele, Nichola, Nichole, Nicki, Nicolette	*English*	People's victory
Nidhi	*Indian*	Treasure
Nidra	*Indian*	Sleep
Niela, Nila	*Gaelic*	Champion
Nighean	*Scottish*	Young woman
Nika	*Russian*	Born on a Sunday

Name	Origin	Definition
Nike	*Greek*	Victory
Nikhita	*Indian*	Sharp
Nimah	*Arabic*	Blessing
Nina, Ninette, Ninya	*Spanish*	Girl
Nira, Niria	*Hebrew*	Plow
Nirvana	*Indian*	Ultimate bliss
Nisha	*Indian*	Night
Nissa, Nissan, Nisse	*Scandinavian*	Elf, fairy
Nita	*Indian*	Serious
Nitza, Nitzana, Nitzanah, Nizana	*Hebrew*	Blossom
Nixie	*German*	Little water sprite
Niyati	*Indian*	Fate, fortune
Noelani	*Hawaiian*	Beautiful girl from heaven
Noele, Noelle	*French*	Christmas
Noemi, Noemie	*Spanish*	Pleasant
Nokomis	*Native American*	Grandmother
Nola	*Celtic*	Kind one
Nolene	*English*	Noble
Nomi	*Hebrew*	Pleasant
Nora, Norabel, Norah	*English*	Honour, light
Norberaht, Norberte	*German*	Bright heroine
Nordica	*German*	From the north
Noreen	*Irish*	Honour, light
Nori	*Japanese*	Doctrine
Norina, Norine	*Latin*	Honour, light
Norma	*Latin*	Model

Name	Origin	Definition
Nova, Novia	*Latin*	New
Noya	*Arabic*	Adorned with beauty
Nuala	*Irish*	Lovely shoulders
Nura	*Arabic*	Light
Nuray	*Arabic*	White moon
Nweh	*Arabic*	Light
Nyad	*Greek*	Water nymph
Nyaga	*African*	Life is precious
Nydia	*Latin*	Refuge, nest
Nyein	*Burmese*	Quiet
Nyx	*Greek*	Night

O

Name	Origin	Definition
Obelia	*Greek*	Pillar of strength
Octavia, Octavie	*Latin*	Eighth child
Oda, Odiana, Odiane	*German*	Elfin spear
Odeda, Odede	*Hebrew*	Strong
Odelette	*French*	Little spring
Odelia, Odelina, Odelinda, Odella, Odelyn, Othili	*Anglo-Saxon*	Little wealthy one
Odera	*Hebrew*	Plough
Odessa	*Greek*	Odyssey, voyage
Odetta	*French*	Melody
Odila, Odile	*German*	Wealthy
Ofelia, Ophelia, Ophelie	*Greek*	Useful, wise

Name	Origin	Definition
Ofra, Ophra, Ophrah	*Hebrew*	Fawn
Ohanna	*Arabic*	God's gracious gift
Oihane	*Spanish*	From the forest
Oksana	*Russian*	Glory be to God
Ola	*African*	Precious
Olathe	*Native American*	Beautiful
Oldwin, Oldwina, Oldwyn	*English*	Special friend
Oleda, Oleta, Olita	*English*	Winged
Olena	*Greek*	Pretty
Olesia	*Polish*	Protector of mankind
Oletha	*English*	Light, nimble
Olexa	*English*	Protector of mankind
Oliana	*Hawaiian*	Oleander
Olinda	*Spanish*	Holy
Olive, Olivette, Olivia, Olivya	*Irish*	Kind one
Oliveria	*Spanish*	Affectionate
Ollie, Olly, Olva	*Latin*	Olive tree
Olwyn	*Celtic*	Daughter of a giant
Olympe, Olympia	*French*	From Olympus
Omah, Omette	*Hebrew*	Cedar tree
Omega	*Greek*	Great
Omie	*Hebrew*	Pleasant
Ona, Oona, Oonagh	*Gaelic*	One, unity
Onde, Ondine	*Latin*	Of the wave
Oni	*African*	Desired

Name	Origin	Definition
Onida	*Native American*	The expected one
Onora	*Irish*	Honour
Opal	*Indian*	Jewel
Ophira	*Greek*	Gold
Ora	*English*	Life
Orabel, Oralie, Orel, Orelda, Oriole	*Latin*	Golden
Orane	*French*	Rising
Orelle, Oriana, Orlanna	*Latin*	Dawn
Orenda	*Native American*	Magic power
Oria	*Latin*	East
Oriel, Orielle	*French*	Angel of destiny
Orla	*Latin*	Golden lady
Orlaith, Orlaithe	*Irish*	Golden
Orlee, Orlena, Orlene, Orlie, Orly	*Hebrew*	Light
Orquidea	*Spanish*	Orchid
Ortensia	*Latin*	Gardener, farmer
Orva	*French*	Brave friend
Otilie, Otthilde, Ottilia, Otylia	*German*	Fortunate heroine
Ove	*Celtic*	Awe
Oz	*Latin*	Detached, free of material things

—∿— **P** —∿—

Name	Origin	Definition
Padma	*Indian*	Lotus
Padraigin	*Irish*	Noble
Page, Paige	*French*	Page
Paili	*Hebrew*	Bitter
Paiva	*Scandinavian*	God of the Sun
Paix	*Latin*	Peace
Pakwa	*Native American*	Frog
Palba	*Spanish*	Blond
Palita, Paloma, Palomina, Palomita	*Spanish*	Dove
Palma, Palmiera, Palmira, Palmyra	*English*	Palm-bearing pilgrim
Pam, Pamela, Pamelina, Pamella, Pamelyn	*Greek*	Honeyed
Pamuy	*Native American*	Water moon
Pan, Pandora	*Greek*	Talented one
Pangi	*African*	Sweet
Pania	*Maori*	Mythological sea maiden
Pansee	*French*	Thoughtful
Panya	*African*	Crown of victory
Panyin	*African*	Older of twins
Paola, Paolina	*Latin*	Petite
Papillon	*French*	Butterfly
Pari	*Indian*	Beauty, fairy

Name	Origin	Definition
Parisa	*Persian*	Angelic face
Parnika	*Indian*	Small leaf
Parvani	*Indian*	Full Moon
Parveen	*Indian*	Star
Pascala, Pascal, Pascaline, Pasclina	*French*	Born at Easter
Pastora	*Spanish*	Shepherdess
Pat, Patia, Patrice, Patricia, Patrizia, Patty	*Latin*	Noble one
Patience	*Latin*	Enduring
Paton, Payton, Peyton	*English*	Royal
Patten, Pattin, Patton	*English*	From the fighter's town
Paula, Paulette, Pauline, Pauly, Pavla, Pavlina	*Latin*	Petite
Pavana	*Indian*	Holy, sacred
Pavati	*Native American*	Clear water
Paxton	*Latin*	Trader
Payne	*Latin*	Petite
Paza, Pazia, Pazice	*Hebrew*	Golden
Peace	*English*	Peace
Pearl, Pearla, Pearle, Perla, Perle	*English*	Pearl
Pedra	*Spanish*	Stone
Peg, Peggy	*Latin*	Child of light
Pelagia, Pelagie, Pelga, Pelgia	*Greek*	From the sea
Pemba	*African*	The force of present existence

Name	Origin	Definition
Penelope	*Greek*	Weaver
Pengana	*Australian Aboriginal*	A hawk
Peni, Peninna, Penny	*Hebrew*	Jewel, coral
Pense, Pensee	*French*	Thoughtful
Penthea	*Greek*	Fifth
Peony	*Greek*	Flower name
Pepi, Pip, Pippi, Pippin	*German*	Persistent, perseverance
Pepin	*German*	Petitioner
Pepper	*English*	From the pepper plant
Perahta	*German*	Glorious
Percy	*Greek*	Pierces
Perdam, Perdea	*Latin*	Lost
Peregrine	*Latin*	Wanderer
Perfecta	*Spanish*	Perfect
Peri, Perri	*English*	Wanderer
Perke, Perzsi	*Hebrew*	Devoted to God
Pernille, Perrine, Petra, Petrina, Petrina, Petronella, Petronia	*Latin*	Rock, stone
Perouze	*Arabic*	Turquoise
Persa, Perse, Persephone	*Greek*	Goddess of the underworld
Peta	*Native American*	Tree
Petula	*Latin*	Impatient
Petunia	*Latin*	Flower

Name	Origin	Definition
Phae, Phaedra, Phaidra, Phedra	*Greek*	Shining one
Phebe, Phoebe, Phoebus	*Greek*	Bright one
Phelia	*Greek*	Wise
Philana, Philantha, Philene, Philia, Philina	*Greek*	Adoring
Philicia, Phylice, Phylicia	*Latin*	Happy
Philida, Phillis, Phyl, Phyllis, Phylys	*Greek*	Dear
Philipinna, Philippa, Philippine	*German*	Loves horses
Philomen, Philomena	*Greek*	Friend, lover of the Moon
Phin, Phineas, Phinny	*Greek*	Oracle
Phoena	*Greek*	Mystical bird
Pia	*Italian*	Devout
Pierah	*Australian Aboriginal*	The Moon
Pierette	*Latin*	Rock, stone
Piksi, Piksy, Pixi, Pixie, Pixy	*Celtic*	Small elf
Piper, Pipere, Pyper	*English*	Piper
Pippa	*Greek*	Loves horses
Pirra	*Australian Aboriginal*	The Moon
Piyali	*Indian*	Tree
Placida	*Spanish*	Tranquil
Polly	*Latin*	Bitter
Poloma	*Native American*	Bow

Name	Origin	Definition
Poppy	*English*	Flower
Porsche, Porsha, Portia	*Latin*	Gift, offering
Prabha	*Indian*	Light, glow
Prabhati, Prachi	*Indian*	Morning
Pragya	*Indian*	Wisdom
Prama	*Indian*	Knowing truth
Pramada	*Indian*	Woman
Pranati	*Indian*	Prayer
Prashanti	*Indian*	Peace
Pratigya	*Indian*	Pledge, vow
Pratima	*Indian*	Icon, idol
Prema	*Indian*	Love
Prerana	*Indian*	Inspiration
Prima	*Italian*	First one
Primavera	*Spanish*	Spring time
Prisca, Priscilla, Priss	*Latin*	From ancient times
Prita	*Indian*	Dear one
Priya, Priyam	*Indian*	Beloved
Pru, Prudence, Prudencia	*Latin*	Foresight
Prue	*Latin*	Valiant one
Prunella	*French*	Colour of plum
Psyche	*Greek*	The soul
Pura, Pureza	*Spanish*	Pure
Purva	*Indian*	East
Purvaja	*Indian*	Elder sister
Purvis	*French*	Provide
Pyrena	*Greek*	Fiery
Pythia	*Greek*	Prophet

Q

Name	Origin	Definition
Qamra	*Arabic*	Moon
Quasha, Quay	*Native American*	Daughter of Ben
Queena, Queenie	*English*	Queen
Quella	*English*	Pacify
Quenby	*Scandinavian*	Womanly
Querida	*Spanish*	Beloved
Quinn	*Latin*	Wise
Quinta, Quintina	*Spanish*	Fifth-born child
Quintessa	*Latin*	Essence
Quirita	*Latin*	Citizen
Quiterie	*French*	Tranquil
Quorra	*Italian*	Heart
Quy	*Vietnamese*	Precious

R

Name	Origin	Definition
Rachael, Rachel, Rachele, Rahel, Raquel	*Hebrew*	One with purity
Rachida	*African*	Righteous
Rachna	*Indian*	Construction, arrangement
Radha	*Indian*	Prosperity
Radhiya	*African*	Agreeable
Rae	*Spanish*	Grace
Raedself	*English*	Elfin counsellor

Name	Origin	Definition
Raeka	*Spanish*	Beautiful, unique
Rafa	*Arabic*	Happy
Rafaella, Raphaella	*Hebrew*	Healer
Rahi	*Arabic*	Spring
Rahil	*Hebrew*	Innocent
Rai	*Japanese*	Doe
Raida	*Hebrew*	Graceful, shining
Rain, Raina, Raine	*Latin*	Ruler
Raisa, Raissa	*French*	Rose
Raja	*Arabic*	Hope
Rajani	*Indian*	Night
Rajata	*Indian*	Silver
Rakhi	*Indian*	Thread of brother-sister bonding
Ramani	*Indian*	Beautiful girl
Ramira	*Spanish*	Judicious
Ramita	*Indian*	Pleasing
Ramla	*African*	Prophetess
Ramona	*Spanish*	Wise protector
Ramya	*Indian*	Elegant, beautiful
Rana	*Latin*	Behold
Rane	*Norwegian*	Queen, pure
Rani	*Indian*	Song
Ranice	*Hebrew*	Lovely tune
Raoghnailt	*Scottish*	Lamb
Raonaid	*Hebrew*	Innocent
Rasha	*Arabic*	Gazelle
Rashida	*African*	Righteous

Name	Origin	Definition
Rasia	*Latin*	Rose
Rathnait	*Irish*	Wealthy, charming
Ratna	*Indian*	Gem
Raven, Ravyn	*English*	Dark-haired
Raya	*Latin*	Trusted by God
Rayna	*Hebrew*	Pure, clean
Rayne	*Latin*	Wise leader
Rayzel	*Hebrew*	Rose
Raziya	*African*	Sweet, agreeable
Rea, Rhea	*Latin*	Mother
Reaghan, Regan	*Celtic*	Regal
Reba, Rebakah, Rebecca, Rebeckah, Rebeque, Ree	*Hebrew*	Captivating
Reena, Riena, Rina	*Indian*	Queen
Regina, Reina	*Spanish*	Queenly
Rehema	*African*	Compassion
Rei, Reiko	*Japanese*	Gratitude
Reign, Rein	*Latin*	Ruler
Reilly	*Gaelic*	Valiant
Reine, Rexy, Reyna	*Latin*	Queenly
Reka	*Maori*	Sweet
Rekha	*Indian*	Straight line
Relle	*Greek*	Bright one
Rena	*Hebrew*	Joyous song
Renata, Rene, Renee, Renette	*Latin*	Reborn
Renita	*Latin*	To be firm
Reta	*Latin*	Child of light

Name	Origin	Definition
Reveka	*Hebrew*	Captivating
Rewa	*Polynesian*	Slender
Rheda	*Anglo-Saxon*	A goddess
Rhiannon, Riana, Rianne	*Welsh*	Great queen, witch
Rhoda, Rhodanthe, Rhodie	*Greek*	Rose
Rhonda	*Celtic*	Good spear
Rhoswen	*Gaelic*	White rose
Ri	*Hebrew*	Bitter
Ria	*Latin*	River
Rica	*Spanish*	Rules the home
Ricarda, Rikki	*English*	Powerful ruler
Rifka	*Hebrew*	Captivating
Riley	*Gaelic*	Valiant
Rilla, Rille, Rillia, Rillie	*German*	Brook
Rima	*Arabic*	White antelope
Rimona	*Hebrew*	Pomegranate
Rini	*Japanese*	Little bunny
Rinna, Rinnah	*Hebrew*	Joyous song
Rio	*Spanish*	River
Rioghnach, Riona	*Irish*	Royal
Risa	*Latin*	Laughing one
Rissa	*Latin*	Of the sea
Rita	*Greek*	Pearl, precious
Riva	*Hebrew*	River
Rivca, Rivka, Rivy	*Hebrew*	Captivating
Rive, Rivi, Reva, Reeva	*French*	River

Name	Origin	Definition
Rizpah	*Greek*	Hope
Roan, Rogan	*Gaelic*	Red-haired
Roana	*Spanish*	Reddish-brown skin
Roanee, Roanna	*Latin*	Rose
Robbin, Roberta, Robin, Robina, Robinette	*English*	Bright, famous
Rochella, Rochelle, Rochette	*French*	From the little rock
Roe, Roesia	*Greek*	Rose
Rohais	*French*	Rose
Rohana	*Indian*	Sandalwood
Rohini	*Indian*	Star
Rois	*Irish*	Horse
Roisine	*Polish*	Rose
Rolande	*German*	Famous soldier
Roma, Romaine, Romana, Romy	*Italian*	From Rome
Romhild, Romhilda, Romhilde	*German*	Glorious battle maiden
Rona, Ronia, Ronli	*Hebrew*	My joy
Ronat	*Celtic*	Seal
Ronica	*Latin*	True image
Ronnie	*Latin*	Powerful, rules with counsel
Rosa, Rosabell, Rosalee, Rosaleen, Rosalia, Rosalie	*Latin*	Rose
Rosalind, Rosalinde, Roselyn	*Spanish*	Little red-haired one

Name	Origin	Definition
Rosamaria, Rosemarie	*Spanish*	Bitter
Rosario	*Spanish*	Rosary
Rose, Rosebud, Rosella, Roselle, Rosellen, Rosemary	*Latin*	Rose
Rosemonde	*Latin*	Noted protector
Rosena, Rosetta, Rosette, Rosey, Rosina, Rosly	*Greek*	Rose
Roshni	*Indian*	Light
Rosselin	*French*	Red-haired
Roux	*French*	Red
Rowana, Rowena	*English*	From the rowan tree
Rox, Roxana, Roxane, Roxie, Roxy	*Persian*	Brilliant
Rubee, Rubia, Rubie, Rubina, Ruby	*French*	Jewel
Rue	*Greek*	Regret
Rufa, Rufina	*Spanish*	Red-haired
Rumer	*English*	Gypsy
Runa	*Scandinavian*	Secret lore
Rupa, Rupali	*Indian*	Beautiful
Ruta	*Hebrew*	Friend
Ruth, Ruthanne, Ruthie	*Hebrew*	Compassionate friend
Ryesen	*English*	Rye
Ryley	*Gaelic*	Valiant

S

Name	Origin	Definition
Sabel	Spanish	Devoted to God
Sabina, Sabine, Sabiny, Sabse, Saidhbhin	Latin	Sabine woman
Sabirah	Arabic	Patience
Sabra	Arabic	To rest
Sabrena, Sabrina	Latin	From the border land
Sachi, Sachiko	Japanese	Bliss-child
Sachita	Indian	Consciousness
Sadbh	Irish	Good
Sade	African	Honour, bestowing of a crown
Sadey, Sadie	Hebrew	Princess
Sadhana	Indian	Fulfilment
Sadhbba, Sadhbh	Irish	Wise
Sadira	Arabic	Ostrich running from water
Safa	Arabic	Innocent
Saffi	Danish	Wisdom
Safia, Safiya, Safiyyah	African	Pure, wise
Sagara	Indian	Ocean, sea
Sagirah	Arabic	Little one
Sahana	Indian	Patience
Sahar	Arabic	Awakening
Sahara	Arabic	The Moon
Saheli, Sakhi	Indian	Friend
Sahiba	Indian	A lady

Name	Origin	Definition
Sahila	*Indian*	Guide
Saida	*Arabic*	Helper
Saidah	*African*	Fortunate
Sairne	*Hebrew*	Princess
Sakari	*Native American*	Sweet
Sakina	*Arabic*	Friend
Sakinah	*Arabic*	Peace of mind, tranquility
Sakti	*Indian*	Energy, goodness
Sakura	*Japanese*	Cherry blossoms
Salaidh, Salli	*Spanish*	Saviour
Salal	*English*	Plant
Saleena, Salina	*French*	By the salt water
Salihah	*African*	Correct
Salila	*Indian*	Water
Sally	*Latin*	Princess
Salma	*African*	Peace, safety
Saloma, Salome	*Hebrew*	Peace
Salva	*Arabic*	Solace, comfort
Salvadora, Salvatora	*Spanish*	Saviour
Samantha	*Hebrew*	Listens well
Samar	*Arabic*	Summer season
Samara	*Hebrew*	Protected by God
Sameh	*Arabic*	Forgiver
Samirah	*Arabic*	Entertaining companion
Samma	*Arabic*	Sky
Samuela, Samuella	*Hebrew*	Asked of God

Name	Origin	Definition
Sancha, Sancia	*Spanish*	Holy
Sanchay	*Indian*	Collection
Sanda, Sandi	*Burmese*	Moon
Sandra, Sandrine	*English*	Protector of mankind
Sandya	*Indian*	Sunset
Sanie	*Greek*	Protector of mankind
Sanjna	*Indian*	Wife of the sun
Saphala	*Indian*	Successful
Saphira, Sapphira, Sapphire	*Greek*	Blue jewel
Sapna	*Indian*	Dream
Sara, Sarah, Sarene, Sarett, Sari, Sarine	*Hebrew*	Princess
Sarafina	*Hebrew*	Burning fire
Sarai	*Hebrew*	Argumentative
Saraid	*Celtic*	Excellent
Sarala	*Indian*	Simple
Sarasa	*Indian*	Swan
Sarea	*Hebrew*	Name of an angel
Saree	*Arabic*	Most noble
Sarisha	*Indian*	Charming, fascinating
Sarita	*Indian*	River
Saryu	*Indian*	The river Sharayu
Sasha	*English*	Protector of mankind
Sashi	*Indian*	Moon
Saturnina	*Spanish*	Gift of Saturn
Sauda	*African*	Black-skinned
Savanna, Savannah	*Spanish*	From the open plain

Name	Origin	Definition
Savarna	*Indian*	Daughter of the ocean
Savita	*Indian*	Sun
Saxona, Saxonia, Saxons	*English*	A Saxon
Scarlet, Scarlett	*English*	Deep red
Schannel	*French*	Channel
Schuyler, Sky, Skye, Skylar	*Dutch*	Shield, scholar
Scota	*Irish*	An Irish woman
Seana	*Irish*	Present
Seanna	*Celtic*	God's grace
Season	*Latin*	Planting time
Sebastiana, Sebastiane, Sebastianne	*Latin*	Revered one
Seema	*Greek*	Limit, border
Segelinde	*German*	Shield of victory
Seina	*Spanish*	Innocent
Sela	*Greek*	Saviour
Selam	*African*	Peace
Selby, Selden, Selwin, Selwyn	*English*	Of the manor-house farm
Selda	*German*	Famous warrior
Sele, Seleta	*Hebrew*	Rock
Selena, Selene, Selia, Selina, Selly	*Greek*	Moon
Selima	*Arabic*	Tranquil
Selin	*Arabic*	Peace
Selma	*Celtic*	Divinely protected

Name	Origin	Definition
Semina, Semine	*Danish*	Goddess of Sun, Moon and stars
Semira	*Hebrew*	From heaven
Sena	*Greek*	Moon
Sennett	*French*	Wise one
Senta	*German*	Wise one
Septima	*Latin*	Seventh born
Sera, Serafina, Serafine, Seraphina	*Hebrew*	Burning fire
Serena, Serene, Serenity	*Spanish*	Peaceful, calm
Serihilde	*German*	Armoured battle maiden
Sevita	*Indian*	Beloved
Shaila	*Indian*	Stone, mountain
Shaili	*Indian*	Style
Shaina	*Hebrew*	Beautiful
Shaine	*Hebrew*	God is gracious
Shalini	*Indian*	Modesty
Shana	*Hebrew*	Gracious, merciful
Shandy	*English*	Rambunctious
Shanen, Shannon	*Irish*	Wise one
Shani	*African*	Marvelous
Shanna	*Hebrew*	Beautiful
Shantay	*French*	Enchanted
Shanti	*Indian*	Peace
Shara, Sharee, Sharen, Shari, Sharon, Sharyn	*Hebrew*	Princess
Sharlene	*English*	Strong

Name	Origin	Definition
Shauna, Shawna	*Irish*	God's grace
Shay	*Swedish*	Majestic
Shayla	*Celtic*	Fairy palace
Shayna, Shaynah	*Hebrew*	Beautiful
Sheela	*Latin*	Blind
Sheena	*Irish*	God's gracious gift
Sheila, Sheilagh	*Latin*	Blind
Shein	*Burmese*	Reflection
Shelby	*English*	Sheltered town
Shelley, Shellie, Shelly	*Anglo-Saxon*	One with purity
Sheri, Sherrill, Sherry, Sherryl	*French*	Beloved, dear
Shifra	*Hebrew*	Beautiful
Shika	*Japanese*	Deer
Shikha	*Indian*	Flame
Shina	*Japanese*	Virtue, good
Shira, Shirah, Shiri	*Hebrew*	Song
Shirlee, Shirleen, Shirleigh, Shirley	*English*	From the country meadow
Shona	*Hebrew*	Gracious, merciful
Shoshana, Shoshanah	*Hebrew*	Rose
Shri	*Indian*	Lustre
Shyla, Shylah	*Celtic*	Loyal to God, strong
Sian, Siana	*Hebrew*	God's grace
Siany	*Irish*	Good health
Sibby, Sibeal, Sibille, Sibyl, Sibyla, Sybil, Sybille	*Greek*	Prophetess, fortune-teller

Name	Origin	Definition
Sidne, Sidney, Sidoney, Sydnee, Sydney	*French*	From the city of St. Denis
Sienna	*Italian*	Reddish brown
Sierra	*Irish*	Dark
Sigfreda, Sigfriede	*German*	Victorious
Signa, Signe	*Scandinavian*	Signal, sign
Sigourney	*French*	Daring king
Sigrath, Sigrid, Sigwald	*Norse*	Winning advisor
Silva, Silvana, Silvia, Silvie, Sylvana, Sylvia, Sylvie	*Latin*	Woodland maid
Silver	*Anglo-Saxon*	White
Sima	*Scottish*	Listener
Simcha	*Hebrew*	Joyous
Simona, Simone	*Hebrew*	One who listens
Simran	*Indian*	God's gift
Sinead	*Hebrew*	Kind
Siobhan	*Irish*	Gracious
Sippora	*Hebrew*	Bird
Siran	*Arabic*	Alluring
Sirena	*Greek*	Siren
Sisi	*African*	Born on Sunday
Sissa	*Greek*	Love, grace
Sissy	*Latin*	Young girl
Siubhan	*Scottish*	Praised
Skena	*Scottish*	From Skene
Skule	*Scandinavian*	Hide
Slaine, Slainie, Slania	*Irish*	Good health
Smriti	*Indian*	Recollection

Name	Origin	Definition
Sofi, Sofia, Sofie, Sophia, Sophie	*Greek*	Wisdom
Sohni	*Indian*	Beautiful
Solace	*Latin*	Comfort
Solaine	*French*	Dignified
Solana	*Spanish*	Sunshine
Solange	*French*	Rare jewel
Soleil	*French*	Sun
Sona	*Indian*	Gold
Sonia, Sonja, Sonya	*Indian*	Wisdom
Sora, Sorano	*Japanese*	Of the sky
Sosanna	*Irish*	Lily
Sparrow	*English*	Bird
Spring	*English*	Spring season
Sraddha	*Indian*	Faith
Stacey, Stacy, Stasia	*Latin*	Stable
Star, Starla, Starling, Starr, Stella, Stellar	*Latin*	Star
Stefa, Stefania, Stephana, Stephanie	*Greek*	Crown
Stockard, Stokkard	*English*	Hardy tree
Storme	*English*	Tempest
Sue, Sueanne, Susan, Suzanne, Susie	*English*	Lily
Suki	*Japanese*	Beloved
Suma	*Japanese*	Born during the summer
Sumi	*Japanese*	Clear, refined

Name	Origin	Definition
Summer	*English*	Born during the summer
Sunny	*English*	Cheerful
Supriya	*Indian*	Beloved
Surya	*Indian*	The Sun
Svetlana	*Russian*	Star
Swann	*Scandinavian*	Swan
Sweta	*Indian*	Fair-complexioned
Syna	*Greek*	Two together
Synne	*Anglo-Saxon*	Gift of the Sun

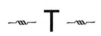

Name	Origin	Definition
Tabatha, Tabbi, Tabbie, Tabitha	*Hebrew*	Beauty, grace
Tabia	*African*	Make incantations
Tablita	*Native American*	Tiara
Tabora	*Spanish*	Plays a small drum
Tacy	*English*	Silence
Taffy	*Welsh*	Beloved
Tahirah	*Arabic*	Chaste, pure
Tahlia, Talia, Taliah	*Hebrew*	Born at Christmas
Tai	*Hebrew*	Talent
Tailor, Tayla, Taylar, Taylor	*English*	Tailor
Taite, Taitum, Tate, Tatum, Tayte	*Anglo-Saxon*	Cheerful, brings joy

Name	Origin	Definition
Taka	*Japanese*	Honorable
Takara	*Japanese*	Treasure, precious
Takoda	*Native American*	Friend to everyone
Tala	*Native American*	Wolf
Talitha, Talya	*Greek*	Dew of heaven
Tallara	*Australian Aboriginal*	Rain
Tallis	*French*	Woodland
Tallulah, Talulah	*Native American*	Leaping water
Talora, Talori	*Hebrew*	Morning's dew
Tamar, Tamara, Tamary, Tammy, Tamryn, Tamra	*Hebrew*	Palm tree
Tamsen, Tamsin, Tamson	*Greek*	Twin
Tanaka	*Japanese*	Dweller
Tandra	*African*	Beauty mark
Tani, Tania, Tanya	*Russian*	Fairy princess
Tansy	*Greek*	Immortality
Tanvi	*Indian*	Delicate girl
Tapanga	*Hebrew*	Unpredictable
Tapti	*Indian*	Name of a river
Tara	*Scottish*	Hill where the kings meet
Tarana	*African*	Born during the day
Taria	*Gaelic*	Tower
Tarin, Taryn, Tarynn	*English*	From the rocky hills

Name	Origin	Definition
Tasha, Tashia, Tassa	*English*	Born at Christmas
Tasia	*Latin*	Stable
Tathra	*Australian Aboriginal*	Beautiful country
Tatiana, Tatjana	*Russian*	Fairy princess
Taura, Taurina	*English*	Born under the sign of Taurus
Taves, Tavia	*English*	Great
Tawia	*African*	First child born after twins
Tawnee, Tawney, Tawni, Tawny	*Irish*	A green field
Tayce	*French*	Silence
Tayen	*Native American*	New Moon
Taylee, Taylie	*Greek*	Blooming, plentiful
Teagan, Tegan, Teige	*Irish*	Good-looking
Teal, Teela	*English*	Blue-green colour
Teara	*Latin*	Flower name
Tedra	*Greek*	Gift of God
Tekla	*Greek*	Divine fame
Telma	*Spanish*	Nursing
Teme	*Hebrew*	Without flaw
Temira	*Hebrew*	Tall
Tempest, Tempeste, Tempestt	*French*	Storm
Teodora	*Spanish*	Gift of God
Teppi	*Greek*	Pretty in face

Name	Origin	Definition
Tera, Terena, Terra, Terrena	*Latin*	Earth, land
Teresa, Theresa, Therese	*Spanish*	Reaper
Teri, Teriana, Terri, Terrin, Terry	*Greek*	Saint's name
Tesia	*Polish*	Loved by God
Tess, Tessa	*English*	Essence
Tessie, Tessy	*English*	Fourth born
Teva	*Scottish*	Twin
Thadina, Thadine	*Hebrew*	Given praise
Thais	*Greek*	The bond
Thalia	*Greek*	Near water
Thara	*Arabic*	Wealth
Thea	*Greek*	Healer, wholesome
Theda, Theodora, Theone, Theophilia, Theora	*Greek*	Gift of God
Thelma	*Greek*	Nursing
Thera	*Greek*	Wild
Thisbe	*Greek*	Where the doves live
Thistle	*English*	Thistle
Thomasa, Thomasina, Thomassa	*Greek*	Twin
Thora, Thordia	*Norse*	Thunder
Thyra	*Greek*	Shield-bearer
Thyrza	*Hebrew*	Sweet-natured
Tia, Tiana, Tianna	*Greek*	Princess
Tiara	*Latin*	Flower name
Tibelde	*German*	The boldest

Name	Origin	Definition
Tierra	*Spanish*	Earth, land
Tiesha	*English*	Joyful
Tifanee, Tiffany, Tiffney, Tiphany	*French*	Appearance of God
Tilda, Tilly	*French*	Battle maiden, strength
Tina	*English*	Heavenly
Tipper	*Irish*	A well
Tira	*Scottish*	Land
Tish	*Latin*	Noble one
Titania	*Greek*	Giant
Titian	*Greek*	Red-gold
Tiva	*Native American*	Dance
Tivona	*Hebrew*	Loves nature
Toa	*African*	Woman of the sea
Toinette, Toni, Tonia	*Latin*	Priceless, flourishing
Topaz	*Latin*	A yellow gemstone
Tora	*Norse*	Thunder
Torey, Tori, Torri	*Latin*	Victory
Tosia	*Latin*	Inestimable
Tracey, Tracie, Tracy, Tressa	*Greek*	Reaper
Treise	*Irish*	Strong
Trella	*Spanish*	Star
Treva, Treve	*Celtic*	Prudent
Tricia, Trish, Trisha	*Latin*	Noble one
Trina	*Greek*	Pure, innocent
Trinity, Triny	*Latin*	The holy three

Name	Origin	Definition
Trishna	*Indian*	Thirst
Trista	*Latin*	Sorrowful
Tristen	*English*	Outcry
Trixie, Trixy	*English*	Cheerful, brings joy
Trudy, True	*Teutonic*	Spear maiden
Tryne	*Dutch*	Pure
Tryphena	*Latin*	Dainty
Tsifira	*Hebrew*	Crown
Tuesday	*English*	Born on Tuesday
Tullia	*Irish*	Peaceful
Twyla	*English*	Woven
Tyna, Tyne	*English*	River
Tyra	*Scottish*	Land
Tzivia	*Hebrew*	Doe

 U

Name	Origin	Definition
Uchenna	*African*	God's will
Udaya	*Indian*	Dawn
Udela, Udele	*Anglo-Saxon*	Wealthy
Ula	*Spanish*	Sea jewel
Ulani	*Polynesian*	Cheerful, light-hearted
Uldwyna	*English*	Special friend
Uli	*German*	Noble leader
Ulla	*English*	Has willpower
Ulrica	*English*	Wolf ruler

Name	Origin	Definition
Ultima	*Latin*	Aloof
Uma	*Japanese*	Horse
Umina	*Australian Aboriginal*	Sleep
Una	*Celtic*	One, unity
Unice	*Greek*	Victorious
Unity	*Irish*	Together
Urania	*Greek*	Heavenly
Urenna	*African*	Father's pride
Uria	*Hebrew*	God is my light
Uriana	*Greek*	The unknown
Urice	*Hebrew*	Light
Ursa, Ursula	*Latin*	Little bear
Urvi	*Indian*	Earth
Usa	*Japanese*	Moon
Uta, Ute	*German*	Fortunate maid of battle
Uttara	*Indian*	Star

V

Name	Origin	Definition
Vail, Vale, Valle, Vayle	*French*	From the valley
Vajra	*Indian*	Diamond
Val, Valarie, Valeraine, Valeria, Valerie	*French*	Brave
Vala	*English*	Chosen
Valborga	*German*	Protecting ruler
Valda	*Norse*	Strong warrior

Name	Origin	Definition
Valeda, Valentiane, Valentina, Valentine, Valina	*Latin*	Good health
Valencia	*Latin*	Brave
Vana	*Indian*	Ultimate bliss
Vanda, Vande	*German*	Wanderer
Vanesa, Vanessa	*Spanish*	Butterfly
Vania, Vanya	*Russian*	God's gift
Vanita	*Indian*	A lady
Vanna	*Greek*	God's gift
Vanora	*Greek*	White wave
Varda, Vardit	*Hebrew*	Rose
Varsha	*Indian*	Rain
Varuni	*Indian*	A goddess
Vasanta	*Indian*	Spring
Vashti	*Persian*	Beautiful
Vedetta, Vedette	*French*	From the guard tower
Veena	*Indian*	A musical instrument
Vega	*Arabic*	Falling star
Velika	*Slavic*	Great
Velvet	*English*	Soft
Venetia	*Italian*	Blessed
Vera, Vere, Verenia, Verin, Verine	*Slavic*	Faith
Verena, Verena, Verina	*Latin*	Protector
Verita, Verity	*English*	Truth
Verna, Verne	*French*	From the alder grove

Name	Origin	Definition
Veronica, Veronique	*Latin*	True image
Verta	*Latin*	Life
Vesna	*Greek*	Goddess of spring
Vespera	*Latin*	Evening
Vesta	*Latin*	Guardian of the sacred fire
Veta	*Spanish*	Intelligent
Vibiana	*Latin*	Lively
Vic, Vicki, Victoria, Victorienne, Vittoria	*Latin*	Victory
Vidette	*Hebrew*	Dearly loved
Vidonia	*Latin*	Vine branch
Vidula	*Indian*	Moon
Vidya	*Indian*	Wisdom, knowledge
Vienna	*Latin*	From wine country
Vieva	*Welsh*	White spirit, white-cheeked
Vignette	*French*	Little vine
Villetta, Vilette	*French*	From the country estate
Vina	*Spanish*	From the vineyard
Vineeta	*Indian*	Humble
Viola, Violet	*English*	Violet
Violetta, Viollette	*French*	Little violet
Virginia, Virginie	*English*	Chaste, maiden
Vita	*Latin*	Life
Viv, Viveca, Vivian, Vivie, Vivien, Vyvyan	*Latin*	Lively
Voleta, Voletta	*French*	Veiled
Vrinda	*Indian*	Virtue, strength

W

Name	Origin	Definition
Walda, Welda	*German*	Ruler
Waleis, Wallis	*English*	From Wales
Waltraud	*Teutonic*	Strength
Wanda, Wande, Wenda, Wendeline, Wendy	*German*	Wanderer
Wanetta, Wann	*English*	Pale
Wania, Wanja, Wanya	*Russian*	God's gift
Warda	*German*	Guardian
Warrina	*Australian Aboriginal*	To give
Welsie, Welss	*English*	From the west
Weslee, Weslia	*English*	From the west meadow
Whitley	*English*	White meadow
Whitney	*English*	From the white island
Wihelma, Wilhelmina, Wilhelmine, Willa	*Teutonic*	Fierce protector
Wila	*Australian Aboriginal*	Woman, wife
Wilda, Wilde	*German*	Wild
Willow	*English*	Willow tree
Wilona	*English*	Hoped for
Winda	*African*	Hunt
Winifred, Winifrid, Winifride, Winn, Winnie	*English*	Peaceful friend

Name	Origin	Definition
Winona, Winonah	*Native American*	First-born daughter
Winter, Winters, Wynter	*English*	Born in the winter
Wyanet	*Native American*	Beautiful
Wyla	*Teutonic*	Woman, wife
Wyn, Wynn, Wynne	*Welsh*	Fair
Wyuna	*Australian Aboriginal*	Clear

X

Name	Origin	Definition
Xalvadora	*Spanish*	Saviour
Xandra, Xandy	*English*	Protector of mankind
Xanthe	*Greek*	Yellow, fair hair
Xavia	*Greek*	Protector of mankind
Xaviera	*Spanish*	Bright, splendid
Xavierre, Xevera, Xeveria	*French*	Owner of a new home
Xena, Xenia	*Greek*	Hospitable
Xetsa	*African*	Twin
Xylia	*Greek*	Wood-dweller
Xylina, Xylona	*Greek*	From the forest

 Y

Name	Origin	Definition
Yachne	*Hebrew*	Kind
Yadra	*Spanish*	Mother
Yaffa	*Hebrew*	Beautiful
Yamini	*Indian*	Night
Yamka	*Native American*	Blossom
Yanamaria, Yanamarie	*Spanish*	Bitter grace
Yani	*Australian Aboriginal*	Peace
Yashila	*Indian*	Famous
Yasmeen, Yasmia, Yasmin, Yasmina	*Arabic*	Jasmine flower
Yayoi	*Japanese*	March
Yedda	*English*	Beautiful voice
Yelena	*Russian*	Shining light
Yepa	*Native American*	Snow woman
Yesenia	*Spanish*	Gypsy
Yesmina	*Hebrew*	Strength
Yetsye	*Hebrew*	Life
Yetta	*English*	Beautiful voice
Yeva	*Russian*	Life-giving
Yindi	*Australian Aboriginal*	The Sun
Ynes, Ynez	*Latin*	Pure
Yoana	*Spanish*	God's gift

Name	Origin	Definition
Yoki	*Native American*	Rain
Yoko	*Japanese*	Positive
Yolanda, Yolande	*Greek*	Modest
Yomaris	*Spanish*	I am the Sun
Yona, Yonina	*Hebrew*	Dove
Yordana	*Hebrew*	Descendent
Yoseba, Yosepha, Yosephina	*Hebrew*	God will multiply
Ysabel	*French*	Devoted to God
Yseult	*French*	Fair
Yumi	*Japanese*	Beautiful
Yumoke	*African*	Everyone loves the baby
Yungara	*Australian Aboriginal*	A wife
Yuri	*Japanese*	To hear
Yuta	*Hebrew*	Praise
Yvette, Yvo, Yvonna, Yvonne	*French*	Archer

~ Z ~

Name	Origin	Definition
Zabrina, Zavrina	*English*	Legendary princess
Zada	*Arabic*	Fortunate
Zahara	*African*	Dazzling
Zahra	*African*	Flower
Zaida, Zayda	*Arabic*	Lucky

Name	Origin	Definition
Zaira, Zaire, Zaria	*Arabic*	Rose
Zakia	*Hebrew*	Bright, pure
Zalika	*African*	Well-born
Zambda	*Hebrew*	Meditation
Zamora	*Hebrew*	Praised
Zandra, Zandria	*English*	Protector of mankind
Zaneta, Zanetta, Zanita	*Spanish*	God's gift
Zara	*French*	Dawn
Zari	*Arabic*	Princess
Zarya	*Slavic*	Golden dawn
Zayna	*Arabic*	Beautiful
Zebina	*Greek*	One who is gifted
Zehave	*Hebrew*	Golden
Zehira	*Hebrew*	Protected
Zelda	*German*	Famous warrior
Zelia	*Greek*	Zealous one
Zelinda	*German*	Shield of victory
Zelma	*English*	Comely
Zelpha, Zilpha	*Hebrew*	Beautiful
Zemira, Zemora, Zimria	*Hebrew*	Praised
Zemirah	*Hebrew*	Joyous song
Zena, Zenais, Zenna, Zinovia	*Greek*	Born of Zeus
Zenia	*Greek*	Hospitable
Zera	*Hebrew*	Seed
Zeva, Ziva	*Greek*	Wolf
Zeya	*Burmese*	Success
Zia	*Hebrew*	Light, splendour

Name	Origin	Definition
Zibia	*Hebrew*	Doe
Zigana	*Hungarian*	Gypsy
Zihna	*Native American*	Spins
Zila, Zili, Zilla	*Hebrew*	Shadow
Zilvia	*Latin*	Woodland maid
Zimra	*Hebrew*	Song
Zina, Zinia, Zinnia	*English*	Flower name
Zinerva	*Celtic*	Fair
Ziona	*Hebrew*	A sign
Zippora	*Hebrew*	Beautiful
Zita	*Hebrew*	Virgin
Zizi	*Arabic*	Rose
Zoe, Zoey	*Greek*	Life
Zohra, Zora, Zorah, Zori, Zoriana, Zorina	*Slavic*	Golden dawn
Zola	*African*	Productive
Zosia, Zotia	*Polish*	Wise one
Zulema, Zulima	*Hebrew*	Peace, tranquility
Zuri, Zuria, Zurie	*French*	White and lovely
Zuriel	*Hebrew*	Stone
Zurina, Zurine	*Spanish*	White
Zuza	*Czech*	Graceful lily
Zwena	*African*	Good
Zylina, Zylona	*Greek*	From the forest
Zysel	*Hebrew*	Sweet

Boys Names

— A —

Name	Origin	Definition
Aaron	*Hebrew*	Revered, sharer
Abakus	*English*	Clever
Abbey	*German*	Bringer of joy
Abbot, Abbott, Abott, Abotte	*Arabic*	Father
Abby	*German*	Firm
Abdul	*Arabic*	Allah's servant
Abel, Abele, Abell, Able	*Spanish*	Naïve, peaceful, vital
Abner	*Hebrew*	Cheerful leader
Abony	*Hungarian*	Father
Abraham, Abrahim, Abram	*Hebrew*	Father of many
Abraxas	*Spanish*	Bright
Acacio, Achazio	*Hebrew*	The Lord holds
Ace, Acey	*Latin*	One, unity
Acharius	*Latin*	Ungrateful
Achilles, Achille	*Greek*	Hero of the Iliad
Ackerley, Ackley	*English*	Meadow of oaks
Acton	*English*	Town with many oaks
Adair	*Gaelic*	Noble, exalted
Adalfrid, Adelfrid, Adelfried	*German*	Protects the descendants
Adalricus	*German*	Noble, powerful and rich
Adam, Adams, Adamson	*Hebrew*	Created by God

Name	Origin	Definition
Adan	*Hebrew*	Little fire
Addie	*Hebrew*	Created by God
Addisen, Adison	*English*	Adam's son
Adelais	*Latin*	Noble
Adele	*Hebrew*	Noble, kind
Adelphos	*Greek*	Brother
Adler	*German*	Eagle
Adley	*Hebrew*	Just
Adolfo, Adolfus	*German*	Noble hero
Adonis	*Greek*	Handsome
Adrian, Adriano, Adrianus	*Greek*	Rich, wealthy
Adrianus	*Latin*	Dark one
Adriel	*Native American*	Skilled
Agostino, Agustin	*Latin*	Exalted
Ahmad, Ahmet	*Arabic*	Praised one
Aidan	*English*	Little fire
Aiken	*Anglo-Saxon*	Sturdy
Ailen	*English*	Made of oak
Aimery, Aimory	*Teutonic*	Industrious ruler
Ajay	*Indian*	Unconquerable, invincible
Akira	*Japanese*	Anchor
Akshay	*Indian*	Name of a god
Alain, Alan	*Celtic*	Cheerful, noble
Alasdair, Alastair, Alastaire, Alistaire, Alister	*Scottish*	Protector of mankind, defender

Name	Origin	Definition
Alban	*Latin*	White, fair
Albert, Alberto, Albertus, Albrecht	*German*	Noble, bright
Alcott	*English*	Old cottage
Aldan	*English*	Wise protector, old friend
Alder	*English*	Birch tree, revered one
Aldous	*German*	Wise
Aldrich, Aldridge, Aldrych	*English*	Old king
Aldwin	*English*	Wise protector, old friend
Alec, Alejandro, Aleksander, Alessandro, Alex, Alexander	*Greek*	Protector of mankind
Alf, Alfie	*English*	Wise counsel
Alfonse, Alfonso, Alphonse	*German*	Noble estate, eager
Alfred, Alfredo	*English*	Wise counsel
Ali	*Arabic*	Noble, truth
Alim	*Arabic*	Wise, learned
Allah	*Arabic*	God
Allard	*English*	Noble, brave
Altair	*Arabic*	Bird, star
Alton	*Anglo-Saxon*	From the old manor
Alvin, Alwyn	*English*	Noble friend
Amadeus	*Latin*	Love of God
Amal	*Indian*	Hope, wish, dream
Ameer	*Arabic*	Prince

Name	Origin	Definition
Amherst	*English*	Place name
Amir	*Arabic*	Commanding
Amistad	*Spanish*	Friendship
Amory	*Latin*	Loving
Amos	*Hebrew*	Troubled
Anatoly	*Greek*	From the East
Anders, Anderson, Andre, Andrew, Andy	*French*	Manly, valiant, courageous
Ang	*Chinese*	Red
Angelo	*Greek*	Angel, heavenly messenger
Angus	*Gaelic*	Superb, unique
Ansel	*German*	Diety
Ansley	*English*	From the pastureland of the noble
Anson	*Anglo-Saxon*	Son of a nobleman
Anthony, Anthoney, Antoine, Antonio, Anton	*Latin*	Priceless, flourishing, flower
Apari	*Australian Aboriginal*	Father
Aquila	*Greek*	Hero of the Iliad
Aram	*Arabic*	High place
Arch	*Anglo-Saxon*	Bold prince
Archer	*Teutonic*	The archer
Archibald, Archie, Archy	*Anglo-Saxon*	Bold prince
Arden, Ardis	*Latin*	Passionate
Ardon	*English*	Bronze

Name	Origin	Definition
Ares	*Greek*	God of war
Argus	*Greek*	Bright, watchful
Ari	*Hebrew*	Lioness of God
Arion	*Greek*	Musician
Aristo	*Greek*	Best
Arkin	*Norwegian*	The eternal king's son
Arland, Arlen, Arliss, Arlyss, Arlo	*Celtic*	Pledge, vow
Arleigh	*Celtic*	Meadow of the hares
Arman, Armand, Armande, Armando	*French*	Of the army
Armen	*Arabic*	Armenian
Armon	*Hebrew*	Castle
Arnold, Arnaud, Arnault, Arnel, Arnell, Arnie	*German*	Eagle, powerful
Aron, Arron	*Hebrew*	Revered, sharer
Arsenio	*Greek*	Manly, virile
Art, Arte	*Welsh*	A rock
Artemis	*Greek*	Source of water
Arthie	*Celtic*	Noble
Arthur	*Celtic*	King
Artie	*Greek*	Moon
Arturo	*Celtic*	Noble
Arun	*Indian*	Sun
Arwin	*Celtic*	Young prince
Asher, Ashe, Asser	*Hebrew*	Fortunate, lucky, blessed
Ashwin	*Indian*	Strong horse

Name	Origin	Definition
Asim	*Indian*	Boundless, limitless
Asztrik	*Hungarian*	Made from ashenwood
Athan	*Greek*	Immortal
Atman	*Indian*	The self
Atul	*Indian*	Matchless
Aubert	*German*	Noble, bright
Aubin, Auburn	*Latin*	Fair
August, Augustin, Augustine, Augusto, Augustus	*Latin*	Exalted
Aurelio, Aurelius	*Latin*	Gold
Austin	*Latin*	Exalted
Averil	*English*	Boar warrior
Avery	*Scottish*	Ruler of the elves
Avram	*Hebrew*	Father of many
Axel	*Swedish*	Divine reward
Azaria	*Hebrew*	God has helped
Azzam	*Arabic*	Determined

 **B**

Name	Origin	Definition
Bae	*Korean*	Inspiration
Bahir	*Arabic*	Sparkling
Bailey, Baileey Baily	*English*	Fortification, able
Bailintin	*Irish*	Valiant
Bainbridge, Bainbrydge	*English*	Lives near the bridge over the white water

Name	Origin	Definition
Baird	*Irish*	Bard
Bairn	*Scottish*	Child
Balamani	*Indian*	Young jewel
Baldev	*Indian*	God-like in power
Baldwin, Baldwyn	*German*	Brave friend
Balfour	*Scottish*	From the pastureland
Ballard	*French*	A dancing song
Balram	*Indian*	Krishna's brother
Balwin	*German*	Brave friend
Bama	*Hebrew*	Son of prophecy
Bancroft	*English*	From the bean field
Banner	*Scottish*	Flagbearer
Banning	*Gaelic*	Son of the slayer
Bao	*Vietnamese*	Protection
Barak	*Hebrew*	Victory against overwhelming odds
Baram	*Hebrew*	Son of the nation
Barclay, Barklay	*Anglo-Saxon*	Birch meadow
Barden	*English*	Lives near the boar's den
Bardon	*English*	A singer and/or poet
Barlow	*English*	Lives on the bare hill
Barnaby	*English*	Son of comfort
Barnard, Barney	*English*	Brave as a bear
Barnett	*English*	Noble man
Baron	*English*	Noble man
Barr	*English*	Noble man
Barrett	*English*	Bear-like
Barrie, Barry, Barrymore	*Welsh*	Spear thrower

Name	Origin	Definition
Bart, Bartholomew	*Hebrew*	Furrow, hill
Bartleigh, Bartley	*English*	From Bart's meadow
Bartlett	*French*	Farmer
Barton	*English*	From the barley farm
Basil, Basile, Basilia	*English*	Brave
Bastian	*Latin*	Revered one
Bates	*Shakespearian*	Furrow, hill
Bax, Baxley, Baxter	*English*	Baker
Baylen	*French*	Auburn-haired
Beacan	*Gaelic*	Small, little one
Beacher, Beecher	*English*	Dweller by the beech tree
Beardsley	*English*	Beard, wood
Bearn	*Anglo-Saxon*	Son
Beau	*French*	Handsome, beautiful
Beaufort	*French*	From the beautiful fortress
Beck	*Swedish*	From the brook
Bela	*Hebrew*	White
Belden	*English*	Child of the unspoiled glen
Bellamy	*French*	Handsome friend
Bem	*African*	Bear
Benedict	*English*	Blessed
Benjamin, Ben	*Hebrew*	Son of the right hand
Bennett	*English*	Blessed
Benoit	*Latin*	Blessed
Benson, Bensen	*Hebrew*	Excellent son
Bentley	*English*	From the moors

Name	Origin	Definition
Benton	*English*	Blessed
Benwick	*Anglo-Saxon*	From Ban
Bercleah	*English*	Lives at the birch tree meadow
Beresford	*English*	From the barley ford
Bergen	*English*	Free citizen
Berk	*Arabic*	Solid, firm
Berkley	*Irish*	From the birch meadow
Berlyn	*German*	Son of Berl
Bernard, Bernardo	*French*	Brave as a bear
Bert	*English*	Bright, famous
Berton	*English*	Fortress
Bertram	*Swedish*	A knight
Bertrand	*French*	Intelligent
Berwyk	*English*	From the barley grange
Beth	*Scottish*	God's oath
Bevin	*Celtic*	Singer
Bevyn	*Celtic*	Young soldier
Bhanu	*Indian*	Sun
Bhaskar	*Indian*	Sun
Bhupen	*Indian*	King
Bialy	*Polish*	White-haired
Bickford	*English*	From the hewer's ford
Bienvenido	*Spanish*	Welcome
Bilal	*Arabic*	First convert of Muhammad
Billy	*English*	Fierce protector

Name	Origin	Definition
Bimisi	*Native American*	Slippery
Bingham	*German*	Kettle-shaped hollow
Birche	*English*	Birch
Birk	*Scottish*	Birch tree
Birkett	*English*	Lives at the birch headland
Bishop	*English*	A bishop
Bjorn	*Swedish*	Bear
Black	*English*	Dark
Blade, Bladen	*English*	Glory
Blaine, Blain, Blane	*Irish*	Source of a river
Blair	*Irish*	Field of battle
Blake, Blakely, Blakemore	*Scottish*	Dark, dark-haired and fair, pale
Blanco	*English*	Blond
Blaze	*English*	Resolute protector
Blythe	*English*	Happy
Bo	*French*	Commanding
Bob, Bobbie, Bobby	*English*	Bright, famous
Bocley	*English*	Lives at the buck meadow
Boden	*French*	Blond
Bodwyn	*Arthurian Legend*	Brother of Mark
Bogart	*German*	Strong as a bow
Bohdan	*Hebrew*	Gift from God

Name	Origin	Definition
Bolton	*English*	Of the manor house farm
Bond	*English*	Farmer
Bonifacio, Bonifaco	*Spanish*	Benefactor
Bono	*French*	Good
Booker	*English*	Beech tree
Boone	*French*	Sweet, good
Boothe	*English*	Lives in a hut
Borak	*Arabic*	The lightning
Bordan	*French*	Cottage
Boris, Borys	*Russian*	Fight, battler
Boswell	*French*	Forested town
Botan	*Japanese*	Peony
Bourn, Bourne	*English*	From the brook
Bowden, Bowdyn	*Celtic*	Messenger
Bowie	*Irish*	Yellow-haired
Bowman	*English*	The archer
Boyce	*French*	Lives near the wood
Boyd, Boyden	*Scottish*	Blond
Brad, Bradley	*English*	From the broad meadow
Bradbourne, Bradburn	*English*	From the brook
Braddock	*English*	Broad-spreading oak
Braden, Bradon, Bradyn, Brayden, Braydon	*Irish*	From the broad meadow
Bradford	*English*	Broad crossing
Bradshaw	*English*	Broad clearing in the wood

Name	Origin	Definition
Brady	*English*	Spirited
Bram	*Irish*	Father of many
Brandan, Brandon, Brandyn	*English*	Sword blade
Brandt	*Teutonic*	Firebrand
Brannen, Branson, Branton, Brantson	*Irish*	Sword blade
Brant	*English*	Fiery hill
Brantley	*English*	Proud
Brasil	*Celtic*	Battle
Braxton	*Anglo-Saxon*	Badger
Brecc	*Anglo-Saxon*	Name of a king
Breen	*Irish*	Fairy palace
Brencis	*Latin*	The crown of victory
Brendt, Brent, Brenton	*English*	Hilltop
Brenn, Brennen, Brennon	*English*	Prince
Brett, Bret, Bretton	*French*	A native of Britain or Brittany
Brewster	*English*	Brewer
Brian	*Celtic*	Strong
Brice	*Scottish*	Son of a nobleman
Brickand	*Celtic*	Swift, quick-moving
Bridger	*English*	Lives at tbe bridge
Brigg	*Celtic*	Swift, quick-moving
Brigham	*English*	Soldier
Brighton	*Hebrew*	The one who is loved
Brinley	*English*	Tawny
Brishen	*English*	Born during a rain

Name	Origin	Definition
Brock	*English*	Badger
Brockley	*English*	From the badger meadow
Broderick	*Irish*	Brother
Brody	*Irish*	Ditch, unusual beard
Brom	*Gaelic*	Raven
Bronson	*German*	Son of the dark man
Brooks	*English*	Son of Brooke
Brougher	*English*	Lives at the fortress
Broughton	*English*	From the fortified town
Brown	*English*	Dark-skinned
Bruce	*Scottish*	Woodlands
Bruno	*English*	Brown
Brutus	*Latin*	Brute
Bryant	*Celtic*	Strong
Bryce	*Celtic*	Swift, quick-moving
Brydger	*English*	Lives at the bridge
Bryston	*Scottish*	Speckled
Buchanan	*Scottish*	From the cannon's seat
Buck, Buckley, Buckner	*English*	Male deer, meadow of deer
Bud, Buddy	*English*	Herald, friend
Bundy	*English*	Free
Burbank	*English*	Lives on the castle's hill
Burdon	*English*	Lives at the castle

Name	Origin	Definition
Burel	*French*	Reddish-brown-haired
Burgess	*Celtic*	Choice
Burghard	*English*	Strong as a castle
Burke	*German*	Fortified hill
Burkett	*French*	From the little stronghold
Burle, Burleigh	*English*	Knotted wood
Burnell	*Irish*	Bear, brown
Burns	*English*	From the brook
Burr	*Swedish*	Youth
Burrell	*French*	Fortified
Burton	*English*	Fortress
Byford	*English*	Lives at the river crossing
Byrd	*English*	Bird
Byrne	*English*	From the brook
Byron	*French*	Bear

 C

Name	Origin	Definition
Cacey	*Irish*	Brave, watchful
Cadby	*English*	From the warrior's settlement
Cadman	*Anglo-Saxon*	Fighter
Cadwell	*English*	Cold spring
Caesar	*Latin*	Hairy child, long-haired

Name	Origin	Definition
Cagney	*Irish*	Surname
Cahya	*Hebrew*	Life
Cailean	*Scottish*	Child
Caillen	*Scottish*	Virile
Caine	*Hebrew*	Warrior
Cal, Cale, Caleb	*Hebrew*	Bold
Calan	*Scottish*	Child
Calbert	*English*	Cowherd, cowboy
Calbex	*English*	Shepherd
Calder	*English*	Rough waters
Caldwell	*English*	From the cold spring
Calhoun	*Irish*	From the forest
Callaghan	*Irish*	Strife
Callum	*Scottish*	Bald dove
Calvin, Calvyn	*Spanish*	Bald
Cam, Cameron	*Scottish*	Bent nose
Camden, Camdin	*Scottish*	From the winding valley
Camillo	*Arabic*	Perfection
Campbell	*Scottish*	From the beautiful field
Candan	*Arabic*	Sincerely
Cane	*Gaelic*	Warrior
Caoimhghin	*Celtic*	Gentle
Carbry	*Celtic*	Charioteer
Carden	*Celtic*	From the black fortress
Carey	*Latin*	Strong

Name	Origin	Definition
Carl	*German*	Strong, manly
Carleton, Carlton	*Scottish*	Free men's town
Carlin	*Irish*	A man
Carlisle, Carlyle	*Teutonic*	Strong, manly
Carlo, Carlos	*French*	Strong
Carmichael	*Scottish*	Friend of Saint Michael
Carr	*Scottish*	Fighter
Carr	*Norwegian*	From the broken mossy ground
Carrington	*Celtic*	Beautiful
Carson	*Scottish*	Son of Carr
Carswell	*English*	Lives at the watercress spring
Carter	*English*	Cart driver
Case, Casey	*Irish*	Brave, watchful
Casmir	*Slavic*	Demands peace
Caspar	*French*	Treasurer
Cass	*Irish*	Curly-haired
Caton	*Spanish*	Knowledgable, wise
Cauley	*Scottish*	Relic
Cayden	*Gaelic*	Spirit of battle
Cedric, Cedrick, Cedrych	*Welsh*	Battle leader, bounty
Cem	*Arabic*	Beautiful
Chace	*English*	Huntsman
Chad, Chadwell, Chadwick	*English*	War-like, warrior

Name	Origin	Definition
Chadburn	*English*	From the wildcat brook
Chan	*Spanish*	God is merciful
Chance, Chancey	*French*	Chancellor
Chander	*Indian*	Moon
Chandler	*French*	Candle maker
Chandrak	*Indian*	Peacock feather
Chandresh	*Indian*	Lord of the Moon
Chane	*African*	Dependability
Chann, Channing, Channon	*Irish*	Young wolf
Chapal	*Indian*	Quick
Chapman	*English*	Merchant
Charles, Charleston, Charlie	*English*	Strong, manly
Chas, Chaz	*English*	Strong, manly
Chase, Chasen	*French*	Hunter
Chatham	*English*	From the soldier's land
Che	*Hebrew*	God will multiply
Chen	*Chinese*	Great, vast
Chester, Chet	*English*	Soldiers' camp
Chetan	*Indian*	Life
Chevy	*French*	Horseman, knight
Chico	*English*	Strength of God
Chin	*Korean*	Precious
Chip	*English*	Gift
Chisholm	*Scottish*	From Chisolm

Name	Origin	Definition
Christian, Chris, Christof, Christophe, Christopher	*Greek*	Servant of Christ
Chuck	*English*	Strong, manly
Churchill	*English*	Lives at the church hill
Cian	*Irish*	Ancient
Ciceron	*Spanish*	Chickpea
Cidro	*Spanish*	Strong gift
Ciel	*Dutch*	Shield, scholar
Cillian	*Irish*	Battle
Ciqala	*Native American*	Little one
Cirilo	*Spanish*	Noble
Cisco	*Spanish*	Free
Clancey	*Celtic*	Offspring of red-headed soldier
Clarence, Clarendon	*Latin*	Bright, shining, clear
Clark, Clarke, Clarkson	*French*	Cleric, scholar
Claude, Claudio	*English*	Lame
Claus	*Greek*	People's victory
Clay, Claybourne, Clayton	*English*	Mortal
Clem, Clemens, Clement	*Latin*	Merciful
Cleveland	*English*	From the cliff
Clifford, Cliff	*English*	Cliff-side
Clint, Clinton, Clintwood	*English*	Hillside town
Clive	*English*	From the cliff

Name	Origin	Definition
Clovis	*French*	Clover
Clyde	*Scottish*	Heard from afar
Coburn	*Scottish*	Place name
Coby	*English*	Place name
Codey, Codie, Cody	*Irish*	Helpful
Colan	*French*	People's victory
Colbert, Colbey	*French*	Dark-haired
Cole, Coley, Colin, Collin	*Greek*	People's victory
Coleman, Colemann	*Irish*	Peace
Collins	*Greek*	Youth, child
Collyer	*English*	Charcoal merchant, coal miner
Colm	*Scottish*	Dove
Colon	*Spanish*	Dove
Colson	*English*	People's victory
Colston, Colten	*English*	Town of colt-breeding
Colt, Colter	*English*	Horse herdsman
Columbo	*Irish*	Dove
Colys	*English*	Son of the dark man
Comhghan	*Irish*	Twin
Con, Conn, Connacht	*Celtic*	Brave counsel, wise
Conan	*Celtic*	Knowledgable, wise
Conley	*Irish*	Ardent, wise
Connell	*Irish*	High, mighty
Conner, Conners, Connor	*Irish*	Desire, wise aid
Connolly	*Irish*	Brave counsel, wise

Name	Origin	Definition
Conrad	*German*	Brave counsel, wise
Conroy	*German*	Persistent
Constantine	*Latin*	Faithful
Consuelo	*Spanish*	Consolation
Conway	*Irish*	Hound of the plains
Cooney	*Irish*	Handsome
Cooper	*English*	Barrel maker
Corben, Corbett, Corbin, Corby	*French*	Raven, black hair
Cord	*Latin*	Honest advisor
Cordell	*English*	Cordmaker
Corey, Cory	*Scottish*	From the hollow
Corlan	*Irish*	Spear-bearer
Cormac, Cormick	*Irish*	Charioteer
Cornel, Cornelius	*Latin*	Horn
Corrado	*German*	Brave counsel, wise
Corran, Corrin	*Irish*	Spear-bearer
Corrick	*Irish*	From the round hill
Cortez	*Spanish*	Courteous
Cortland	*French*	Court attendant
Corvin, Corwin	*English*	Raven-haired
Cosmo	*Greek*	Order, universe
Costello	*Irish*	Surname
Coughlan	*Irish*	Hooded
Coulter	*English*	Horse herdsman
Court	*English*	From the court
Courtenay, Courtland	*French*	Court attendant
Courtnay	*French*	Dweller by the dark stream

Name	Origin	Definition
Covell	*English*	Lives at the cave slope
Cowan, Cowen	*Irish*	Twin
Coyne	*French*	Modest
Cradawg	*Celtic*	Mythical son of Bran
Craig	*Scottish*	From near the crag
Crandall, Crandell	*English*	From the crane valley
Cranston	*English*	From the crane estate
Crawford	*English*	From the crow's ford
Crayton	*Scottish*	Border dweller
Cree, Creigh, Crichton	*English*	Lives at a town near a creek
Creedon	*Irish*	Belief, guiding principle
Crespin, Crispin	*English*	Curly-haired
Cretien	*French*	Annointed, follower of Christ
Cristobal	*Spanish*	Christ-bearer
Croften	*English*	From the enclosed town
Cromwell	*English*	From the crooked well
Cronan	*Irish*	Little dark one
Crosby	*English*	Lives near the town crossing
Crosley	*English*	From the cross meadow
Cruz	*Spanish*	Cross
Cuinn	*Irish*	Intelligent
Culbert	*English*	Seaman

Name	Origin	Definition
Cullan, Cullen, Cullin	*Irish*	Good-looking
Culver	*English*	Dove
Cunningham	*Scottish*	From Cunningham
Curcio	*French*	Courteous
Curran, Curren, Currey	*Irish*	Churn
Currito, Curro	*Spanish*	Free
Curt, Curtis, Curtys	*English*	Courteous
Cuthbert	*English*	Noted splendor
Cutler	*English*	Makes knives
Cy, Cyra, Cyril	*English*	Lordly, proud
Cyneric	*English*	Royal
Cyrus	*Persian*	The Sun

 **D**

Name	Origin	Definition
Dace, Dacey, Dacian	*French*	Of the nobility
Daeg, Daegan	*Irish*	Black-haired
Dael, Dale	*English*	Valley
Daelan, Dalen	*English*	Angel from God
Dag, Dagny	*Norwegian*	Brightness, new day
Dagan	*Hebrew*	Grain, corn
Dagen	*Irish*	Black-haired
Dagwood	*English*	From the bright one's forest
Dahy	*Irish*	Quick and agile
Dailey, Daley	*Anglo-Saxon*	From the valley
Daimen	*Greek*	Divine power, fate

Name	Origin	Definition
Dain, Daine	*English*	From Denmark
Daire	*Irish*	Wealthy
Daiton	*English*	Bright town
Dakarai	*African*	Happiness
Dakota	*Native American*	Friend
Dalan	*Irish*	Blind
Dalbert	*English*	Proud
Dallas	*Celtic*	Wise
Dalton	*English*	Valley
Daly	*Gaelic*	Small valley
Dalziel	*Scottish*	Little field
Damek	*Czech*	Earth
Damian	*Spanish*	Tame
Damon	*Irish*	Constant
Dan, Daniel, Daniels, Danny	*Hebrew*	Judge is the Lord
Dante	*Spanish*	Lasting
Danton	*French*	Priceless, flourishing
Daran	*English*	Great
Darby	*Irish*	Free
Darcy	*French*	Dark
Darek, Daric, Darick	*English*	Gifted ruler
Darell, Darrel, Darrell, Darroll, Darryl	*English*	Beloved
Daren	*English*	Born at night
Darence	*English*	Beloved
Darian	*Persian*	King
Dariel	*French*	Dearly loved

Name	Origin	Definition
Darin, Daron, Darren, Darron	*English*	Great
Dario	*Spanish*	King
Darius	*Persian*	King
Darnel, Darnell	*English*	Hidden
Darold, Darrold	*English*	Beloved
Darpak	*Indian*	God of love
Darrance, Darrence	*English*	Beloved
Darrick, Darroch	*Irish*	Gifted ruler
Darshan	*Indian*	A God's name
Dartagnan	*French*	Leader
Dartmouth	*English*	Port's name
Darton	*English*	From the deer park
Darvell	*French*	Town of eagles
Darwin, Darwyn	*English*	Beloved friend
Dary	*Irish*	Wealthy
Dave, Davey, Davi, David	*Scottish*	Beloved one
Davian	*English*	Beloved
Davidson	*Hebrew*	David's son
Daviel	*English*	Beloved
Davin	*Hebrew*	Dearly loved
Davion	*English*	Beloved
Davis	*Hebrew*	David's son
Davison	*English*	Beloved
Dawayne	*Irish*	Dark
Dawes, Dawson	*Hebrew*	Beloved one
Dax	*French*	Place name
Daxter	*Latin*	Dexterous

Name	Origin	Definition
Daxton	*English*	Place name
Daylan, Daylen, Daylin	*English*	Angel from God
Dayne	*French*	From Denmark
Dayson	*English*	Beloved
Dayton	*Norwegian*	Bright town
Deacon, Deakin	*Greek*	Servant, messenger
Dean, Deane	*English*	Presiding official
Dearborn, Dearbourne	*English*	From the deer brook
Deavon	*English*	Place name
Declan	*Irish*	Servant, messenger
Dedrick	*English*	Gifted ruler
Deegan	*Irish*	Black-haired
Deepak	*Indian*	Lamp, kindle
Deke	*English*	Dusty one, servant
Del	*French*	Sea
Delaney	*Irish*	Descendant of the challenger
Delbert	*English*	Proud, noble, bright
Delling	*Scandinavian*	Scintillating
Delman	*English*	From the valley
Delmar, Delmer	*French*	Mariner
Delmon, Delmont	*French*	Of the mountain
Delray, Delron	*French*	Of the king
Delsin	*Native American*	Alive
Delton	*English*	From the town in the valley
Delvin, Delvon	*English*	Godly friend

Name	Origin	Definition
Demeter, Demetrius, Demitri	*Greek*	Lover of the Earth
Demothi	*Native American*	Talks while walking
Dempsey	*Gaelic*	Proud
Dempster	*English*	Judge
Denis	*French*	Of Dionysus
Denisc	*Anglo-Saxon*	Danish
Denley	*English*	From the valley meadow
Denney, Dennie, Dennis, Dennison	*English*	Greek god of wine
Denton	*English*	From the valley farm
Denver	*English*	Green valley
Denzel	*English*	Of Dionysus
Deo	*Greek*	God-like
Deon	*French*	Of Dionysus
Derald	*English*	Beloved
Derek, Derick, Derik, Derrek	*English*	Gifted ruler
Derex	*German*	Ruler
Derian	*Anglo-Saxon*	Harm
Dermod, Dermot	*Irish*	Free
Derrian	*English*	Great
Derry	*Irish*	Great lover
Derwyn	*English*	Gifted friend
Des, Desi	*Latin*	Man of the world
Desmond	*Anglo-Saxon*	Happy defender
Destan	*French*	By the still waters

Name	Origin	Definition
Deston	*French*	Destiny
Devan, Devon	*English*	Divine
Devante	*Spanish*	Fighter of wrong
Deverick	*French*	Place name
Devery	*French*	To speak kind words
Deviprasad	*Indian*	Gift of goddess
Devland	*Irish*	Misfortune
Devlin	*Irish*	Beloved one
Devry	*French*	Place name
Dewain	*Celtic*	Song
Dewey	*Welsh*	Beloved one
Dewitt	*Welsh*	Blond
Dex, Dexter	*Latin*	Dexterous
Dhanesh	*Indian*	Lord of wealth
Dhaval	*Indian*	Fair-complexioned
Diamont	*English*	Bridge protector
Diandre	*French*	Divine protector
Dick, Dicken, Dickens, Dickenson	*French*	Powerful ruler
Diederich, Deiderick, Dietrich	*German*	People's ruler
Diego	*Spanish*	Supplanter
Digby	*English*	Settlement near a ditch
Dilan, Dillen, Dillon	*Irish*	Like a lion
Dimitri, Dimitry	*Greek*	Lover of the Earth
Dinkar	*Indian*	Sun
Dirk	*German*	Ruler
Divakar	*Indian*	Sun

Name	Origin	Definition
Dixon	English	Powerful, rich ruler
Doane	English	From the down hill
Dobbs	English	Bright, famous
Dobry	Polish	Good
Dohosan	Native American	Bluff
Dolan	Irish	Dark, bold
Dolphus	German	Noble hero
Domenico, Domenic, Dominique	Spanish	Of the Lord
Domingo	Spanish	Born on Sunday
Dominy	Latin	Of the Lord
Don	English	Ruler of the world
Donaghy	Celtic	Strong warrior
Donahue	Irish	A brave black man
Donald	Scottish	Great chief
Donaldson	English	Ruler of the world
Donatello	Spanish	Gift from God
Donato	French	Gift
Donavan, Donavon, Donovan	Irish	Brown-haired chieftain
Donnally	Celtic	Brave
Donnan	Irish	Brown
Donnelly	Irish	A brave black man
Donnelly	Celtic	Surname
Donny	English	Ruler of the world
Dontell	English	Enduring
Dorak	Australian Aboriginal	Lively

Name	Origin	Definition
Dorian, Dorrian	*Greek*	Place name
Dorrance	*Irish*	Stranger
Dorset	*English*	Tribe near the sea
Doug, Doughlas	*Scottish*	From the dark water
Dougal, Doughal, Douglas	*Irish*	Dark stranger
Dover	*English*	Water
Doyle	*Irish*	Dark stranger
Drago, Drake	*French*	Dragon
Drefan	*Anglo-Saxon*	Trouble
Drew	*French*	Manly, valiant, courageous
Driscol, Driscoll	*Celtic*	Mediator
Dristan	*Arthurian Legend*	An advisor to Arthur
Drudwyn	*Celtic*	A knight
Drummond	*Celtic*	Lives on the hill top
Dryden	*English*	From the dry valley
Duane, Duayne	*Irish*	Dark
Duardo	*Spanish*	Wealthy guardian
Dudley	*English*	People's meadow
Duffy	*Irish*	Dark-faced
Duke	*Latin*	Leader of the seas
Dumont	*French*	Of the mountain
Duncan	*Celtic*	Brown warrior
Dunley	*English*	From the hill meadow
Dunmore	*Scottish*	From the great hill fortress

Name	Origin	Definition
Dunn, Dunne	*English*	Dark-skinned
Dunston	*German*	Valiant fighter
Durand, Durant, Durante	*French*	Enduring
Durango	*French*	Strong
Dureau	*French*	Strong
Durwald	*English*	Gatekeeper
Durwin, Durwyn	*Anglo-Saxon*	Dear friend
Dustan, Dustin, Dusty	*English*	Valiant fighter
Duval	*French*	Of the valley
Dwade	*English*	Dark traveller
Dwayne	*Irish*	Dark
Dwenn	*English*	One of originality
Dwight	*English*	Fair
Dwyer	*Irish*	Black
Dwyght	*English*	Fair
Dyami	*Native American*	Eagle
Dylan	*Welsh*	Sea god, son of the waves
Dyre	*Scandinavian*	Dear heart

 **E**

Name	Origin	Definition
Eachan	*Irish*	Horseman
Eadger	*English*	Wealthy spear
Eadmund	*English*	Happy defender

Name	Origin	Definition
Eadward, Eduard, Edward	*Anglo-Saxon*	Guardian
Eadwine, Eadwyn, Edwin	*English*	Wealthy friend
Eagan, Eagon	*Irish*	Fiery, forceful
Ealdian	*Anglo-Saxon*	Long-lived
Ealdun, Eldan, Elden	*English*	From the elves' valley
Eallard	*English*	Brave
Eames	*Irish*	Prosperous guardian
Eammon	*African*	The hidden
Earie	*Scottish*	From the East
Earl, Earle	*Anglo-Saxon*	Chief
Earnan	*Irish*	Knowing
Earnest, Ernest	*German*	Serious, determined
Earvin	*English*	Friend
Easton	*English*	From East town
Eaton, Eatun	*English*	From the riverside village
Eban, Eben, Ebenezer	*Hebrew*	Rock
Eberhard	*English*	Resolute
Eckerd	*German*	Sacred
Ector	*Arthurian Legend*	Father of Arthur
Ed, Eddie, Eddy	*English*	Prosperous warrior
Edan	*Celtic*	Delightful, perfect, pleasure
Edbert	*English*	Wealthy
Edelmar	*English*	Noble
Edgar, Edgarton	*Gaelic*	Prosperous warrior

Name	Origin	Definition
Edie	*Hebrew*	Rich gift, happy
Edison	*English*	Son of Edward
Edlin	*German*	Wealthy friend
Edmond, Edmund	*English*	Wealthy defender
Edmondo	*English*	Happy defender
Edred	*Anglo-Saxon*	Name of a king
Edric, Edrick	*Anglo-Saxon*	Power and good fortune
Edsel	*German*	Rich
Edson	*English*	Son of the prosperous warrior
Edwald, Edwaldo	*English*	Wealthy ruler
Efraim, Ephraim	*Hebrew*	Very fruitful
Efrat	*Hebrew*	Honored
Efron	*Hebrew*	Young stag
Egan, Eghan	*Irish*	Ardent, little fire
Egbert	*Anglo-Saxon*	Intelligent
Egerton	*English*	From the town on the ridge
Eginhard, Eginhardt	*German*	Strong with a sword
Egmont	*German*	Weapon, defender
Egor	*Greek*	Farmer
Egyed	*Hungarian*	Shield-bearer
Ehren	*German*	Honorable
Eilis	*Hebrew*	God's oath
Eimar	*Irish*	Swift
Eimhin	*Irish*	Swift
Einar	*Norwegian*	Warrior, leader
Eisa	*Arabic*	God will help

Name	Origin	Definition
Eisig	*Hebrew*	He who laughs
Ekalinga	*Indian*	Shiva
Ekanga	*Indian*	Bodyguard
Elam	*Hebrew*	One of the five sons of Shem
Elan	*Hebrew*	Tree
Elary, Elery, Ellary	*German*	Cheerful
Elazar	*Hebrew*	God has helped
Elbert	*German*	Bright, famous
Elbridge	*English*	Old counsel
Eldrian, Eldridge, Eldwin	*English*	Old and wise rule
Elfred	*English*	Wise counsel
Elgan	*Welsh*	Bright circle
Elgin, Eljin	*Celtic*	Noble
Eli	*Hebrew*	Jehovah is God
Elias	*Spanish*	Jehovah is God
Elijah	*Hebrew*	Jehovah is God
Eliot, Eliott	*French*	Believes in God
Elisha	*Hebrew*	God is salvation
Ellard	*English*	Brave
Ellis	*English*	Jehovah is God
Ellsworth	*Hebrew*	Jehovah is God
Ellwood	*English*	From the old forest
Elmer	*English*	Noble
Elne	*Anglo-Saxon*	Courage
Eloy	*French*	Chosen
Elrad	*Hebrew*	God rules
Elrod	*English*	The king

Name	Origin	Definition
Elroy	*Irish*	Red-haired youth
Elson	*English*	From the old town
Elsu	*Native American*	Flying falcon
Elsworth	*English*	From the noble's estate
Elton	*English*	From the old town
Elvern, Elvin	*English*	Noble friend
Elvey	*English*	Elf warrior
Elvis	*English*	Wise friend
Elwell	*English*	From the old spring
Ely	*German*	Famous warrior
Eman	*Irish*	Serious
Emanuel	*Hebrew*	With God
Emerson, Emery, Emmyrson	*English*	Brave, powerful
Emile	*French*	Industrious
Emilio	*Spanish*	Flattering
Emir	*Arabic*	Charming prince
Emmott	*English*	Hard worker
Emst	*German*	Serious
Enando	*German*	Bold venture
Eneas	*Spanish*	Praised
Engel, Englebert	*German*	Angel
Eno	*German*	Strong with a sword
Enoch	*Hebrew*	Trained, dedicated
Enrico, Enrique	*Spanish*	Ruler of an estate
Eoghan	*Irish*	God's gift
Eoin	*Celtic*	Young
Eran	*Hebrew*	Roused, awakened

Name	Origin	Definition
Erasmo	*Spanish*	Friendly
Erek, Eric, Erik	*Polish*	Lovable
Erhard, Erhardt	*German*	Honor
Eri	*Hebrew*	From Ireland
Erikson	*Scandinavian*	Ever-powerful
Ernie, Ernst, Erny	*German*	Earnest, vigorous
Eron	*Spanish*	Revered, sharer
Errol, Erroll	*Scottish*	Nobleman
Ervin, Erving	*English*	Friend
Esau	*Hebrew*	Hairy
Esben	*Scandinavian*	God
Escott	*English*	From Scotland
Esmond	*English*	Protected by God
Espen	*Scandinavian*	God bear
Estcott	*English*	From the east cottage
Esteban, Estevan	*Spanish*	Crown
Estefan	*Spanish*	Crowned in victory
Estes	*Latin*	Estuary
Estmund	*English*	Protected by God
Etan	*Hebrew*	Strong, firm, constant
Ethan, Ethen	*Latin*	Strong, firm, constant
Ethelred	*Hebrew*	Noble
Etienne	*French*	Crown
Etu	*Native American*	Sun
Euan, Ewan	*Irish*	God is merciful
Eudor	*Greek*	Good gift
Eugene	*French*	Born lucky, well-born

Name	Origin	Definition
Eustace	*English*	Fruitful
Eustace	*Greek*	Fruitful
Evadeam	*Arthurian Legend*	Dwarf
Evan, Evans, Evanston	*Celtic*	Young warrior
Evander	*Greek*	Benevolent ruler
Ever	*English*	Strong as a boar
Everard	*English*	Brave
Everett, Evert, Everton	*English*	Hardy, brave
Everhard	*English*	Strong as a boar
Everil, Everill	*English*	Boar-warrior
Evian	*English*	Young warrior
Evzen	*Czech*	Of noble birth
Ewald	*English*	Powerful
Ewing	*English*	Youth
Eyou	*Hebrew*	Symbol of piety
Ezekiel, Ezekyel	*Hebrew*	Strength of God
Ezer, Ezra	*Hebrew*	Helper, salvation
Ezhno	*Native American*	Solitary
Ezio	*Hebrew*	Friend, lover

F

Name	Origin	Definition
Faber, Fabian, Fabien, Fabio	*English*	Bean grower
Fadil	*Arabic*	Generous
Faegan, Fagan	*English*	Joyful

Name	Origin	Definition
Faer	*English*	Traveller
Faerrleah, Fairlie, Farley	*English*	From the bull's pasture
Faerwald, Farold	*English*	Powerful traveller
Fairfax	*Anglo-Saxon*	Blond
Fairleigh, Fairley	*English*	Distant meadow
Fakhir	*Arabic*	Proud
Falken	*German*	Falconry
Fallon	*Irish*	Ruler
Faraji	*African*	Consolation
Farar	*Latin*	Blacksmith
Farid	*Arabic*	One of a kind
Fariel	*Persian*	Star
Faris	*English*	A knight
Farlan	*Scottish*	Son of the furrows
Farnham	*English*	From the fern field
Faron	*Spanish*	Blacksmith
Farquharson	*Scottish*	Son of the dear one
Farran, Farren	*Irish*	Adventurous
Farrel, Farrell	*Celtic*	Courageous
Farris	*English*	Strong as iron
Farrow	*Celtic*	Man of valour
Farson	*English*	Son of Farr
Faruq	*Arabic*	Wise
Faxon	*Teutonic*	Long-haired
Fearghus, Ferghus, Fergus	*Celtic*	Strong, manly
Federico	*Spanish*	Peaceful ruler
Fedor	*Greek*	Gift of God

Name	Origin	Definition
Felding	*English*	Lives in the field
Feldon, Feldun	*English*	From the field estate
Feliciano	*Spanish*	Happy
Felipe, Felippe, Filbert, Filip	*Spanish*	Loves horses
Felix	*Spanish*	Lucky
Feran	*Anglo-Saxon*	Advances
Ferde, Ferdy	*German*	Courageous traveller
Ferdinand, Fernando	*Spanish*	Adventurer
Ferguson	*Celtic*	Son of the first choice
Ferrel, Ferrell	*Celtic*	Rock, iron
Ferris, Ferrys	*Latin*	Rock, iron
Fidel	*Spanish*	Faithful
Fido	*Spanish*	Sincere
Fielder	*English*	Field
Fielding	*English*	Lives in the field
Filbert	*English*	Brilliant
Filmore	*English*	Famous
Finghin	*Irish*	Handsome
Finian, Finnegan	*Irish*	Fair
Finlay, Finley, Finn	*Scottish*	Fair hero
Firth	*Scottish*	Arm of the sea
Fisk	*Swedish*	Fisherman
Fitz	*French*	Son
Fitzgerald	*French*	Son of Gerald
Fitzgibbon	*English*	Son of Gilbert
Fitzhugh	*English*	Son of Hugh
Fitzjames	*English*	Son of James

Name	Origin	Definition
Fitzpatrick	*English*	Son of Patrick
Fitzsimmons	*English*	Son of Simon
Flanagan	*Irish*	Ruddy
Flannan	*Irish*	Ruddy
Flannery	*Irish*	Flat land
Flavio	*Spanish*	Blond
Fleming	*English*	From Flanders
Fletcher	*French*	Arrow maker
Flinn, Flyn, Flynn	*Irish*	Son of a red-haired man
Flint	*English*	A stone to start a fire
Florentino	*Spanish*	Blooming
Florus	*French*	Flower
Floyd	*Welsh*	Gray
Flynn	*Irish*	Ruddy
Flynt	*English*	Stream
Fodor	*Hungarian*	Curly-haired
Fogarty	*Irish*	Exiled
Foley	*Irish*	Plunders
Folkus	*Hungarian*	Famous
Fonda	*Spanish*	Profound
Fontaine, Fontayne	*French*	Fountain
Fonzie	*German*	Eager
Forbes	*Scottish*	Headstrong
Forde	*English*	A shallow place used to cross a river or stream
Forest, Forrest, Forster	*English*	Out of the woods

Name	Origin	Definition
Fortun	*French*	Lucky
Foster	*French*	Forest keeper
Fowler	*English*	Game warden
Francis, Francisco, Franco, Frank, Franklyn	*French*	Free
Fraser, Frasier	*French*	Strawberry
Frayne	*English*	Foreigner
Fred, Freddy, Frederick	*English*	Peaceful friend
Freeland	*English*	From the free land
Freeman	*Anglo-Saxon*	Free man
Fremont	*German*	Noble protector
Fresco	*Spanish*	Fresh
Frey	*Scandinavian*	God of weather
Freyne	*English*	Foreigner
Frigyes	*Hungarian*	Peace, might
Fritz	*German*	Peaceful ruler
Fujita	*Japanese*	Field
Fuller	*English*	Cloth thickener
Fulton	*English*	From the people's estate
Fyfe	*Scottish*	From Fifeshire
Fyodor	*Greek*	Gift of God
Fytch	*English*	Ermine

—⁓— G —⁓—

Name	Origin	Definition
Gabe, Gable, Gabor	*Hebrew*	God is my strength

Name	Origin	Definition
Gabrian	*Hebrew*	God's able-bodied one
Gabriel, Gabriele, Gabriello, Gavriel	*Spanish*	God is my strength
Gadi	*Arabic*	My wealth
Gael	*Irish*	Joyful
Gaetan	*French*	From Gaete
Gaffney	*Irish*	Calf
Gagan	*Indian*	Sky, heaven
Gage	*French*	Pledge, oath
Gahan	*Celtic*	Eager aide
Gai	*French*	Merry
Galen	*Gaelic*	Festive party
Galip	*Arabic*	Winner
Gallagher	*Irish*	Eager aide
Galloway	*Latin*	From Gaul
Galton	*English*	From the town on the high ground
Galvin, Galvyn	*Irish*	Sparrow
Gamal	*Arabic*	Camel
Gamba	*African*	Warrior
Ganan	*Australian Aboriginal*	From the west
Ganesh	*Indian*	A Hindu god
Gannon	*Irish*	Fair
Gara	*Irish*	Goshawk (bird)
Garan, Garen, Garin, Garrin	*French*	Guardian
Garcia	*Spanish*	Brave in war

Name	Origin	Definition
Gardener, Gardner	*Danish*	Gardener
Garet, Garett	*English*	Brave with a spear
Gareth	*French*	Gentle, watchful
Garey	*English*	Spear
Garfield	*English*	Promontory
Garlan, Garlon	*French*	Wreath, prize
Garland	*French*	Crowned in victory
Garmond	*English*	Spear protector
Garnell	*French*	Keeper of grain
Garner	*French*	Granary
Garnet, Garnett	*English*	Armed with a spear
Garold	*Teutonic*	Rules by the spear
Garrard	*English*	Brave with a spear
Garrey, Garrie, Garry, Gary	*English*	Spear
Garrick	*English*	Rules by the spear
Garrison, Garryson	*English*	Son of Gary
Garrod	*Teutonic*	Rules by the spear
Garrson	*English*	Son of Gar
Garth	*French*	Garden
Garton	*English*	Lives in the triangular farm stead
Garvan	*Irish*	Rough
Garvey, Garvie	*Latin*	Spear bearer
Garvin	*English*	Rough, rugged
Gaspar, Gaspard	*French*	Treasure
Gaston	*French*	From Gascony
Gauthier, Gautier	*French*	Powerful ruler
Gavan, Gavin, Gavyn	*Welsh*	White hawk

Name	Origin	Definition
Gavi	*Hebrew*	God is my strength
Gavrie	*Russian*	Man of God
Gaye	*French*	Merry
Gayelord	*French*	Brave strength
Gaynor	*Gaelic*	Son of the fair-haired one
Gedeon	*Hungarian*	Destroyer
Geffrey, Geoff, Geoffrey	*French*	Peaceful
Gehard	*English*	Spear hard
Gene	*English*	Born lucky
Genesis	*Hebrew*	Origin, birth
Geol	*English*	Born at Christmas
Geordie, George, Georges, Georgio	*Greek*	Farmer
Gerald, Geraldo	*German*	Rules by the spear
Gerard, Gerardo, Gerhard	*French*	Rules by the spear
Gere	*English*	Rules by the spear
Gergely	*Latin*	Vigilant watch
Gerik	*Polish*	Prosperous spearman
Gerlach	*German*	Marksman
Germain	*French*	From Germany
Geron	*French*	Guardian
Geronimo	*Spanish*	Sacred
Gerrell	*English*	Rules by the spear
Gerrit	*English*	Rules by the spear
Gerry	*English*	Rules by the spear
Gersham	*Hebrew*	Exiled
Gerson	*Hungarian*	Stranger

Name	Origin	Definition
Gervais, Gervaise, Gervis	*English*	Spear bearer
Giacomo	*Hebrew*	Replaces
Giaffar	*Arabic*	January, enlightened
Gian, Giannes	*Hebrew*	Gift from God
Gibbesone, Gibson	*English*	Gilbert's son
Gideon	*Hebrew*	Mighty warrior
Gifford	*English*	Gift of bravery
Gijs	*English*	Bright
Gikhrist	*Irish*	Serves Christ
Gil	*French*	Happiness
Gilbert, Gilberto	*French*	Bright lad
Gildas	*English*	Serves God
Gilibeirt, Gilleabart	*Irish*	Pledge, vow
Gilleasbuig	*Scottish*	Brave
Gilli	*Hebrew*	Happiness
Gillivray	*Scottish*	Servant of judgment
Gilmer	*English*	Sword bearer
Gilmore	*Celtic*	Sword bearer
Gilpin	*English*	Trusted
Gilroy	*Scottish*	Serves the king
Gilvarry	*Irish*	Serves Christ
Ginton	*Arabic*	A garden
Giovanni	*Hebrew*	Gift from God
Giselbert	*English*	Trusted
Giuseppe	*Hebrew*	God will multiply
Givon	*Arabic*	Hill, heights
Gladwin	*English*	Happy friend

Name	Origin	Definition
Glen, Glenn, Glyn	*Celtic*	From the valley
Goddard	*German*	Hard spear
Godfrey	*Irish*	God's peace
Godric	*Anglo-Saxon*	Rules with God
Godwin, Godwine	*English*	God's friend
Gofried	*German*	Peaceful god
Golden	*English*	Blond
Golding	*English*	Son of gold
Goldwin	*English*	Golden friend
Golligan	*Irish*	Surname
Goodwin, Goodwine	*English*	Good friend
Gopal	*Indian*	Lord Krishna
Gopan	*Indian*	Protection
Gordie, Gordon, Gordy	*Anglo-Saxon*	From the cornered hill
Gormley	*Irish*	Sad
Gottfried	*German*	Peaceful god
Govannon	*Anglo-Saxon*	God of the forge
Govind	*Indian*	Cowherd
Gowan	*Scottish*	A smith
Gowyn	*English*	God's friend
Graden	*English*	Son of the Gray family, son of Gregory
Grady	*Irish*	Noble
Graeham, Graeme, Graham	*Anglo-Saxon*	Farm home
Graent, Grant	*English*	Great
Granger	*English*	Farmer

Name	Origin	Definition
Grantham	*English*	From the great meadow
Grantland, Grantley	*English*	From the large meadow
Granville	*French*	From the large town
Gray, Graysen	*English*	Grey-haired
Grayvesone	*English*	Son of the reeve
Greagoir, Greg, Gregorio, Gregory	*Irish*	Watchful
Greeley, Greely	*English*	From the grey meadow
Gregson	*English*	Son of Gerald
Gremian	*Anglo-Saxon*	Enrages
Gresham, Grisham	*English*	From the grazeland
Gretel	*German*	Pearl
Griff, Griffie	*Welsh*	Fierce chief, ruddy
Griffin	*Irish*	Surname
Griffith	*Welsh*	A murderer
Grimbold	*Anglo-Saxon*	Fierce, bold
Grimm	*Anglo-Saxon*	Fierce
Grindan	*Anglo-Saxon*	Sharp
Griswald, Griswold	*German*	From the grey forest
Grosvenor	*French*	Great hunter
Grover	*English*	Lives in the grove
Gualterio	*Spanish*	Strong warrior
Gui	*French*	Guide
Guido	*Spanish*	Guide
Guillaume, Guillermo	*French*	Resolute protector
Guiseppe	*Hebrew*	God will multiply

Name	Origin	Definition
Gulab	*Indian*	Rose
Gunn	*Scottish*	White
Gunnar	*Teutonic*	Brave warrior
Gunter, Gunther	*Scandinavian*	Battle, warrior
Gurdayal	*Indian*	Compassionate guru
Gurdeep	*Indian*	Lamp of the guru
Guri	*Hebrew*	My lion cub
Gurmeet	*Indian*	Friend of the guru
Guru	*Indian*	Teacher, master, priest
Gus, Gussie	*Latin*	Exalted
Gustav, Gustave, Gustavo	*French*	Royal staff
Guy	*English*	Lively
Guyapi	*Native American*	Frank
Gwen	*Celtic*	White, fair
Gwri	*Celtic*	Blond
Gyula	*Hungarian*	Name of honour

H

Name	Origin	Definition
Habib	*Hebrew*	Beloved one
Hackett	*German*	Little woodsman
Hadar	*Hebrew*	Glory
Haddad	*Arabic*	Smith
Hadden, Haddon, Haden	*English*	Child of the heather-filled valley
Hadi	*Arabic*	To the light

Name	Origin	Definition
Hadley	*English*	Field of heather
Hadrian, Hadrianus	*Swedish*	Dark one
Hadwin, Hadwyn	*English*	War friend
Haefen	*English*	Safety
Haele	*English*	Lives in the hall
Hagalean, Hagley	*English*	From the hedged enclosure
Hagan	*Teutonic*	Strong defence
Hahn	*German*	Rooster
Haim	*Hebrew*	Life
Hakan	*Native American*	Fiery
Hakeem, Hakim	*Arabic*	Wise
Halbart, halbert	*English*	Brilliant hero
Halden	*English*	From Denmark
Hale	*English*	Hero
Haley	*Irish*	Field of hay
Halford	*English*	From the hall by the ford
Halig	*Anglo-Saxon*	Holy
Halim	*Arabic*	Gentle
Halliwell, Hallwell	*English*	Lives by the holy spring
Halsey, Halsig	*English*	From Hal's island
Halstead	*English*	From the manor house
Halton, Helton	*English*	From the hill estate
Hamad, Hamden, Hamid	*Arabic*	Praised one

Name	Origin	Definition
Hamal	*Arabic*	Lamb
Hamilton	*French*	Beautiful mountain
Hamlett	*German*	From the little home
Hamlin	*German*	Loves the little home
Hampton	*English*	Place name
Han, Hann, Hans	*German*	Gift from God
Hanan	*Hebrew*	Grace
Hanford	*English*	From the high ford
Hank	*German*	Rules the home
Hanley, Hanly	*English*	From the high meadow
Hanlon	*Irish*	Surname
Hansel	*Hebrew*	God is gracious
Hansen, Hanson	*Anglo-Saxon*	Son of a nobleman
Harbin	*French*	Famous warrior
Harcourt	*French*	From the fortified farm
Harden, Hardin, Harding	*English*	From the hare's valley
Hardtman	*German*	Strong
Hardwin, Hardwyn	*English*	Brave friend
Hardy	*German*	Strong
Harel	*Hebrew*	Mountain of God
Haresh	*Indian*	Shiva
Harford	*English*	From the hare's ford
Hargrove	*English*	From the hare's grove
Hari	*Indian*	Sun
Harilal	*Indian*	Son of Hari
Harish	*Indian*	Vishnu

Name	Origin	Definition
Harith	*African*	Cultivator
Harlan	*English*	From the hare's land
Harland, Harley, Harlon, Harlow	*English*	Meadow of the hares
Harman, Harmen, Harmon	*English*	Soldier
Harold, Herold	*English*	Army commander
Harper	*English*	Harpist
Harrington	*Irish*	Surname
Harris, Harrison	*English*	Son of Harry
Harrod	*Hebrew*	Heroic
Harry	*English*	Army man
Harsha	*Indian*	Joy
Hart, Harte	*English*	Strong, brave
Hartford	*English*	From the stag's ford
Hartley	*English*	From the deer pasture
Hartman, Hartmann	*English*	Strong
Hartwell	*English*	Lives near the stag's spring
Hartwood	*English*	From the stag's forest
Haru	*Japanese*	Born in the spring
Harun	*Arabic*	Superior
Harvey	*English*	Eager to fight
Hashim	*Arabic*	Destroys evil
Haslet, Haslett	*English*	From the hazel-tree land
Hassan	*Arabic*	Handsome

Name	Origin	Definition
Hassun	*Native American*	Stone
Hastin	*Indian*	Elephant
Hastings	*English*	Swift one
Havard	*Scandinavian*	Guardian of the home
Haven	*English*	Place of safety
Haverhil, Haverl	*English*	Boar warrior
Hawley, Hawly	*English*	From the hedged meadow
Hayden	*English*	From the hay meadow
Hayes	*Irish*	From the hedged place
Hayle	*English*	Lives in the hall
Hayward	*English*	Keeper of the hedged enclosure
Haywood	*English*	From the hedged forest
Healy	*English*	From the slope land
Heanford	*English*	From the high ford
Hearne	*English*	Mythical hunter
Heath	*English*	Untended land where flowering shrubs grow
Heathcliff, Heathclyf	*English*	From the heath cliff
Heathley	*English*	From the heath-covered meadow
Hector	*Spanish*	Steadfast
Hegarty	*Irish*	Unjust

Name	Origin	Definition
Heli	*German*	Protector, courage
Heller	*German*	The Sun
Helmut	*German*	Brave
Hemaraj	*Indian*	Lord of gold
Henderson, Henson	*Scottish*	Son of Henry
Hennessy	*Irish*	Surname
Henning	*Teutonic*	Ruler of an estate
Henri, Henrik, Henrique, Henry	*German*	Rules the home
Heramba	*Indian*	Boastful
Herb, Herbert, Herbie	*English*	Strong army
Herman, Hermann	*German*	Soldier
Hernan, Hernandez, Hernando	*Spanish*	Adventurous
Herrick	*German*	Army commander
Herschel, Hershel	*Hebrew*	Deer
Hewett, Hewitt, Hewlett	*German*	Little Hugh
Hezekiah	*Hebrew*	God is my strength
Hiatt	*English*	From the high gate
Higgins	*Irish*	Intelligent
Hilario	*Spanish*	Happy
Hildbrand	*German*	War sword
Hillock, Hillocke	*English*	From the small hill
Hilton	*English*	Manor of the hill
Hiram	*Hebrew*	Exalted
Hiroshi	*Japanese*	Generous
Hobart, Hobbard	*German*	Bright
Hogan	*Irish*	Youth

Name	Origin	Definition
Holbrook	*English*	From the brook
Holcomb	*English*	From the deep valley
Holden, Holdin	*Teutonic*	Kindly, gracious
Hollis	*English*	Lives by the holly trees
Holman	*English*	From the valley
Holmes	*English*	From the river island
Holt	*Anglo-Saxon*	Son of the unspoiled forest
Holwell	*English*	Lives by the holy spring
Homer	*Greek*	Promise
Honi	*Hebrew*	Gracious
Horado	*Spanish*	Timekeeper
Hori	*Polynesian*	Farmer
Horton	*English*	From the grey estate
Hoshi	*Japanese*	Star
Hotah	*Native American*	White
Houghton	*English*	From the estate on the bluff
Houston	*English*	Hill town
Howard, Howe, Howie	*English*	Guardian of the home
Howi	*Native American*	Turtle dove
Howland	*English*	From the chief's land
Hring	*English*	Ring
Hrocby	*English*	From the crow's estate

Name	Origin	Definition
Hrytherford	*English*	From the cattle ford
Htway	*Burmese*	Youngest
Hubbard	*German*	Graceful
Hubert	*German*	Brilliant
Hud	*English*	Hooded
Hudson	*English*	Son of the hooded man
Huey, Hugh	*English*	Intelligent
Hughes	*Irish*	Surname
Hugo	*English*	Intelligent
Hulbard, Hulbart	*German*	Graceful
Humberto	*Spanish*	Bright
Humphrey	*German*	Peaceful
Hunt	*English*	Pursuer
Hunter	*English*	Hunter
Huntingden	*English*	From the hunter's hill
Huntington	*English*	From the hunting farm
Huntley	*English*	From the hunter's meadow
Hurley	*Irish*	Sea tide
Hurst	*English*	Lives in the forest
Husain	*Arabic*	Handsome, good
Hutton	*English*	From the estate on the ridge
Huxeford	*English*	From Hugh's ford
Huxley, Huxly	*English*	From Hugh's meadow
Hwitcomb	*English*	From the white hollow

Name	Origin	Definition
Hwitford	*English*	From the white ford
Hyatt	*English*	From the high gate
Hyde	*English*	From the hide

Name	Origin	Definition
Iacob, Iacobe	*Hebrew*	Held by the heel
Iago, Iakovos	*Spanish*	Supplanter
Iain, Ian	*Scottish*	Gift from God
Ibila	*Arabic*	Breath, child
Ibrahim	*Hebrew*	Father of many
Ichabod	*Hebrew*	The glory has departed
Idal	*English*	From the yew-tree valley
Iden	*Celtic*	Wealthy
Igasho	*Native American*	Wanders
Ignacio, Ignatios, Ignatius, Ignazio	*Latin*	Lively
Igor	*Norse*	Hero
Ike	*English*	Laughing one
Iksander, Ixsander	*Greek*	Protector of mankind
Ikshu	*Indian*	Sugarcane
Ilesh	*Indian*	Lord of Earth
Ilias, Ilja, Illias, Ilya	*Latin*	Jehovah is God
Imanuel, Immanuel	*Hebrew*	God is with us
Imre	*German*	Great king

Name	Origin	Definition
Incendio	*Spanish*	Fire
Indeever	*Indian*	Blue lotus
Indra	*Indian*	God of rain and thunder
Inesh	*Indian*	King of kings
Ingall, Ingalls, Ingel	*German*	Angel
Ingar, Ingmar	*Scandinavian*	Famous son
Inglebert	*German*	Divinely brilliant
Ingram	*Teutonic*	Ing's raven
Iniss, Innes, Innis, Inys	*Irish*	From the river island
Inteus	*Native American*	Has no shame
Iosef, Ioseph	*Hebrew*	God will multiply
Ira	*Hebrew*	Descendant
Irv	*Anglo-Saxon*	Lover of the sea
Irven, Irvin, Irving, Irvyn	*Celtic*	Friend
Irwin, Irwyn	*English*	Sea lover
Isaac, Isaak	*Hebrew*	Laughing one
Isadoro	*Spanish*	Strong gift
Isaiah, Isaias	*Hebrew*	God's helper
Isen	*Anglo-Saxon*	Iron
Isenham, Isham	*English*	From the iron one's estate
Ishan	*Indian*	Sun
Ishmael, Ismael	*Spanish*	God listens
Ishwar	*Indian*	Powerful
Isidoro, Isidro	*Spanish*	Gifted with many ideas

Name	Origin	Definition
Israel, Isreal, Izreal	*Hebrew*	God perseveres
Istaqa	*Native American*	Coyote man
Istu	*Native American*	Sugar
Itai	*Hebrew*	Friendly
Ittamar	*Hebrew*	Island of palms
Ivan, Ivar, Iver, Ives	*Spanish*	Archer
Ivey	*English*	Ivy
Ivo	*English*	Archer's bow

J

Name	Origin	Definition
Jabari	*African*	Brave, fearless
Jabbar	*Arabic*	Mighty
Jabin	*Hebrew*	God has built
Jabir	*Arabic*	Comforts
Jacan	*Hebrew*	Troubled
Jacinto	*Spanish*	Hyacinth flower
Jack, Jackie, Jackson	*English*	God is gracious
Jacob, Jacques	*Hebrew*	Supplanter
Jacy	*English*	Beautiful
Jaden, Jadon, Jaedon	*Hebrew*	Jehovah has heard
Jae	*English*	Bluejay
Jaecar	*German*	Hunter
Jael	*Hebrew*	Mountain goat
Jafar	*Indian*	Little stream
Jagger	*English*	Teamster

Name	Origin	Definition
Jago	*English*	Supplanter
Jahmal	*Arabic*	Handsome
Jai	*English*	Healer
Jaime, Jamie, Jamieson	*Scottish*	Supplanter
Jairo	*Spanish*	Jehovah enlightens
Jake, Jakob	*English*	Supplanter
Jakeem	*Hebrew*	Raised up
Jaleel	*Arabic*	Great
Jamaal, Jamal	*Arabic*	Handsome
James, Jameson	*Hebrew*	Supplanter
Jamil	*Arabic*	Handsome
Jan	*Hebrew*	Gift from God
Jansen	*German*	God is merciful
Janvier	*French*	Enlightened
Jared	*Hebrew*	Ruler
Jarek	*Polish*	Born in January
Jarel, Jarell	*English*	Strong, open-minded
Jaren, Jarin, Jaron, Jeren	*English*	Singing
Jarett	*Teutonic*	Ruler
Jarret, Jarrett, Jarrod, Jerret	*English*	Strong spear
Jarvis	*English*	Spearman
Jason	*Greek*	Healer
Jaspar, Jasper	*Arabic*	Treasurer
Javan	*Latin*	Angel of Greece
Javier	*French*	Born in January
Jawahar	*Indian*	Jewel
Jax, Jaxon	*English*	God is gracious

Name	Origin	Definition
Jay, Jaye, Jayar, Jayron	*English*	Healer
Jaycee, Jayvee	*English*	Beautiful
Jean	*French*	Gift from God
Jeb	*Hebrew*	Held by the heel
Jed, Jedd, Jedi	*Hebrew*	Beloved by God
Jedadiah, Jedediah	*Hebrew*	Beloved of Jehovah
Jedrek	*Polish*	Strong, manly
Jeevan	*Indian*	Life
Jeff, Jeffery, Jeffrey	*English*	Peaceful
Jefferson	*English*	Son of Geoffrey
Jefford	*English*	Place name
Jelani	*African*	Mighty
Jem	*English*	Supplanter
Jenda	*Hebrew*	Gift from God
Jennis	*English*	God is gracious
Jens	*Hebrew*	Gift from God
Jeorg	*Greek*	Farmer
Jeraldo	*Spanish*	Rules by the spear
Jeramie, Jeramy, Jeremiah, Jeremy	*English*	Exalted of the Lord
Jerard	*French*	Rules by the spear
Jerel	*English*	Strong, open-minded
Jeri, Jerie, Jerri, Jerry	*Teutonic*	Rules by the spear
Jericho	*Hebrew*	City of the Moon
Jerick	*English*	Strong
Jermain, Jermaine, Jermayne	*French*	From Germany
Jerold, Jerrald	*Teutonic*	Rules by the spear

Name	Origin	Definition
Jeronimo	*Spanish*	Sacred
Jervis	*English*	Spearman
Jerzy	*Greek*	Farmer
Jesiah	*Hebrew*	God is salvation
Jesper	*French*	Jasperstone
Jess, Jesse, Jessie	*Hebrew*	Gift from God
Jesus	*Hebrew*	Named for Jesus
Jethro	*Hebrew*	Abundance
Jim, Jimmy	*English*	Supplanter
Jin	*Chinese*	Truth, treasure
Jiri	*Greek*	Farmer
Jiro	*Japanese*	Second male
Jishnu	*Indian*	Triumphant
Jivin	*Indian*	To give life
Joachim, Joakim	*Hebrew*	The Lord will judge
Joaquin	*Spanish*	Jehovah has established
Job, Jobe, Joby	*Hebrew*	Persecuted
Jock	*Scottish*	God is gracious
Jodoc	*Celtic*	Joy
Jody	*English*	God will multiply
Joe, Joey	*English*	God will multiply
Joel	*Hebrew*	Strong-willed
Johan, Johann, Johannes	*German*	Gift from God
John, Johnathan, Johnny, Johnson	*English*	God is merciful
Johnston	*Scottish*	From John's farm
Jokin	*Hebrew*	God will establish

Name	Origin	Definition
Jolie	*French*	Beautiful
Jonah, Jonas	*Hebrew*	Dove
Joop	*Hebrew*	God will multiply
Jordain, Jorden, Jordell, Jordi	*English*	To descend, to flow
Jorge, Jorgen, Jorges	*Spanish*	Farmer
Jorie	*Hebrew*	God will uplift
Jorim	*Hebrew*	Jehovah is exalted
Jorrin	*Greek*	Farmer
Jose, Joseph	*Spanish*	God will multiply
Josh, Joshua	*Hebrew*	Jehovah is salvation
Josiah	*Hebrew*	Jehovah has healed
Josias	*Spanish*	God is salvation
Joss	*Hebrew*	Jehovah is salvation
Juan, Juanito	*Spanish*	Gift from God
Jud, Judas, Judd	*Hebrew*	Praised
Judah, Jude	*Hebrew*	The praised one
Jules, Julian, Julio	*Latin*	Youthful
Juliano, Julius	*Spanish*	Jove's child
Juma	*African*	Born on Friday
Jung	*Korean*	Righteous
Junien	*Hebrew*	God will uplift
Jurek, Jurgi	*Greek*	Farmer
Jurgen	*German*	Farmer
Jussey, Just	*Latin*	Justice
Justain, Justin, Justino, Justus	*English*	Justice
Jyll	*English*	Youthful

—∞— K —∞—

Name	Origin	Definition
Kaarle, Kaarlo, Karl	*French*	Strong, manly
Kabos	*Hebrew*	Swindler
Kadar	*Arabic*	Strong
Kade	*Scottish*	From the wetlands
Kadeen, Kaden, Kadin	*Arabic*	Friend, companion
Kadir	*Arabic*	Green
Kaga	*Native American*	Chronicler
Kagan, Kagen	*Irish*	Intelligent
Kahill	*Arabic*	Good friend
Kahleil, Kahlil, Kailil	*Arabic*	Friend
Kai	*Scottish*	Fire
Kain, Kaine, Kane, Kayne	*Gaelic*	Warrior
Kajika	*Native American*	Walks without sound
Kal, Kalisto	*Greek*	Most beautiful
Kale	*Hawaiian*	Strong
Kalen	*English*	Keeper of the keys
Kaliq	*Arabic*	Creative
Kalman	*French*	Manly
Kalti	*Australian Aboriginal*	Spear
Kam	*Scottish*	Bent nose
Kamadev	*Indian*	God of love
Kamal	*Indian*	Perfection

Name	Origin	Definition
Kamden	*Scottish*	From the winding valley
Kameron, Kamron	*Scottish*	Bent nose
Kamil, Kamillo	*Arabic*	Perfection
Kamlesh	*Indian*	God of lotus
Kanak	*Indian*	Gold
Kanaye	*Japanese*	Zealous one
Kanen, Kannen, Kannon	*Polynesian*	Free
Karcsi	*French*	Joy
Kardos	*Hungarian*	Swordsman
Kareef, Karif	*Arabic*	Born during autumn
Kareem, Karim	*Arabic*	Generous
Karmel	*Hebrew*	Song
Karney	*Celtic*	Fighter
Karsa	*Hungarian*	Falcon
Karsten, Karston	*Greek*	Blessed
Kasch	*German*	Blackbird
Kaseeb, Kasib	*Arabic*	Fertile
Kaseem	*Arabic*	Divided
Kasen	*Latin*	Protected with a helmet
Kasey	*Irish*	Brave, watchful
Kasim, Kassim	*Arabic*	Divided
Kasimir	*Slavic*	Demands peace
Kaspar	*Persian*	A treasured secret
Kassi	*English*	Protector of mankind
Kateb	*Arabic*	Writer
Kauri	*Polynesian*	A New Zealand tree

Name	Origin	Definition
Kaushal	*Indian*	Clever, skilled
Kavan, Kaven	*Irish*	Handsome
Kavi	*Indian*	A wise man
Kay	*Scottish*	A knight
Kayin	*African*	Celebrated child
Keagan, Keegan	*Irish*	Intelligent
Kealan	*Irish*	Slender
Kean, Keanan, Keane	*Irish*	Ancient
Kear, Kearn, Kearney, Keary	*Celtic*	Father's dark child
Keaton	*English*	Place of the hawks
Kedar	*Arabic*	Powerful
Keddrick, Kedric, Kedrick	*English*	Bounty
Keefe, Keefer	*Irish*	Handsome
Keeland	*Gaelic*	Little
Keever	*Gaelic*	Lovable, handsome
Keifer	*German*	Barrel maker
Keiran	*Irish*	Dark-haired
Keith	*Irish*	From the battlefield
Kel, Kelly	*Celtic*	Warrior
Kelan	*Irish*	Slender
Kelby	*German*	Dark-haired
Kele	*Native American*	Sparrow
Keleman, Kelemen	*Hungarian*	Gentle, kind
Kelian, Kilian, Killian	*Dutch*	Fight, strife
Kell	*English*	From the spring
Kellach	*Irish*	Strife

Name	Origin	Definition
Kellen	*German*	Swamp
Kelson, Kelton	*Scandinavian*	Beautiful island
Kelvan, Kelven, Kelvyn, Kelwyn	*Gaelic*	River man
Kem	*English*	Champion
Kemal	*Arabic*	Beautiful
Kemen	*Spanish*	Strong
Kemp, Kempe, Kemper, Kempson	*English*	Warrior
Ken	*Scottish*	Born of fire
Kendal, Kendale, Kendall	*Celtic*	Royal valley
Kende	*Hungarian*	Name of an honour
Kendreague	*Celtic*	Loving male
Kendrew	*Scottish*	Valiant, courageous
Kendric, Kendrick, Kendrik, Kendrix	*Scottish*	Royal chieftain
Kenelm	*English*	Defends the family
Kenley	*Welsh*	Chief hero
Kennady, Kennedy	*Gaelic*	Helmeted chief
Kennard	*English*	Strong
Kennet, Kenneth, Kenney	*English*	Handsome
Kennon	*Scottish*	Good-looking, fair
Kenric, Kenrick, Kenrik, Kenryk	*Anglo-Saxon*	Fearless leader
Kent, Kentigem	*Anglo-Saxon*	Chief
Kenton	*English*	From Kent
Kentrell	*English*	Royal chieftain

Name	Origin	Definition
Kenward	*English*	Bold guardian
Kenway	*Anglo-Saxon*	Brave in war
Kenyon	*Gaelic*	Blond
Kenzie	*Scottish*	Fair
Keon	*Irish*	Gracious, merciful
Keowynn	*Hawaiian*	God's gracious gift
Kermit, Kermode	*Celtic*	Free of envy
Kern	*Gaelic*	Small, dark-skinned
Kerr	*Scottish*	Man of strength
Kerrick	*English*	King's rule
Kerrigan	*Irish*	Dusk, dark
Kerrin	*Gaelic*	Beautiful
Kerry	*Celtic*	Dear
Kers	*Indian*	Name of a plant
Kerwin, Kerwyn	*Irish*	Dark eyes
Kester	*English*	Christ bearer
Kev, Kevan, Kevin, Kevyn	*Gaelic*	Gentle, lovable
Keve	*Hungarian*	Stone
Kevion	*Irish*	Handsome child
Key	*English*	Guiding
Khaldun	*Arabic*	Eternal
Khaled, Khalid	*Arabic*	Immortal
Kharim	*Arabic*	Generous
Kharouf	*Arabic*	Lamb
Khin	*Burmese*	Friendly
Khoury	*Arabic*	Priest
Kian	*Irish*	Ancient

Name	Origin	Definition
Kiefer	*German*	Barrel maker
Kieon	*English*	Leading
Kieran, Kieron	*Irish*	Dark-skinned
Kim, Kimball	*Anglo-Saxon*	Chief
Kimm	*Vietnamese*	The golden one
Kin	*Japanese*	From the top of the cliff
Kindall	*Celtic*	Ruler of the valley
Kingdon	*English*	From the king's hall
Kingsley	*English*	From the king's meadow
Kingston	*English*	From the king's town
Kingswell	*English*	From the king's well
Kinney	*Scottish*	Good-looking, fair
Kinsey, Kinsley	*English*	Victorious
Kintan	*Indian*	Wearing a crown
Kip, Kipling, Kipp, Kippar	*English*	Cures salmon or herring
Kirby	*Irish*	Church farm
Kirk, Kirkland, Kirkley, Kirklin	*English*	From the church
Kirkwood	*Norse*	From the church's forest
Kisho	*Japanese*	Knows his own mind
Kit	*English*	Christ bearer
Kitchi	*Native American*	Brave
Klaus	*German*	People's victory
Klemens	*Latin*	Merciful

Name	Origin	Definition
Knight	*English*	Noble, soldier
Knocks, Knoll, Knox	*English*	From the hills
Knoton	*Native American*	Wind
Koby	*German*	Dark-haired
Koen	*German*	Honest advisor
Kolby	*English*	Dark-haired
Kolet	*Australian Aboriginal*	A dove
Kolt, Kolten, Koltin	*German*	Coal town
Kon, Konrad	*German*	Brave counsel, wise
Konstantin	*Latin*	Faithful
Kontar	*African*	Only child
Korbin	*English*	Raven-haired
Kord, Kordell	*German*	Honest advisor
Korrigan	*English*	Spearman
Korvin	*Latin*	Crow
Kosmos	*Greek*	Order, universe
Kozma	*Greek*	Decoration
Kris, Kristo, Kristofer	*Greek*	Christ bearer
Krischnan, Krister, Kristian	*Greek*	Christian
Krispen	*Latin*	Curly haired
Kuhlbert, Kulbert	*German*	Calm, bright
Kulan	*Australian Aboriginal*	A possum
Kuno	*German*	Honest advisor
Kurt	*English*	Courteous
Kurtis	*German*	Wise

Name	Origin	Definition
Kwahu	*Native American*	Eagle
Kyi	*Burmese*	Clear
Kyine	*Burmese*	Smell sweet
Kylan, Kylar, Kylen	*Irish*	Church
Kyle	*Irish*	Handsome
Kyn	*Vietnamese*	The golden one
Kyne	*English*	Royal
Kyran	*Irish*	Dark
Kyril	*Greek*	Proud
Kyrksen	*Scottish*	Church

L

Name	Origin	Definition
Label	*Hebrew*	Lion
Labhras	*Latin*	Crown of victory
Lache, Laec	*English*	Lives near water
Lachlan	*Scottish*	From the land of lakes
Lad, Ladde	*English*	Attendant
Ladbroc, Laibrook	*English*	By the path by the brook
Ladd	*English*	Young man
Ladislav	*Czech*	Famous ruler
Laefertun	*English*	From the rush farm
Laidley, Laidly	*English*	From the creek meadow
Laine	*Scottish*	Narrow road

Name	Origin	Definition
Laird	*Scottish*	Lord
Lakeland	*Irish*	Home of the Norse
Lakota	*Native American*	Friend
Lam	*Vietnamese*	Knowledge
Lamar, Lamarr	*French*	Land
Lambart, Lambert, Lambrecht	*German*	Light of land
Lamont	*Scottish*	Lawyer
Lance, Lancelot	*French*	Knight's attendant
Lancelin	*French*	Servant
Landan, Landen, Landon	*English*	Long hill
Lander, Landers, Landis, Landman	*English*	Lion man
Lando	*Latin*	Bright sun
Landry	*Greek*	Ruler
Lane, Lanny	*English*	Fair, beautiful
Lang, Langdon, Langer, Langford	*English*	Long, tall
Langley	*French*	Englishman
Lani	*Polynesian*	Peace, hope
Lantos	*Hungarian*	Lute player
Laoidhigh	*Irish*	Poetic
Lapidoth	*Hebrew*	Torch
Larcwide	*Anglo-Saxon*	Counsel
Laren	*Scottish*	Serves Lawrence
Larenzo, Larry, Lars, Larson	*German*	Honour, victory

Name	Origin	Definition
Larue, Leroux	*French*	The red-haired one
Lasalle	*French*	The hall
Laszlo	*Hebrew*	God's help
Latham	*Scandinavian*	Division
Lathrop	*English*	From the farm with the barn
Latimer	*French*	Interprets Latin
Laughlin, Loughlin	*Irish*	Servant
Laughton	*Latin*	Crown of victory
Launder	*English*	From the grassy plain
Laurence, Laurent, Lawrence	*Scottish*	Honour, victory
Lavan	*Hebrew*	White
Law	*English*	From the hill
Lawford	*English*	From the ford at the hill
Lawler	*Latin*	Soft-spoken
Lawley, Lawson, Lawton	*Latin*	Crown of victory
Layne	*English*	Narrow road
Layton	*English*	From the meadow farm
Lazar, Lazarus	*Hebrew*	God will help
Lear	*English*	Of the meadow
Leary	*Irish*	Cattle keeper
Leathan	*Scottish*	River
Leax	*Anglo-Saxon*	Salmon
Lee	*English*	Poet

Name	Origin	Definition
Leeland	*English*	Pasture ground
Leeroy	*French*	The king
Lehel	*Hungarian*	Breathes
Lei	*Gaelic*	Handsome
Leicester	*English*	From Leicester
Leif	*Norse*	Beloved
Leighton, Leland	*English*	From the meadow land
Leith	*Celtic*	River
Leman	*English*	From the valley
Lemuel	*Hebrew*	Devoted to God
Len, Lenard, Lennie, Lenny, Leonard	*German*	Lion-hearted
Lenin, Lennon	*Gaelic*	Cloak
Lenix, Lennox, Lenox	*Scottish*	From the field of elm trees
Lensar	*English*	With his parents
Leo, Leon, Leone	*Spanish*	Lion
Leof	*Anglo-Saxon*	Beloved
Leopold, Leopoldo	*English*	Bold leader
Leroi, Leroy	*French*	The king
Leron	*French*	The circle
Les	*Latin*	Small meadow
Lester	*English*	Fortified
Leverett	*French*	Young rabbit
Levi	*Hebrew*	United
Lew	*German*	Shelter
Lewes, Lewis, Lewy	*German*	Warrior
Lex	*English*	Protector of mankind

Name	Origin	Definition
Leyman	*English*	From the meadow land
Li	*Chinese*	Strength
Liam	*Irish*	Resolute protector
Lidmann	*Anglo-Saxon*	Sailor
Lifton	*English*	From tbe hillside town
Lincoln	*English*	Lakeside
Lindberg, Linden, Lindley, Linton	*German*	Linden tree
Linley, Linly	*English*	From the flax field
Linus	*French*	Flaxen-haired
Lionel, Lionell	*English*	Lion
Lisandro	*Spanish*	Liberator
Lisle	*English*	From the island
Litton	*English*	From tbe hillside town
Livingstone	*Scottish*	From Livingston
Lloyd	*Celtic*	Grey-haired
Lochlann	*Irish*	Home of the Norse
Locke	*English*	Lives by tbe stronghold
Lockwood	*English*	From the enclosed wood
Logan, Logen	*Scottish*	Little hollow
Loki	*Scandinavian*	Trickster god
Loman	*Irish*	Bare
Lon, Lonny	*Gaelic*	Fierce

Name	Origin	Definition
London	*English*	Fierce ruler of the world
Lonell	*French*	Young lion
Lonzo	*Spanish*	Eager
Lorimar, Lorimer	*English*	Saddle maker
Loring	*French*	Famous in battle
Loritz	*German*	Laurel
Lorne	*Celtic*	Crown of victory
Lotario, Lothair	*German*	Warrior
Lou	*German*	Light
Louie, Louis	*German*	Warrior
Lovell, Lowell	*French*	Dearly loved
Lowan	*Australian Aboriginal*	A mallee fowl
Lowe	*French*	Little wolf
Luc, Luca, Lucan, Lucas, Lucien, Lucius	*French*	Bringer of light
Lucky	*English*	Fortunate, lucky
Ludlow	*English*	From the prince's hill
Luduvico, Ludvig, Ludwig, Ludwik	*German*	Warrior
Lufti	*Arabic*	Kind
Lundie	*Scottish*	From the island grove
Lundy	*Scottish*	Monday
Lunn	*Irish*	Strong
Luxovious	*Celtic*	Mythical god of Luxeuil

Name	Origin	Definition
Lwin	*Burmese*	Outstanding
Lyall	*Scottish*	Loyal
Lyfing	*English*	Dearly loved
Lyman	*English*	From the valley
Lyndon, Lynford	*English*	Lives by the linden tree
Lyon	*French*	Young lion
Lyre	*English*	A fork from river
Lysander	*Greek*	Liberator
Lytton	*English*	Hillside town

 M

Name	Origin	Definition
Maarten	*Dutch*	Fondness of war
Mac, Mack, Max, Maxfield, Maximo	*Latin*	The greatest
Macalister	*Scottish*	Son of Alasdair
Macario	*Spanish*	Happy
Macarthur	*Scottish*	Son of Arthur
Macaulay, Maculey	*Scottish*	Son of Olaf
Macbain	*Scottish*	Son of Beathan
Maccallum	*Scottish*	Son of Callum
Macclennan	*Scottish*	Son of Finnian's servant
Maccoll	*Scottish*	Son of Coll
Maccormack	*Irish*	Son of Cormac
Maccus	*Celtic*	Hammer

Name	Origin	Definition
Macdonald, Macdonell	*Scottish*	Son of the world's ruler
Macdougal	*Scottish*	Son of Dougal
Mace	*English*	Aromatic spice
Macewen	*Scottish*	Son of Ewen
Macey	*English*	Gift of God
Macfarlane	*Scottish*	Son of Farlan
Macgowan	*Scottish*	Son of the smith
Macgregor	*Scottish*	Son of a shepherd
Machar	*Scottish*	Plain
Machau	*Hebrew*	Gift from God
Machk	*Native American*	Bear
Machum	*Hebrew*	Comfort
Macinnes	*Scottish*	Son of the unique choice
Macintosh	*Scottish*	Son of the thane
Maciver	*Scottish*	Son of an archer
Mackendrick	*Scottish*	Son of Henry
Mackenzie	*Gaelic*	Son of the wise leader
Mackinley	*Scottish*	Son of Kinley
Mackinnon	*Scottish*	Son of the fair born
Macklin	*Celtic*	Son of Flann
Maclachlan	*Scottish*	Son of Lachlan
Macmillan	*Scottish*	Son of the bald man
Macnaughton	*Scottish*	Son of the pure one
Macneill	*Scottish*	Son of the champion
Macnicol	*Scottish*	Son of the conquering people

Name	Origin	Definition
Macon, Makon	*English*	To make
Macpherson	*Scottish*	Son of the parson
Macquaid	*Irish*	Son of Quaid
Macquarrie	*Scottish*	Son of the proud
Macqueen	*Scottish*	Son of the good man
Macrae	*Scottish*	Son of grace
Madan	*Indian*	Cupid
Maddock, Maddox	*Celtic*	Good fortune
Maeret	*English*	Little famous one
Magee	*Irish*	Child of light
Magne	*Norse*	Mighty warrior
Magnum, Magnuson	*Scandinavian*	Large
Mago	*Irish*	Great
Mahadev	*Indian*	Most powerful god
Maher	*Irish*	Generous
Mahesh	*Indian*	Shiva
Mahir	*Arabic*	Skilled
Mahkah	*Native American*	Earth
Mahmoud, Mahmud	*Arabic*	Praised one
Mahon	*Irish*	Bear
Mai	*Hebrew*	Pearl
Maitland	*English*	From the meadow
Major, Majors	*Latin*	Greater
Maka	*Australian Aboriginal*	A small fire
Makarand	*Indian*	Honey bee
Makeen, Makin	*Arabic*	Strong
Makis	*Hebrew*	Gift from God

Name	Origin	Definition
Maks, Maksim	*Latin*	The greatest
Makya	*Native American*	Eagle hunter
Malachai	*Hebrew*	Messenger of God
Malcolm	*Scottish*	Servant of Saint Columba
Maldwyn	*German*	Brave friend
Malik	*Arabic*	Master
Malin	*English*	Army counsellor
Malone, Maloney	*Irish*	Serves Saint John
Malvin, Malvyn	*Celtic*	Leader
Malyn	*English*	Little warrior
Mamoru	*Japanese*	Earth
Manasses	*Hebrew*	Forgetful
Manchester, Manheim, Mansfield, Manton	*English*	Man of the meadow
Mandar	*Indian*	Flower
Mandek	*Polish*	Army man
Mandel	*French*	Almond
Mander	*English*	From me
Mandhatri	*Indian*	Prince
Mane	*Irish*	Great
Manfred, Manfried	*German*	Peaceful
Manley	*English*	Hero
Mannie, Manolo, Manuel	*Spanish*	God is with us
Manning	*English*	Son of a hero
Mannix	*Irish*	Monk
Manny	*Spanish*	Man of peace

Name	Origin	Definition
Manprasad	*Indian*	Calm
Mansur	*Arabic*	Divinely aided
Manus	*Irish*	Large
Manville	*French*	From the great estate
Marc, Marco, Marcus, Marek, Marilo, Mark	*French*	Defender
Marcas, Marceau, Marcel, Marcellus, Markey	*Irish*	Of Mars, god of war
Marchland, Marchman	*English*	From the march
Marcin	*Polish*	Warlike
Marden, Mardon	*English*	From the valley with the pool
Mardyth	*English*	Field near water
Mariano, Mariel, Mario, Marius	*Spanish*	Bitter
Marid	*Arabic*	Rebellious
Mariner	*Celtic*	Lives by the sea
Marji	*English*	Pearl
Marlan, Marland, Marlen, Marlon	*English*	Famous
Marley, Marlow, Marlowe, Marsden	*English*	From the marsh valley
Marlys	*French*	Little hawk
Marmaduke	*Celtic*	Leader of the seas
Marmion	*French*	Small one
Marnin	*Hebrew*	Brings joy
Marron	*Australian Aboriginal*	A leaf
Marschall, Marshall	*French*	Steward

Name	Origin	Definition
Mart, Martel, Martie, Martin, Martins, Martinson	*Latin*	Of Mars, god of war
Martand	*Indian*	Sun
Marus	*Latin*	Defender
Marv, Marvin, Marvyn	*Celtic*	Good friend
Marwood	*English*	From the lake forest
Marx	*German*	Defender
Maryse, Maurice, Maury	*French*	Dark-skinned
Mase, Masen, Mason, Masson	*French*	Stone worker
Maska	*Native American*	Strong
Maslen, Maslin	*French*	Little twin
Massey	*Hebrew*	Gift of God
Massimiliano	*Latin*	The greatest
Matai	*Hebrew*	Gift of God
Matari	*Australian Aboriginal*	A man
Mateo, Mateus, Mathew, Mathius, Mats, Matt, Matthew	*Spanish*	Gift of God
Mathe	*Scottish*	Bear
Mather	*English*	Strong army
Matherson	*English*	Son of Mather
Matheson	*Scottish*	Bear's son
Matin	*Arabic*	Strong
Maughold	*Irish*	Name of a saint
Maui	*Polynesian*	A legendary hero

Name	Origin	Definition
Maunfeld	*English*	From the field by the small river
Maverick, Mavrick	*English*	Independent
Maxwell	*Anglo-Saxon*	Capable
Mayank	*Indian*	Moon
Mayer	*German*	Bringer of light
Mayfield	*English*	From the warrior's field
Mayhew	*French*	Gift of God
Maynard	*French*	Firm
Mayne, Maynor	*German*	Powerful
Mayr, Meier, Meir	*Latin*	Farmer
Mead, Meade	*English*	Meadow
Medwin, Medwyn	*English*	Strong friend
Mehemet, Mehmet	*Arabic*	Praised one
Mehul	*Indian*	Rain
Meinhard	*German*	Firm
Meka	*Hawaiian*	Eyes
Mel	*Hebrew*	Smooth snow
Melborn, Melbourne, Melbyrne	*English*	From the mill stream
Meldrick, Meldrik	*English*	From the powerful mill
Melton	*English*	From the mill town
Melville, Melvin, Melvyn	*French*	Leader
Menahem, Mendel, Mendelssohn	*English*	Repairer
Mercer	*French*	Merchant

Name	Origin	Definition
Merewood	*English*	From the lake forest
Meril, Merral, Merrel, Merv, Mervin	*English*	Famous
Merle	*French*	Blackbird
Merlin	*French*	Falcon
Merlow	*English*	From the hill by the lake
Merritt	*English*	Deserving
Merwyn	*English*	Good friend
Micah, Michael, Michel, Mick, Mickey, Miguel	*Hebrew*	Like God
Mihir	*Indian*	Sun
Mika	*Hebrew*	New Moon
Miki	*Australian Aboriginal*	Beautiful tree
Mila, Milah, Milan, Miles, Milo	*German*	Merciful
Milap	*Native American*	Charitable
Milford	*English*	From the mill's ford
Millard, Millen, Miller	*French*	One who grinds grain
Millson	*English*	One who mills
Milton	*English*	From the mill town
Miner	*Latin*	Youth
Miron	*Hebrew*	Holy place
Miroslav	*Slavic*	Famous
Mitali	*Indian*	Friend
Mitch, Mitchell	*Irish*	Like God

Name	Origin	Definition
Mitesh	*Indian*	One with few desires
Mladen	*Slavic*	Forever in youth
Modraed	*English*	Brave
Moe, Moishe	*Hebrew*	Saved
Mohammed, Muhammad	*Arabic*	Praised one
Mohan	*Indian*	Fascinating
Mohin	*Indian*	Attractive
Moki	*Native American*	Deer
Molloy	*Irish*	Noble chief
Monohan	*Irish*	Monk
Monroe	*Scottish*	From the river's mouth
Montae	*Spanish*	Steep mountain
Montaigu	*French*	From the pointed hill
Montaine, Monte, Montel	*French*	Mountain
Montgomery	*English*	Mountain hunter
Mooney	*Irish*	Wealthy
Moore	*Irish*	Dark-skinned
Moran	*Irish*	Great
Moray	*Celtic*	Sailor
Mordecai, Mordechai	*Hebrew*	Warrior
Moreland, Moreley,	*English*	From the moors
Morey, Moritz, Morley, Morrey, Morrison	*French*	Dark-skinned
Morgan	*Irish*	Dweller of the sea
Morogh	*Scottish*	Man of the sea

Name	Origin	Definition
Morrissey	*Irish*	Choice of the sea
Mort	*French*	City on the moor
Mort, Morten, Morty	*Anglo-Saxon*	Still water
Morvyn	*Celtic*	Lives by the sea
Moses, Moshe, Mosheh, Moss	*Hebrew*	Saved
Moukib	*Arabic*	Last of the prophets
Moulton	*English*	From the mule farm
Mowan	*Australian Aboriginal*	The Sun
Mukhtar	*Arabic*	Chosen
Muller	*English*	Grinder
Mullyan	*Australian Aboriginal*	Eagle
Mungo	*Celtic*	Lovable
Munin	*Scandinavian*	Memory
Munir	*Arabic*	Sparkling
Munro, Munroe	*Scottish*	From Ro
Murdoch, Murdock	*Scottish*	Protector of the sea
Murphee, Murphey, Murphy, Murrough	*Gaelic*	Sea warrior
Murray	*Scottish*	Dark-skinned
Musa	*Arabic*	Song
Myerson	*Latin*	Farmer
Myo	*Burmese*	Relative

~~ **N** ~~

Name	Origin	Definition
Naal	*Irish*	Name of a saint
Naaman	*Hebrew*	Pleasant
Nabil	*Arabic*	Noble
Nachik	*Indian*	Fire
Nachman, Nahum	*Hebrew*	Compassionate
Nachton	*Scottish*	Pure
Nadav, Nadiv	*Hebrew*	Nobel
Nadim	*Arabic*	Friend
Nadir	*Arabic*	Dearly loved
Naeem	*African*	Benevolent
Naftali	*Hebrew*	Wreath
Nahele	*Native American*	Forest
Nairne	*Scottish*	From the alder-tree river
Naldo	*Spanish*	Powerful
Nalin	*Indian*	Water
Namdev, Narsi	*Indian*	Poet
Nanda	*Indian*	River
Nandi	*Indian*	One who pleases
Nandin	*Indian*	Delightful
Nann	*French*	Grace
Nansen	*Scandinavian*	Son of Nancy
Nantan	*Native American*	Spokesman
Napoleon	*Greek*	Lion of the woods
Narciso	*Latin*	Lily

Name	Origin	Definition
Narcissus, Narcisus	*Greek*	Self-love
Nardo	*German*	Strong
Naresh	*Indian*	Lord of man
Narmad	*Indian*	Bringing delight
Nartan	*Indian*	Dance
Nas, Nasir	*Arabic*	Protector
Nash, Nashe	*English*	Cliff
Nasim	*Arabic*	Fresh
Nasser	*Arabic*	Victorious
Natal, Natale	*French*	Born at Christmas
Natan, Natanael, Nate, Nathan	*Hebrew*	Gift from God
Naughton	*Scottish*	Pure
Navarre	*French*	Plains
Naveen, Navin	*Indian*	New
Nawat	*Native American*	Left-handed
Nayan	*Indian*	Eye
Neal, Neale, Nealon, Neil, Niall	*Celtic*	Champion
Nealson, Neilson, Nelson	*Celtic*	Son of a champion
Neason	*Irish*	Name of a saint
Nechtan	*Scottish*	Pure
Ned	*English*	Guardian of prosperity
Neelam	*Indian*	Emerald
Neeraj	*Indian*	Lotus
Neese	*Celtic*	Choice

Name	Origin	Definition
Nefen	*German*	Nephew
Nemiah	*Hebrew*	God's compassion
Nemo	*Latin*	No name
Neo	*Greek*	New
Neron	*Spanish*	Strong
Ness	*Scottish*	From the headland
Nesto, Neto	*Spanish*	Serious
Nestor	*Greek*	Wise
Neuman, Newman	*English*	Newcomer
Nevada	*Spanish*	Snow-clad
Nevan	*Irish*	Holy
Nevelson, Nevil, Neville, Newland	*French*	New village
Nevins	*English*	Middle
Newall, Newgate, Newlin, Newton	*French*	From the new manor
Nichol, Nicholai, Nick, Nicky, Nicolo, Nicholson	*Greek*	People's victory
Nicson	*English*	Son of Nick
Nigan	*Native American*	Ahead
Nigel	*Latin*	Dark one
Nihar	*Indian*	Mist, fog
Nike	*Greek*	Victory
Nikhil	*Indian*	Complete
Niko, Nikos, Nykko	*English*	People's victory
Nilay	*Indian*	Heaven
Niles	*English*	Champion

Name	Origin	Definition
Nilson	*Celtic*	Son of a champion
Nimbus	*Latin*	Halo
Nino, Ninoshka	*Italian*	God is gracious
Nira, Nirel, Niria, Niriel	*Hebrew*	God's field
Nirad	*Indian*	Given by water
Niranjan	*Indian*	Simple
Nirav	*Indian*	Without sound
Nirmal	*Indian*	Pure
Nishan	*Arabic*	Sign
Nisi	*Hebrew*	Emblem
Nissim	*Hebrew*	Wonders
Nixen	*English*	Son of Nick
Nixon	*English*	People's victory
Noa, Noah, Noam	*Hebrew*	Comfort
Nobel, Noble	*Latin*	Honourable one
Noel	*Hebrew*	Comfort
Nolan, Noland, Nolen, Nolyn, Nowlan	*Irish*	Noble
Norbert, Norberto	*English*	Shining from the north
Noreis	*French*	Caretaker
Norman, Normand, Norris, Norville	*French*	From the north
Northclif, Northclyf	*English*	From the north cliff
Northrop, Northrup, Nortin, Norton	*English*	From the north farm
Norval	*Scottish*	From the north valley
Norwood, Norwyn	*English*	From the north

Name	Origin	Definition
Nowell	*French*	Christmas
Nuri	*Hebrew*	Fire
Nye	*English*	Island
Nyein	*Burmese*	Quiet
Nyle	*Celtic*	Desire
Nyree	*Hebrew*	God's field

 O

Name	Origin	Definition
Oakden, Oakes, Oakley, Ogden	*English*	From the oak-tree valley
Obadiah, Obed, Obie	*Hebrew*	Servant of God
Obelix	*Greek*	Pillar of strength
Ochen	*African*	One of the twins
O'Conner, O'Connor	*Irish*	Desire
Octavian, Octavio, Octavius, Octavus	*Latin*	Eighth child
Odakota	*Native American*	Friend
Odale, Odalye	*English*	Of the valley
Odbart, Odhert	*German*	Wealthy
Oddvar	*Norse*	The spear's point
Odell	*Irish*	Little wealthy one
Odern	*Australian Aboriginal*	By the sea
Odhran, Odran, Oran	*Irish*	Pale green
Odie, Odis	*German*	Ode
Odion	*African*	First of twins

Name	Origin	Definition
Odo	*French*	Acute
Odon	*Hungarian*	Wealthy defender
Odwolf, Odwolfe	*English*	Wealthy wolf
Odysseus	*Greek*	Full of wrath
Oegelsby, Ogelsvie	*English*	Fearsome
Ofer	*Hebrew*	Fawn
Ogilvie, Ogilvy	*Scottish*	From the high peak
Ojas	*Indian*	Body strength
O'Keefe	*Irish*	Surname
Olaf, Olav, Olen	*Norse*	Talisman
Oldrich	*Czech*	Rich, powerful
Oleg	*Slavic*	Holy
Oliphant	*Scottish*	Great strength
Oliver, Olivero, Olivier, Olley, Ollie	*French*	Kind one
Olney	*English*	Holy
Omar, Omer	*German*	Famous
Omeet, Omet	*Hebrew*	My light
Ommar	*Arabic*	First son
O'Neill	*Gaelic*	Champion
Onslow, Onslowe	*English*	From the zealous one's hill
Oojam	*Indian*	Enthusiasm
Ora	*Polynesian*	Gold
Orad	*Australian Aboriginal*	Earth
Oram	*Gaelic*	Pale one
Ordwald	*English*	Spear strength

Name	Origin	Definition
Ordway	*Anglo-Saxon*	Warrior armed with a spear
Ordwin	*English*	Spear friend
Oren, Orin	*Gaelic*	Pine tree
Orest, Orestes	*Greek*	Mountain
Orford	*English*	From the cattle ford
Orham	*English*	From the riverbank enclosure
Ori	*Hebrew*	My light
Orien, Orion	*Greek*	The hunter
Oris	*Greek*	Tree
Orlan, Orland	*German*	From the pointed hill
Orlando, Orly	*Latin*	Bright sun
Orlege	*Anglo-Saxon*	Battle strife
Orman, Ormand, Ormund	*English*	Spearman
Ormos	*Hungarian*	Like a cliff
Oro	*Spanish*	Gold
Oros	*Hungarian*	Educated
Orran, Orren, Orrie	*Gaelic*	Pine
Orsen, Orsin, Orsini, Orson	*English*	Bear
Orton	*English*	From the shore farm
Orval, Orville	*French*	From the golden village
Orvin, Orvyn	*Anglo-Saxon*	Brave friend
Os, Osbart, Osbeorht, Oz	*English*	Divine, brilliant

Name	Origin	Definition
Osaze	*Hebrew*	Favoured by God
Osbourne, Osburn	*English*	Divine warrior
Oscar, Oskar	*Celtic*	Divine spear
Osgood	*Norse*	Divine spear
Osip	*Hebrew*	God will multiply
Osman, Osmar, Osmond, Ossie	*English*	Glorious, inspired
Osraed, Osred	*English*	Divine counsellor
Osric, Osrick	*English*	Divine ruler
Ossian	*Latin*	Fawn
Oswald, Oswaldo, Oswall	*English*	Divinely glorious, inspired
Otello, Othello, Otho, Otis, Otto	*German*	Acute
Othman, Othmann	*German*	Wealthy
Ottokar	*German*	Happy fighter
Ouray	*Native American*	Arrow
Oved, Ovid	*Hebrew*	Worker
Owen, Owens, Owyn	*Welsh*	Warrior
Oxford, Oxton, Oxley	*English*	From the ox farm
Oxon	*English*	From where the oxen ford
Ozi, Ozzi, Ozzie, Ozzy	*Hebrew*	Strong

—ᵐ— **P** —ᵐ—

Name	Origin	Definition
Pablo	*Spanish*	Little one
Pace, Pascal, Pascha, Pasqual	*French*	Born on Easter
Pachem, Paix	*Latin*	Peace
Pacho, Pancho	*Spanish*	Free
Packard	*English*	One who packs
Paco	*Spanish*	Bald eagle
Paddy	*Latin*	Noble one
Paden, Padruig	*Scottish*	Royal
Padgett	*French*	Young attendant
Padraic, Padraig	*Irish*	Noble one
Paella	*English*	Mantle
Page, Paget	*French*	Attendant
Paine, Payne	*English*	Pagan
Palban, Palden	*Spanish*	Blond
Pallaton	*Native American*	Warrior
Pallav	*Indian*	Young leaves
Palmer	*English*	Bearing a palm branch
Palmere	*English*	Pilgrim
Palti	*Hebrew*	God liberates
Pankaj	*Indian*	Lotus flower
Panos	*Greek*	Rock
Panyin	*African*	Older twins
Paolo	*Latin*	Little one
Parag	*Indian*	Pollen grains

Name	Origin	Definition
Paramjeet	*Indian*	Highest success
Paras, Parees	*Indian*	Touchstone
Paresh	*Indian*	Supreme spirit
Paris	*English*	Name of a god
Parisch, Parrish	*English*	Lives near the church
Paritosh	*Indian*	Contentment
Parke, Parker	*English*	Keeper of the forest
Parkin, Parkins, Parkinson, Perkins	*Latin*	Rock, stone
Parkley	*English*	Cultivated land
Parlan	*Scottish*	Farmer
Parnall, Parnell	*English*	Little rock
Parr	*English*	From the stable
Parri	*Australian Aboriginal*	Stream
Parry, Perin, Perrin	*Welsh*	Pear tree
Parsefal, Parsifal, Perce, Percival, Percy	*French*	Pierce the veil
Pat, Paterson, Patrice, Patrick	*Latin*	Noble one
Paton, Patten, Patton, Payden, Peyton	*Scottish*	From the fighter's farm
Patwin	*Native American*	Man
Paul, Pauley, Paulo, Paulson, Pavel	*French*	Little one
Pavan	*Indian*	Wind
Pax, Paxton	*Latin*	Peace
Payatt	*Native American*	He is coming

Name	Origin	Definition
Paytah	*Native American*	Fire
Paz	*Spanish*	Golden
Pearce, Pears, Pearson, Peirce, Pierce, Pierre	*Irish*	Rock
Peder, Pedro	*Greek*	Stone
Pelham, Pelton	*English*	Mantle
Pelle	*Latin*	Rock, stone
Pellegrin	*Hungarian*	Pilgrim
Pembroke	*Welsh*	Rocky hill
Penda	*Anglo-Saxon*	Love
Penley, Penton	*English*	From the enclosed pasture meadow
Penn, Penrod	*German*	Esteemed commander
Pentele	*Hungarian*	Merciful
Pepe, Pepillo	*Spanish*	God will multiply
Pepin	*German*	Persistent
Pepper	*English*	From the pepper plant
Pepperell	*French*	Piper
Peppi	*German*	Petitioner
Peri, Perri	*English*	Wanderer
Peril	*Latin*	Trial, test
Pert, Perth	*Celtic*	From the thicket
Pete, Peter, Peterson, Petr, Petrus	*English*	Rock
Phelan	*Irish*	Joyful
Phelps	*English*	Loves horses

Name	Origin	Definition
Pherson	*Scottish*	Parson
Phil, Philby, Philip, Philippe, Phillips	*Greek*	Loves horses
Philly	*Greek*	Dear
Phineas	*Hebrew*	Oracle
Phoebus	*Greek*	Bright one
Phoenix	*Greek*	Mystical bird
Picford, Pickford, Pickworth	*English*	From the woodcutter's ford
Pierpont	*French*	Lives by the stone bridge
Pindari	*Australian Aboriginal*	From the high ground
Pinochos	*Hebrew*	Dark-skinned
Piper	*English*	Piper
Pippin	*French*	Name of a king
Pirro	*Spanish*	Red-haired
Pitney	*English*	From the preserving land
Placido	*Spanish*	Tranquil
Platon	*Spanish*	Broad-shouldered
Platt	*French*	From the flat land
Pollock	*English*	Little rock
Pomeroy	*French*	Lives near the apple orchard
Ponce	*Spanish*	Born fifth
Porfirio	*Spanish*	Purple
Porter, Portier	*French*	Gatekeeper
Powell	*Welsh*	Little one

Name	Origin	Definition
Prabhat	*Indian*	Dawn
Prabir	*Indian*	Brave one
Pradeep	*Indian*	Light, shine
Prahlad	*Indian*	Eternal joy
Prajeet	*Indian*	Victorious
Pramesh	*Indian*	Master of knowledge
Pranay	*Indian*	Romance
Pranet	*Indian*	Leader
Prashant	*Indian*	Calm
Pratosh	*Indian*	Extreme delight
Pravar	*Indian*	Chief
Praveen	*Indian*	Expert
Prem	*Indian*	Love
Prentice, Prentiss	*English*	Apprentice
Prescot, Prescott, Presley, Preston, Priestly	*English*	Priest's cottage
Prewitt, Pruet	*French*	Valiant one
Primo	*Italian*	First one
Prince, Princeton	*English*	First
Prue	*French*	Foresight
Pryce	*Welsh*	Urgent
Pryor	*French*	Head of the priory
Pueblo	*Spanish*	From the city
Puneet	*Indian*	Pure
Pusan	*Indian*	A sage
Puskara	*Indian*	Fountain
Putnam	*Anglo-Saxon*	Dwells by the pond
Putney	*English*	From the sire's estate

~ Q ~

Name	Origin	Definition
Qadir	*Arabic*	Capable
Qaseem	*Arabic*	Divides
Qorbin	*Greek*	A gift devoted to God
Quaid	*Irish*	Powerful ruler
Quan, Quann	*Vietnamese*	Soldier
Quany, Quarrie	*Scottish*	Proud
Quasim	*Arabic*	One who helps people
Quennel, Quesnel	*French*	Dweller by the oak tree
Quent, Quentin, Quenton, Quentrell	*French*	Fifth-born child
Queran	*Irish*	Dark
Quigley	*Irish*	Unruly hair
Quillan	*Gaelic*	Club
Quin, Quinn	*French*	Intelligent
Quinby	*Scandinavian*	From the queen's estate
Quincey, Quincy, Quint	*French*	Fifth-born child
Quinlan	*Irish*	Graceful
Quy	*Vietnamese*	Precious

~~ R ~~

Name	Origin	Definition
Raanan	*Hebrew*	Fresh
Rab	*English*	Bright
Rabi	*Arabic*	Breeze
Rad	*English*	Wise
Radbert, Radburt, Readman	*English*	Red-haired counsellor
Radbourne, Radburn, Radbyrne	*English*	Lives by the red stream
Radcliff, Radcliffe, Radclyf, Radford, Radley	*English*	From the red cliff
Radman	*Slavic*	Joy
Radmund	*English*	Red-haired defender
Radolf	*English*	Red wolf
Radolph	*English*	Red wolf
Rae	*Scottish*	Beautiful
Raeburn	*Teutonic*	Dweller by the stream where deer drink
Raed	*English*	Red
Raedan	*Anglo-Saxon*	Advises
Raedford	*English*	From the red ford
Raedleah	*English*	From the red meadow
Raedpath	*English*	Lives near the red path
Rafael, Rafaello, Rafe, Rafer, Rafferty	*Hebrew*	Healed by God
Raff, Raffi	*Hebrew*	Wolf

Name	Origin	Definition
Raghnall	*Irish*	Strong
Ragnar	*English*	Wise leader
Rai	*English*	Trust
Raighne	*Irish*	Mighty
Raimond	*French*	Guards wisely
Rainart, Rainhard	*German*	Strong judgment
Rainer, Rainier	*Latin*	Ruler
Raj, Rajan	*Indian*	King
Rajani	*Indian*	Night
Rajeev	*Indian*	Blue lotus
Rajesh	*Indian*	God of kings
Rajiv	*Indian*	Striped
Rakesh	*Indian*	Lord of the night
Rakin	*Arabic*	Respectful
Rald	*German*	Leader
Raleigh, Raley, Rawley	*English*	Dweller by the deer meadow
Ralf, Ralph, Ralston	*English*	Wolf
Raman	*Indian*	Beloved
Rambert, Ramhart	*German*	Mighty
Ramey, Rami, Ramy	*Arabic*	Loving
Ramirez	*Spanish*	Judicious
Ramiro	*Spanish*	Great judge
Ramm	*Anglo-Saxon*	Ram
Ramon, Ramond	*English*	Wise protector
Ramsay, Ramsey, Ramzi	*Scottish*	Ram's island
Ramsden	*English*	From the ram's valley

Name	Origin	Definition
Ranald	*Scottish*	Powerful
Rance, Ranson	*English*	Son of the shield
Rand, Randal, Randie, Randolf, Randy	*English*	Wolf, protector
Randkin	*English*	Little shield
Rane, Raner, Ranier	*English*	Ruler
Ranell	*English*	Strong counsellor
Ranfield, Renfield	*English*	From the raven's field
Rangey	*English*	From raven's island
Rangford, Ransford	*English*	From the raven's ford
Rangley, Ransley	*English*	From the raven's meadow
Ranit	*Hebrew*	Lovely tune
Ranjan	*Indian*	Pleasing
Ranjeet	*Indian*	Victor in wars
Rankin	*Anglo-Saxon*	Little shield
Ranon	*Hebrew*	Joyful
Raoul, Raul	*French*	Wolf
Rapere	*English*	Maker of rope
Rase	*Welsh*	Enthusiastic
Rashad, Rasheed	*Arabic*	Thinker, counsellor
Rashid	*African*	Integrity
Rashne	*Persian*	Judge
Raulo	*Spanish*	Wise
Ravi	*English*	Benevolent
Ravid	*Hebrew*	Wanderer
Rawiri	*Maori*	Beloved
Rawling	*English*	Son of Rawley

Name	Origin	Definition
Rawlings, Rawlins, Rawson	*English*	Son of Rolfe
Ray	*English*	Grace
Rayburn, Rayfield, Rayhourne	*English*	From the deer's stream
Rayce, Rayder, Raydon, Rayford	*French*	Counsellor
Rayghun	*Gaelic*	Little king
Raymond, Raymund, Raymundo	*French*	Worthy protector
Raynard	*French*	Brave one
Razi	*African*	Secret
Reace, Reece, Reese	*Welsh*	Enthusiastic
Read, Reade, Reading, Reed, Reid	*English*	Red-haired
Reagan, Reagen, Reaghan, Regan	*Celtic*	Little king
Reamonn	*English*	Worthy protector
Reardon	*Gaelic*	Poet
Reave, Reeve, Reeves	*English*	Steward
Redd, Redding, Redfield, Redford, Redgrave	*Scottish*	From the red ford
Redley	*English*	From the red meadow
Redmond	*Irish*	Adviser
Reg, Reggie, Reginald, Reinald, Reinhold	*English*	Strong counsellor
Regent	*Gaelic*	Little king
Reginhard	*German*	Brave, powerful

Name	Origin	Definition
Regis	*Latin*	Kingly
Reidar	*Scandinavian*	Warrior
Reilley, Reilly	*Irish*	Island meadow
Reiner	*German*	Counsel
Reinhard, Reinhart	*Norse*	Brave one
Reja	*Indian*	King
Rell	*English*	Bright one
Remi, Remington, Remmy	*French*	From the raven's farm
Remus	*Latin*	Swift oarsman
Ren	*English*	Water lily
Renaldo	*Spanish*	Counsellor
Renard, Renaud	*French*	Brave one
Renato	*English*	Reborn
Rendor	*Hungarian*	Policeman
Rene	*French*	Reborn
Renfred, Renfrew	*Welsh*	From the still waters
Renke	*German*	Strong judgment
Renne, Renny	*French*	To rise again
Renshaw	*Welsh*	From the raven forest
Renton	*Welsh*	From the raven's farm
Reod	*English*	Ruddy-coloured
Rett, Rhett, Rhys	*Welsh*	Enthusiastic
Reuben, Reuhen, Reuven, Rouvin, Ruben, Rubin	*Hebrew*	Behold: a son
Reuel	*Hebrew*	Friend of God
Reve	*French*	Dream
Rex, Rexford	*Latin*	King

Name	Origin	Definition
Rexton	*English*	Ruler
Rey	*French*	Brave one
Reyhurn	*English*	From the deer's stream
Reymond	*French*	Guards wisely
Reynald, Reynold, Reynolds	*German*	Counsellor
Reynard, Reynart, Reynaud, Reyner	*German*	Strong, brave
Rhodes	*Greek*	Rose
Rian, Ryan, Ryen, Ryon	*Irish*	Kingly
Ricard, Ricardo, Rich, Richardson, Richmond	*French*	Powerful ruler
Rick, Rickie, Ricky	*French*	Noble one
Riddock	*Irish*	From the smooth field
Rider	*English*	Horseman
Ridge, Rigg	*English*	From the ridge
Ridgely	*English*	Lives at the meadow's ridge
Ridley	*English*	Reed clearing
Rigby	*English*	Valley of the ruler
Rigel	*Arabic*	Foot
Rikard, Rikkert	*German*	Powerful ruler
Riley	*Gaelic*	Valiant
Rimon	*Arabic*	Pomegranate
Rinan	*Anglo-Saxon*	Rain
Rinehart	*German*	Brave one

Name	Origin	Definition
Ringo	*Japanese*	A ring
Rio	*French*	River
Riobard	*Irish*	Bright, famous
Riordain, Riordan	*Irish*	Bright
Rip, Ripley, Rypley	*English*	Dweller in the noisy meadow
Rishi	*Indian*	Ray of light
Rishley	*English*	From the wild meadow
Rishon	*Hebrew*	First
Risley	*English*	From the brushwood meadow
Riston	*English*	From the wild meadow
Ritter	*German*	Horseman
River, Rivers	*French*	River
Riyad	*Arabic*	Garden
Ro	*Spanish*	Red-haired
Roald	*Teutonic*	Fame, power
Roan, Roane	*Gaelic*	Red-haired
Roarke	*Gaelic*	Ruler
Rob, Robb, Robbins, Robert, Robert, Robertson	*French*	Bright, famous
Rocco	*Italian*	Powerful ruler
Roch	*French*	Glory
Roche, Rock, Rockford, Rockwell, Rocky	*French*	Rock
Rod, Roddrick, Roddy, Roderich, Roderigo	*English*	Ruler

Name	Origin	Definition
Rodes	*English*	Lives near the crucifix
Rodger, Rodgers,	*German*	Spearman
Rodhlann	*German*	Soldier
Rodor	*Anglo-Saxon*	Sky
Rodwell	*English*	Lives by the spring near the road
Roe	*English*	Red-haired
Rogan, Rohan	*Irish*	Red-haired
Rohit	*Indian*	Red
Roibin	*Irish*	Robin
Roland, Rolando, Roldan, Rollan, Rolland, Rollo	*French*	Soldier
Rolf	*Scandinavian*	Wolf
Romain, Roman, Romeo	*Italian*	From Rome
Romney	*English*	From Romney
Ron	*Hebrew*	Song
Ronan	*Irish*	An oath
Rongo	*Maori*	God of rain and fertility
Roni	*Hebrew*	Joyous song
Ronin	*Japanese*	Samurai without a master
Ronnie	*Norse*	True image
Ronson	*English*	Son of Ronald
Rook	*English*	Raven
Roon, Roone, Rooney	*Gaelic*	Red-haired

Name	Origin	Definition
Roosevelt	*Dutch*	Field of roses
Roper	*English*	Maker of rope
Rorey, Rorry, Rory	*Irish*	Red
Rorke, Rourke	*Irish*	Ruler
Ros, Ross, Roswald	*Scottish*	From the peninsula
Roscoe	*English*	From the deer forest
Rossiter	*Scottish*	Red
Roswell	*German*	Horseman
Roth	*Scottish*	Red
Rousse, Rousset	*French*	Red-haired
Rover	*English*	Wanderer
Rowan, Rowe, Rowen, Rowin, Rowson	*English*	Red-haired
Rowley	*Gaelic*	Red-haired
Rowyn, Royan	*Irish*	Red-haired
Roxbury	*English*	From the raven's fortress
Roy	*French*	Red
Royal, Royale, Royall	*French*	Noble one
Royce	*French*	Famous
Royden	*French*	From the king's hill
Royse	*English*	Royal
Ruark	*Irish*	Famous ruler
Rubert	*English*	Bright, famous
Rudd	*English*	Ruddy-coloured
Rudi, Rudy	*German*	Wolf
Rudiger	*German*	Spearman
Rudyard	*English*	From the rough enclosure

Name	Origin	Definition
Ruff	*French*	Red-haired
Rufus	*English*	Red-haired
Rune	*German*	Secret
Rupak	*Indian*	Sign
Rupert	*English*	Bright, famous
Rupesh	*Indian*	Lord of beauty
Rusk, Ruskin, Russ, Russel, Rusty	*French*	Red-haired
Rutherford, Ruthren	*English*	From the cattle ford
Rutledge	*English*	From the red pool
Rutley	*English*	From the root meadow
Ryce	*Anglo-Saxon*	Powerful
Rycroft, Rygecroft, Rygeland, Rylan	*English*	Dweller in the rye field
Ryder	*English*	Horseman
Rydge	*English*	From the ridge
Rye, Ryleigh, Ryley	*Irish*	Island meadow
Rysc	*English*	Rush

S

Name	Origin	Definition
Saber	*French*	Sword
Sabino	*Spanish*	A Sabine tribe member
Sabir	*Arabic*	Patience
Sacha, Sascha, Sasha	*Russian*	Protector of mankind

Name	Origin	Definition
Sachiel	*Hebrew*	Angel of water
Sadiq	*Arabic*	Friend
Saeger, Seager	*English*	Seaman
Saelig, Sealey, Seely	*English*	From the happy meadow
Saewald, Sewald, Sewall	*English*	Powerful sea
Safford, Salford, Salhford	*English*	From the willow ford
Sagar	*Indian*	Wise
Sage	*French*	Wise
Saghir	*Arabic*	Short
Sagiv	*Hebrew*	Mighty
Sahen	*Indian*	Falcon
Sahib	*Indian*	Sir
Sahir	*Arabic*	Wakeful
Sal, Salbatore, Salvador, Salvatore	*Spanish*	Saviour
Salamon, Salmon, Saloman, Soloman	*Hebrew*	Peaceful
Saleem, Salem	*Arabic*	Peaceful
Salhtun, Salton	*English*	Lives near the willow farm
Salim	*African*	Peace
Sallsbury	*English*	From the fortified keep
Sam, Samelle, Sammy, Sampson, Samuel	*Hebrew*	Asked of God
Samarjit	*Indian*	Victorious in war
Sami	*Arabic*	All hearing

Name	Origin	Definition
Samir	*Indian*	Wind
Samman, Sammon	*Arabic*	Grocer
Samoel	*Hebrew*	Name of God
Samrat	*Indian*	Emperor
Sanborn, Sanbourne, Sandford, Sandy, Sanford	*English*	Dweller at the sandy ford
Sancho	*Spanish*	Saint
Sanda, Sandi	*Burmese*	Moon
Sandeep	*Indian*	A lighted lamp
Sander, Sanders, Sanderson, Saunders	*English*	Alexander's son
Sandor	*Greek*	Protector of mankind
Sani	*Native American*	The old one
Santi, Santiago	*Spanish*	Supplanter
Santo, Santos	*Italian*	A saint
Santosh	*Indian*	Happiness
Sapan	*Indian*	Dream
Sarang	*Indian*	Spotted deer
Sarge	*French*	Officer
Sarkis	*Arabic*	Royalty
Sarojin	*Indian*	Lotus-like
Sarosh	*Persian*	Prayer
Sasson	*Hebrew*	Joy
Saul	*Spanish*	Asked of God
Saurav	*Indian*	Divine
Sauville, Saville	*French*	From the willow farm
Sawyer	*Celtic*	Cuts timber

Name	Origin	Definition
Sawyers	*English*	Son of Sawyer
Saxon	*English*	Large stone
Sayer, Sayers, Sayre, Sayres	*Welsh*	Carpenter
Sayyid	*Arabic*	Master
Scaffeld	*English*	From the crooked field
Scanlan, Scanlon	*Irish*	Scandal
Scead	*Anglo-Saxon*	Shade
Schaeffer, Schaffer	*German*	Steward
Schuyler, Sky, Skye, Skyelar, Skylar, Skylor	*Dutch*	Scholar
Scolaighe, Scully	*Irish*	Herald
Scot, Scott, Scottas, Scotty	*Scottish*	From Scotland
Sea, Seabert, Seabright	*English*	Glorious sea
Seabrook	*English*	From the brook by the sea
Seadon	*English*	From the hill by the sea
Seamus, Shamus	*Irish*	Supplanter
Sean, Seanan, Shaughn, Shawn	*Irish*	Gift from God
Searlas	*French*	Manly
Seaton, Seeton	*English*	From the town by the sea
Seaver, Sever	*Anglo-Saxon*	Fierce stronghold
Seaward, Seward	*English*	Sea guardian
Sebastiano, Sebastien	*Spanish*	Revered one

Name	Origin	Definition
Secgwic, Sedgewick, Sedgeley	*English*	From the swordsman's meadow
Sefton	*English*	From Sefton
Segar, Seger	*English*	Seaman
Selby	*English*	From the manor house
Selden	*English*	From the willow valley
Selig, Selik	*English*	Blessed
Selwin, Selwyn	*English*	Good friend
Senen	*Hebrew*	Gift from God
Senet, Sennet	*French*	Wise
Septimus	*Latin*	Seventh-born
Serafim, Serafin, Seraphim	*Hebrew*	An angel
Serge, Sergei, Sergio	*Latin*	Attendant
Seth	*Hebrew*	Annointed
Seung	*Korean*	Successor
Severin, Severn, Sevrin	*English*	Strict
Seymour	*English*	Tailor
Shaddoc, Shaddock, Shattuck	*English*	Shad fish
Shai, Shaylon, Shea	*Irish*	Majestic
Shaine	*Irish*	Beautiful
Shakar	*Arabic*	Grateful
Shalom	*Hebrew*	Peaceful
Shaman	*Native American*	Holy man
Shanahan	*Irish*	Wise one

Name	Origin	Definition
Shandon	*Irish*	God is gracious
Shane	*Hebrew*	God is merciful
Shanley	*Irish*	Child of the old hero
Shareef, Sharif	*Arabic*	Illustrious
Shashikant	*Indian*	Moonstone
Shashwat	*Indian*	Everlasting
Shaw	*English*	Terse
Sheehan, Sheen	*Irish*	Peaceful one
Sheffield	*English*	From the crooked field
Sheiling	*Scottish*	From the summer pasture
Shelby	*English*	From the manor house
Shelden, Sheldon, Shelton	*English*	Deep valley
Shelley, Shelly	*Anglo-Saxon*	Clearing on a bank
Shelny	*Anglo-Saxon*	From the ledge farm
Shem	*Hebrew*	Protected by God
Shep, Shepard, Shepley, Sheppard	*English*	Shepherd
Sherbourn, Sherbourne	*English*	From the clear brook
Shereef, Sherif	*Arabic*	Illustrious
Sheridan, Sheridon	*Celtic*	Untamed
Sherlock	*English*	White-haired
Sherman, Shermon, Sherwin	*English*	Wool cutter
Sherwood	*English*	From the bright forest

Name	Origin	Definition
Shet	*Hebrew*	Compensation
Shilo, Shiloh	*Hebrew*	Belonging
Shimon	*Hebrew*	One who listens
Shipley, Shipton	*English*	From the deep meadow
Shwe	*Burmese*	Gold
Shyamal	*Indian*	Dark blue
Sian	*Celtic*	God's grace
Sid, Sidney, Syd, Sydney	*English*	From St. Denis
Siddael, Siddel, Siddell	*English*	From the wide valley
Siegfried, Sigfrid, Sigfried	*German*	Victorious
Siegmund, Sigmund	*Teutonic*	Victory protector
Silas	*English*	Forest
Silvano, Silvester	*English*	Trees
Silvio	*Latin*	Silver
Sim	*Scottish*	Listener
Simcha	*Hebrew*	Joy
Simen, Simeon, Simon, Symeon	*Hebrew*	Obedient
Simpson	*Hebrew*	Son of Simon
Sinai	*Hebrew*	From the clay desert
Sinclair, Sinclaire	*Scottish*	St. Clair
Singh	*Indian*	Lion
Sinjin	*French*	St. John
Sinley	*Anglo-Saxon*	Friendly
Siranno, Sirano, Syranno	*Greek*	From Cyrene
Sivan	*Hebrew*	Ninth month

Name	Origin	Definition
Skeat, Skeet, Skeeter, Sketes	*English*	Swift
Skelton	*English*	From the estate on the ledge
Skene	*Scottish*	From Skene
Skip, Skipp, Skipper, Skippy	*Norse*	Captain
Skipton	*English*	From the sheep estate
Slade, Slaed	*English*	Child of the valley
Slaton, Slayton	*English*	From the valley farm
Slean	*Anglo-Saxon*	Strikes
Slevin	*Gaelic*	Mountaineer
Sloan, Sloane	*Scottish*	Fighter
Sly	*Latin*	Woodsman
Smedley	*English*	From the flat meadow
Smith, Smits, Smitty, Smythe	*English*	Blacksmith
Snowden	*English*	From the snow-covered hill
Sohan	*Indian*	Good-looking
Sol	*Hebrew*	Sun
Somer	*French*	Born in summer
Somerset	*English*	From the summer settlers
Somerton, Somerville	*English*	From the summer estate
Sonnagh	*Welsh*	Rampart
Sonnie, Sonny	*English*	Son

Name	Origin	Definition
Sophronio	*Greek*	Self-controlled
Sorel, Sorrell	*French*	Reddish-brown hair
Soren	*Norse*	Thunder
Sorley	*Irish*	Viking
Southwell	*English*	From the south spring
Spalding, Spaulding, Spelding	*English*	From the split meadow
Spangler, Spengler	*German*	Tinsmith
Sparke	*English*	Gallant
Spear, Spere	*English*	Spear
Spence, Spencer, Spenser	*English*	Keeper of provisions
Spike	*English*	Long, heavy nail
Sproul, Sproule, Sprowle	*English*	Active
Squier, Squire	*English*	Shield-bearer
Staerling, Starling	*English*	Bird
Staffan	*Swedish*	A garland
Stafford	*English*	From the landing ford
Stamford	*English*	From the stony ford
Stan	*English*	Glory
Stan	*Polish*	Lives by the stony grove
Stanbeny, Stanburh	*English*	From the stone fortress
Stanberry, Stanbury, Stanfield, Stanford, Stanhope	*English*	From the rocky meadow

Name	Origin	Definition
Stancliff, Stanclyf	*English*	From the rocky cliff
Stanislas, Stanislav, Stanislaw	*Polish*	Glory
Stantun, Staunton	*English*	From the stony farm
Stanweg	*English*	Lives by the stony road
Stanwic, Stanwik, Stanwyk	*English*	From the stony village
Stanwood	*English*	From the stony forest
Starbuck	*English*	Star deer
Stasio	*Polish*	Glory
Stasya	*Latin*	Stable
Steadman	*Anglo-Saxon*	Dwells at the farm
Stearn, Stearne	*English*	Serious-minded
Steele	*English*	Durable
Steen, Stein, Steinbeck, Steinberg, Steinway	*German*	Stone
Stefan, Stefano, Steffan, Stefford, Stefn, Stephen, Steven	*German*	Crown
Sterling, Sterlyn, Stirling	*English*	Pure, valued
Stew, Steward, Stewart, Stewert, Stuart	*Teutonic*	Keeper of the estate
Stian	*Scandinavian*	Swift
Stiles	*English*	Stiles
Stilleman, Stillman	*English*	Quiet
Stilwell	*Anglo-Saxon*	From the tranquil stream

Name	Origin	Definition
Stock, Stockley, Stockman, Stockton, Stokley	*English*	From the tree stump
Stockwell	*English*	From the tree-stump spring
Stod, Stoddard	*English*	Horse
Storm	*English*	Stormy weather
Stowe	*English*	Place name
Strahan	*Irish*	Poet
Stratford	*English*	From the river ford
Strom	*German*	Stream
Strong	*English*	Powerful
Stroud, Stroude	*English*	From the thicket
Struthers	*Irish*	From the stream
Sudama	*Indian*	Meek
Sudarshan	*Indian*	Good-looking
Sudhakar	*Indian*	Mine of nectar
Sudhir	*Indian*	Resolute, brave
Sudhish	*Indian*	Excellent intellect
Suffield, Sundy, Sutherland, Sutton	*Norse*	From the southern land
Sujit	*Indian*	Victory
Sukumar	*Indian*	Handsome
Sullivan, Sullyvan	*Irish*	Dark eyes
Sumenor, Sumner	*French*	Summoner
Sundar	*Indian*	Beautiful
Sunday, Sunnee	*English*	Bright, cheerful
Sunil	*Indian*	Dark blue
Suresh, Surya	*Indian*	Sun

Name	Origin	Definition
Sutclyf, Sutcliff, Suttecliff	*English*	From the south cliff
Suthfeld	*English*	From the south field
Suthleah	*English*	From the south meadow
Sven, Svenson	*Scandinavian*	Youth
Swain, Swaine, Swayne	*English*	Knight's attendant
Swapnil	*Indian*	Seen in a dream
Sweeney, Sweeny	*Irish*	Little hero
Swift	*Anglo-Saxon*	Swift
Swinton	*English*	From the swine farm
Sylvanus, Sylvester, Szilveszter	*English*	Forest
Szemere	*Hungarian*	Demolisher

T

Name	Origin	Definition
Taavi	*Hebrew*	Dearly loved
Tab, Tabbert, Tabor	*English*	Brilliant
Tabansi	*African*	One who endures
Tabar, Taber	*Irish*	A well
Tad, Taddy, Tadeo, Tadeusz	*English*	Courageous
Tadhg	*Celtic*	Poet
Tadi	*Native American*	Wind
Tadleigh	*Irish*	Bard
Tag	*Irish*	Handsome

Name	Origin	Definition
Tahir	*Arabic*	Chaste, pure
Tahu	*Arabic*	Pure
Tai	*English*	Blooming
Taillefer, Telfer, Telford	*French*	Works in iron
Tailor, Taylan, Tayler	*English*	Tailor
Taima	*Native American*	Thunder
Tait, Tate	*Irish*	Cheerful
Tajo	*Spanish*	Day
Takoda	*Native American*	Friend to everyone
Taksony, Tas	*Hungarian*	Well-fed
Tal	*English*	Dew of heaven
Talbert, Talbot, Talbott, Talford	*English*	Tall
Taliesin	*Celtic*	Poet
Tallie, Tally	*French*	Born at Christmas
Tama	*Polynesian*	Boy, son
Tamas	*Hebrew*	Twin
Tamir	*Arabic*	Owns palm trees
Tamsin, Taveon, Tavey	*Scottish*	Twin
Tamtun, Tanton	*English*	From the quiet river farm
Tancrede, Tancredo	*Italian*	Of thoughtful counsel
Tanek	*Polish*	Immortal
Taneli	*Hebrew*	Judged by God
Tanguy	*Celtic*	Fighter
Tanmay	*Indian*	Engrossed
Tanner	*English*	Leather maker

Name	Origin	Definition
Tao	*Chinese*	Long life
Tapan	*Indian*	Sun, summer
Tapani	*Hebrew*	Victorious
Tapas	*Indian*	Heat
Tarak	*Indian*	Star
Taran	*Indian*	Heaven
Tarang	*Indian*	Wave
Tardos	*Hungarian*	Bald
Taree	*Australian Aboriginal*	A wild fig
Tareec, Tareek, Tareeq, Tariq	*Arabic*	Morning star
Taro	*Japanese*	First-born male
Taron, Tarrin, Terran, Terron	*English*	Earthman
Tarrence	*English*	Roman clan name
Tarun	*Indian*	Youth
Taurin, Taurino, Tauro, Toro	*Latin*	Born under the sign of Taurus
Tavin, Tavio	*Scottish*	Hillside
Tay	*English*	Great
Teaghue, Teague	*Irish*	Poet
Tearlach	*Scottish*	Strong
Tedd, Teddy, Tedman, Tedric	*English*	Gift of God
Tee, Tonio, Tony	*Latin*	Priceless, flourishing
Teerth	*Indian*	Holy place
Tegan	*Celtic*	Good-looking
Tej	*Indian*	Light, lustrous

Name	Origin	Definition
Tejas	*Indian*	Sharpness
Tellan	*Anglo-Saxon*	Considers
Teman	*Hebrew*	Right hand
Tempeltun, Templeton	*English*	From the temple farm
Tennessee, Tennison, Tennyson	*English*	Son of Dennis
Teo, Teodor, Teodoro	*Spanish*	God
Teppo	*Hebrew*	Victorious
Terance, Terrence	*Latin*	Polished, tender
Terciero	*Spanish*	Born third
Terell, Terrall	*English*	Powerful
Teri, Terry	*Latin*	Reaper
Teris, Terriss	*Irish*	Son of Terrence
Tevin, Tevis	*Irish*	Hillside
Teyen	*English*	From the enclosure
Thacher, Thacker, Thatcher, Thaxter	*English*	Roofer
Thad, Thaddaus	*Latin*	Courageous
Thaman	*Indian*	Name of a god
Than	*Burmese*	Brilliant
Thane, Thayne, Theyn	*English*	Follower
Thanos	*Greek*	Noble
Thebault, Theo, Theobold, Thibaut	*German*	The boldest
Theomund	*English*	Wealthy defender
Theophilus	*Greek*	Beloved by God
Theron, Therron	*French*	Hunter
Thet	*Burmese*	Calm
Thierry	*French*	People's ruler

Name	Origin	Definition
Thom, Thomas, Thomson, Tom, Tomkin	*English*	Twin
Thomkins	*English*	Little Tom
Thor, Thodis, Thordis	*Norse*	Thunder
Thorn, Thorne, Thorndike	*English*	Town of thorns
Thornley, Thornton	*English*	Thorn tree
Thorp, Thorpe	*English*	From the village
Thurl, Thurle	*Irish*	Strong fort
Thuza	*Burmese*	Angel
Thwaite	*Scandinavian*	Clearing, enclosure
Tie	*English*	Tailor
Tiegh, Tigh, Tighe	*English*	Enclosed
Tier, Tiernan, Tiernay, Tierney	*Irish*	Regal
Tilden	*English*	From the fertile valley
Tilford	*English*	From the fertile ford
Tilian	*Anglo-Saxon*	Strives
Tillman	*English*	Virile
Tilton	*English*	From the good estate
Tim, Timmy, Timo, Timon, Timothy	*English*	One who honours God
Timeus	*Greek*	Perfect
Timin	*Indian*	Large fish
Timur	*Hungarian*	Iron
Tine	*English*	River
Tinh	*Vietnamese*	Mindful, aware

Name	Origin	Definition
Tipper	*Irish*	A well
Titan, Tito, Titus	*Greek*	Of the giants
Titusz	*Hungarian*	Dove
Tivon	*Hebrew*	Loves nature
Tobey, Tobiah, Tobias, Tobin, Tobit, Toby	*English*	Goodness of God
Tobrecan	*Anglo-Saxon*	Destroys
Tocho	*Native American*	Mountain lion
Tod, Todd	*English*	Clever, wily
Tolan, Toland	*Anglo-Saxon*	From the taxed land
Toli	*Spanish*	Farmer
Tomor	*Hungarian*	Iron
Tong	*Vietnamese*	Fragrant
Tor, Toran, Torean, Toren, Torion, Torran	*Irish*	From the rocky hills
Torey, Torr, Torrance	*Scottish*	From the low hills
Tormaigh, Tormey	*Irish*	Thunder spirit
Torn	*English*	From the thorn tree
Torsten	*English*	Little Tom
Toryn	*Irish*	Chief
Tostig	*English*	Name of an earl
Tova	*Hebrew*	Goodly
Tovi	*Hebrew*	Goodness of God
Towley	*English*	From the town meadow
Towne, Townes, Townley, Townsend	*English*	From the end of the town
Toyo	*Japanese*	Plentiful

Name	Origin	Definition
Trace, Tracy	*French*	Brave
Trahaearn, Trahern, Tray	*Welsh*	Strong as iron
Traigh	*Irish*	Strand
Tramaine, Tremain, Treymayne	*English*	From the big town
Travers, Travis	*French*	From the crossroads
Treacy, Treasigh	*Irish*	Fighter
Treadway, Tredway	*English*	Strong warrior
Treffen	*German*	Meets
Trefor, Trevor	*Celtic*	Cautious
Trennen	*German*	Divides
Trent, Trenton	*Latin*	Torrent
Tretan	*German*	Walks
Trevan, Treven, Trevian, Trevyn	*English*	Fair town
Trey	*English*	Third born
Trip, Tripp, Tripper, Trypp	*English*	Traveller
Tristan, Tristen, Tristian, Tristin	*English*	Outcry
Tristram	*Welsh*	A knight
Troi, Troy, Troye	*English*	The city of Troy
Trowbrydge	*English*	From the tree bridge
Trueman, Truesdale, Truman, Trumen	*English*	Disciple, loyal
Trumbald, Trumble	*English*	Strong, brave
Trymian	*Anglo-Saxon*	Encourages
Tu	*Vietnamese*	Star
Tuck, Tucker, Tuckman	*English*	Tailor

Name	Origin	Definition
Tulio	*Spanish*	Lively
Tully	*Irish*	Peaceful
Tungar	*Indian*	High, lofty
Tungesh	*Indian*	Moon
Tunleah	*English*	From the town meadow
Tupper	*English*	Ram herder
Turi	*Celtic*	Bear
Turio	*Celtic*	Privileged birth
Turner	*French*	Carpenter
Tushar	*Indian*	Fine drops of water
Tuvya	*Hebrew*	Goodness of God
Twain	*English*	Two pieces
Twiford, Twyford	*English*	From the double-river ford
Twitchel, Twitchell	*English*	Lives on a narrow passage
Ty, Tyrus	*Latin*	From Tyre
Tyce, Tyeson	*French*	Fiery
Tye	*English*	Enclosed
Tyfiell, Tyreece, Tyrel, Tyrelle	*Irish*	Scandinavian god of battle
Tyg	*English*	From the enclosure
Tyler, Tylere, Tylor	*English*	Tiler, roofer
Tymon	*Greek*	Honours God
Tynan	*Irish*	Enclosed
Tyne	*English*	River
Tyrnan	*Gaelic*	Regal
Tyron, Tyrone	*Greek*	King

Name	Origin	Definition
Tyson	*English*	Son of Tye
Tzadok	*Hebrew*	Just
Tzion	*Hebrew*	Sunny mountain
Tzvi	*Hebrew*	Deer

U

Name	Origin	Definition
Uaid	*Irish*	Powerful ruler
Ualtar	*German*	Strong warrior
Ubel	*German*	Evil
Udale, Udall, Udayle	*English*	From the yew-tree valley
Uday	*Indian*	To rise
Udeep	*Indian*	Flood
Udeh	*Hebrew*	Praise
Udo	*Teutonic*	Prosperous
Udolf, Udolph, Ulger	*English*	Wolf ruler
Ugo	*Italian*	Intelligent
Ugor	*Hungarian*	Hungarian
Ujesh	*Indian*	Gives light
Uland, Ulandus	*Teutonic*	Noble country
Ulani	*Polynesian*	Cheerful
Ulhas	*Indian*	Joy
Ulises, Ulysses	*Spanish*	Full of wrath
Ullock, Ullok	*English*	Wolf sport
Ulmar	*English*	Famous wolf
Ulrich, Ulrick	*English*	Noble leader

Name	Origin	Definition
Ulu	*English*	Second born
Ulz	*German*	Noble leader
Unni	*Norse*	Modest
Unwin, Unwine	*English*	Unfriendly
Upchurch	*English*	From the upper church
Upshaw, Upton	*English*	From the upper town
Upwood	*English*	From the upper forest
Urbaine, Urban, Urbano	*Latin*	From the city
Uri, Uriah, Urie, Uriel	*Hebrew*	God is my light
Urien	*Arthurian Legend*	Privileged birth
Uros	*Hungarian*	Little lord
Urquhart	*Scottish*	From the fount on the knoll
Utpal	*Indian*	Water lily
Uttam	*Indian*	Best
Uwan	*Australian Aboriginal*	To meet
Uzziah	*Hebrew*	God is mighty

V

Name	Origin	Definition
Vachel	*French*	Little cow
Vaclav	*Slavic*	Wreath, glory
Vahe	*Arabic*	Victor
Vail, Vale, Vayle	*English*	Lives in the valley

Name	Origin	Definition
Val	*English*	Good health
Valdemar	*Scandinavian*	Famous ruler
Valen, Vallen	*English*	Strong
Valente, Valentin, Valentino	*Latin*	Good health
Valiant	*French*	Brave
Vallis	*French*	A Welshman
Vance	*English*	Dweller at the windmill
Vandan	*Indian*	Salutation
Vannes	*English*	Grain fans
Vardan, Vardenm Vardon, Varton, Verddun	*French*	From the green hill
Vareck, Varek, Varik	*English*	From the fortress
Varney	*Celtic*	From the alder grove
Varun	*Indian*	Lord of the waters, Neptune
Vasily, Vassily	*Greek*	Royal
Vasu	*Indian*	Wealth
Vasuman	*Indian*	Born of fire
Vaughan, Vaughn	*Celtic*	Little, small
Vayk	*Hungarian*	Rich
Veda, Vedis	*Indian*	Eternal knowledge
Veer	*Indian*	Brave
Vencel, Venceslas	*Slavic*	Wreath, glory
Verda	*French*	From the alder grove, spring-like
Verdell	*French*	Green, flourishing

Name	Origin	Definition
Verel, Verrall	*French*	True
Vern, Vernal, Vernay, Verne, Verney, Vernon	*French*	From the alder grove, spring-like
Veto	*Spanish*	Intelligent
Vial	*French*	Lively
Vic, Vicente, Vicq	*French*	From the village
Victor, Victorio, Victoro, Viktor	*Spanish*	Victor
Vida	*German*	Dearly loved
Vidal, Videl	*French*	Life
Vidar	*Scandinavian*	Lumberjack
Vidor	*Hungarian*	Happy
Vidur	*Indian*	Wise
Vidvan	*Indian*	Scholar
Vijay	*Indian*	Victory
Vikram	*Indian*	Valorous
Vilem, Vilhelm, Viliam	*Teutonic*	Valiant protector
Vince, Vincent, Vincente	*English*	Conqueror
Vinnie, Vinson	*English*	Conqueror
Vipan	*Indian*	Sail, petty trade
Viplav	*Indian*	Drifting about, revolution
Vipul	*Indian*	Plenty
Viraj	*Indian*	Resplendent, splendour
Virgil	*English*	Flourishing
Vishal	*Indian*	Huge, broad, great

Name	Origin	Definition
Vishnu	*Indian*	Lord Vishnu, root, To pervade
Vishwas	*Indian*	Faith, trust
Vital	*French*	Lively
Vito, Vittorio	*Spanish*	Conqueror
Vivek	*Indian*	Judgment
Vlad, Vladimir, Vladislav	*Slavic*	To rule with peace, regal
Volker	*German*	People's guard
Vyacheslav	*Slavic*	Wreath, glory

W

Name	Origin	Definition
Wade, Wadley	*Anglo-Saxon*	A ford
Wadsworth	*English*	From Wade's estate
Waggoner, Wagner, Wainwright	*English*	Wagon maker
Wain	*English*	Craftsman
Wait, Waite	*English*	Guard
Wake	*English*	Alert
Wakefield	*English*	From Wake's field
Wakeley	*English*	From Wake's meadow
Wakeman	*English*	Watchman
Wakler	*English*	Thickener of cloth
Walbridge	*English*	From the Welshman's bridge
Walcot, Walcott	*English*	Old cottage

Name	Origin	Definition
Walden, Waldo, Waldron	*English*	Divinely powerful
Waldorf	*Teutonic*	Powerful
Waleis	*English*	From Wales
Walford	*English*	From the Welshman's ford
Walfred	*Teutonic*	Peaceful ruler
Walker	*English*	Cloth worker
Wallace, Wallach, Wallas, Wallis, Walsh, Welch, Welsh	*English*	Welshman
Waller	*German*	Mason
Walt, Walten, Walter, Walton	*German*	Powerful ruler
Wann	*Anglo-Saxon*	Dark
Wapi	*Native American*	Lucky
Ward, Warde, Warden, Warford, Warley, Warton	*English*	Guardian
Warner	*English*	Defender
Warren, Warrener	*German*	Guardian
Warrick, Warwyk	*English*	Fortress
Washbourne, Wahburne	*English*	From the flooding brook
Washington	*English*	From the wise man's estate
Wasily	*Greek*	Regal
Wasim	*Arabic*	Handsome
Watford	*English*	From the hurdle ford

Name	Origin	Definition
Watkins, Watson	*English*	Warrior
Watt, Wattekinson, Watts	*English*	Son of Walter
Waverly	*English*	From the tree-lined meadow
Wayde, Waylan, Wayland, Waylon	*English*	Angel from God
Wayne	*Celtic*	Dark
Wayte	*English*	Guard
Wazlaw	*Slavic*	Glory
Weatherby, Wetherby, Wethrby	*English*	From the wether-sheep farm
Weatherly, Wetherly	*English*	From the wether-sheep meadow
Webb, Webbe, Webber, Webbestre, Weber	*English*	Weaver
Weiford	*English*	From the farm by the weir
Weirley	*English*	From the weir meadow
Welborn, Welborne, Welby	*English*	From the spring brook
Weldon, Welford, Weller, Welles	*English*	Lives by the spring
Wellington	*Anglo-Saxon*	From the wealthy estate
Wendale, Wendall, Wendell, Windell	*English*	Wanderer
Wentworth	*English*	From the white one's estate

Name	Origin	Definition
Werner	*Teutonic*	Defender
Wes, Wesley	*English*	From the west meadow
West, Westby, Westley	*English*	From the west
Westbroc, Westbrook, Westcott	*English*	From the west brook
Westen, Westin	*English*	West town
Weyland	*English*	From the land by the highway
Weylin	*Celtic*	Son of the wolf
Wharton	*English*	From the estate at the hollow
Wheatley	*English*	From the wheat meadow
Wheaton	*English*	Wheat town
Wheeler	*English*	Wheel maker
Whelan	*Irish*	Joyful
Whistler	*English*	Piper
Whit, Whitby, Whitcomb, Whitfield, Whitman, Whittaker	*English*	White
Wiatt	*English*	Guide
Wickam, Wickley	*English*	From the village meadow
Wigman	*English*	Warrior
Wilber, Wilbert, Wilbur, Wilburn	*English*	Wilful, bright
Wilbur	*Anglo-Saxon*	Bright resolve
Wildon	*English*	From the wooded hill
Wiley	*English*	Enchanting

Name	Origin	Definition
Wilford, Wilfred, Wilfredo, Wilfried	*English*	Desires peace
Wilhelm, Wilkes, Wilkie, Will, Willem, William, Wilton	*Teutonic*	Resolute protector
Willard	*English*	Bold
Williams, Willimson, Wilson	*Teutonic*	Son of William
Willis, Wilmer	*English*	Resolute protector
Willoughby	*English*	From the willow farm
Win, Winn, Wyn, Wyndell, Wyne	*English*	Peaceful friend
Wincel	*English*	From the bend in the road
Winchell	*Anglo-Saxon*	Drawer of water
Windgate	*English*	From the winding gate
Windham, Wyndam	*English*	The field with the winding path
Windsor, Winfield, Winfred, Winfrey, Wingate, Winslow	*English*	From Windsor
Winefield	*English*	From a friend's field
Winston, Wystan	*Anglo-Saxon*	Battle stone
Winters	*English*	Born in the winter
Winton	*Teutonic*	Valiant protector
Winwood	*English*	From Wine's forest
Witt, Witton	*English*	Wise
Wodeleah, Woodley	*English*	From the wooded meadow

Name	Origin	Definition
Woden	*Anglo-Saxon*	King of gods
Wolcott	*Teutonic*	Wolf strife
Wolfe	*English*	Wolf
Wolfgang	*German*	Wolf strife
Wolfram	*Teutonic*	Wolf raven
Wolfrick	*German*	Wolf ruler
Woodman	*English*	Hunter
Woodrow, Woodruff, Woodward, Woody	*English*	Forester
Woolsey	*English*	Victorious wolf
Worcester	*English*	From the alder-forest army camp
Wordsworth	*English*	World guardian
Worth	*English*	From the farm
Worthington	*Anglo-Saxon*	From the river's side
Wray	*English*	Worthy protector
Wregan	*Anglo-Saxon*	Accuses
Wren	*Welsh*	Chief
Wright	*Anglo-Saxon*	Craftsman
Wyatt, Wyeth	*French*	Little warrior
Wyclyf, Wycliff	*English*	From the white cliff
Wylie	*English*	Enchanting
Wylkes	*Teutonic*	Valiant protector
Wyman	*Anglo-Saxon*	Fighter
Wynthrop	*English*	From Wine's estate
Wynton	*English*	From Windsor
Wynward	*English*	From Wine's forest
Wyth	*English*	From the willow tree

─ X ─

Name	Origin	Definition
Xabat, Xalbador, Xalvador	*Spanish*	Saviour
Xander	*Greek*	Protector of mankind
Xarles	*French*	Manly
Xaver, Xavier, Xever	*Arabic*	Enlightened
Xenos	*Greek*	Stranger
Xerxes	*Persian*	Prince
Xever	*Arabic*	Owns a new house
Ximen	*Hebrew*	Obedient
Xiomar	*German*	Famous in battle
Xuan	*Vietnamese*	Spring

─ Y ─

Name	Origin	Definition
Yaakov, Yakov	*Hebrew*	Held by the heel
Yadon	*Hebrew*	He will judge
Yael, Yale	*German*	One who produces
Yagil	*Hebrew*	He will rejoice
Yago	*Spanish*	Supplanter
Yahto	*Native American*	Blue
Yair	*Hebrew*	Enlighten
Yan, Yann, Yanni, Yannis, Yanis	*Hebrew*	God's grace
Yaphet	*Hebrew*	Handsome

Name	Origin	Definition
Yardley, Yardly	*English*	From the enclosed meadow
Yarin	*Hebrew*	To understand
Yaron	*Hebrew*	Singing
Yarran	*Australian Aboriginal*	Acacia tree
Yas	*Native American*	Snow
Yash	*Indian*	Victory
Yashpal	*Indian*	Protector of fame
Yasin, Yasir	*Arabic*	Rich
Yasuo	*Japanese*	Peaceful one
Yates	*English*	Gatekeeper
Yavin	*Hebrew*	Understanding
Yegor, Yoyi, Yura, Yurchik, Yuri	*Greek*	Farmer
Yehuda, Yehudi	*Hebrew*	Praise God
Yeoman, Yoman	*English*	Retainer
Yerik	*Russian*	Appointed by God
Yeshaya	*Hebrew*	God lends
Yigol	*Hebrew*	Redeemed
Yiska	*Native American*	Night has passed
Yisreal	*Hebrew*	God's peace
Yitzchak	*Hebrew*	Humorous
Yoel	*Hebrew*	God prevails
Yogesh	*Indian*	God of Yoga
Yogi	*Indian*	Master of oneself
Yonah	*Hebrew*	Dove

Name	Origin	Definition
Yorick	*Scandinavian*	Farmer
York	*English*	Yew tree
Yoshi	*Japanese*	Best
Youri	*Australian Aboriginal*	To hear
Yudhajit	*Indian*	Victor in war
Yuka	*Australian Aboriginal*	Tree
Yukio	*Japanese*	Gets what he wants
Yule	*English*	Born at Christmas
Yuma	*Native American*	Chief's son
Yuri	*Russian*	Farmer
Yurik, Yurko, Yusha	*Greek*	Farmer
Yusef, Yusuf	*Hebrew*	God shall multiply
Yvan, Yves, Yvo	*Teutonic*	Archer

⸺ Z ⸺

Name	Origin	Definition
Zacarias, Zaccaria, Zaccheo, Zach, Zachary, Zackry	*Spanish*	Remembered by God
Zacchaeus, Zakai	*Hebrew*	Clean, pure
Zadok	*Hebrew*	Just
Zafir	*Arabic*	Victorious
Zahid	*Arabic*	Altruistic
Zahir	*Arabic*	Sparkling
Zahur	*African*	Flower

Name	Origin	Definition
Zaid	*African*	Growth
Zain, Zane, Zayne	*English*	God is merciful
Zaki	*Arabic*	Intelligent
Zander	*English*	Protector of mankind
Zani	*Hebrew*	Gift from God
Zaniel	*Latin*	Angel of Mondays
Zanipolo	*Italian*	Little gift of God
Zarad, Zared	*Hebrew*	Ambush
Zarek	*Greek*	May God protect the king
Zayit	*Hebrew*	Olive
Zazu	*Hebrew*	Movement
Zdenek	*French*	Follower of Saint Denys
Zeb	*Hebrew*	Servant of God
Zebadiah	*Hebrew*	Gift from God
Zebulon	*Hebrew*	Home
Zed, Zedekiah	*Hebrew*	God's justice
Zefferino, Zefiro	*Greek*	Wind of spring
Zeke	*English*	Strength of God
Zelig	*German*	The blessed one
Zen, Zeno, Zenos	*Greek*	Gift of Zeus
Zenon	*Spanish*	Living
Zephan	*Hebrew*	Treasured by God
Zephyr	*Greek*	Wind
Zero	*Greek*	Empty
Zeth, Zetico, Zeticus	*Greek*	Investigator
Zev	*Hebrew*	Deer
Zeyar	*Burmese*	Success

Name	Origin	Definition
Ziff	*Hebrew*	Wolf
Ziggy	*Teutonic*	Victory protector
Zion	*Hebrew*	A sign
Ziv	*Hebrew*	Very bright
Ziva	*Hebrew*	Splendid
Ziven	*Slavic*	Alive
Zoello, Zoellus	*Greek*	Son of Zoe
Zohar	*Hebrew*	Sparkles
Zorro	*Slavic*	Golden dawn
Zotico, Zoticus	*Greek*	Lively
Zsolt	*Hungarian*	An honour
Zuriel	*Hebrew*	God is my rock
Zvi	*Hebrew*	Wolf

BABY NAMES
WORKSHEETS

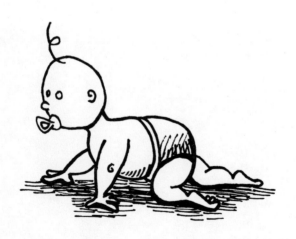

How to Use the Baby Names Worksheets

The following baby names worksheets provide spaces for Mom and Dad to write down their top picks for boys and girls. After they grade the names based on their preferences (A being the best and F the worst), both parents trade lists and grade each other's choices. Once this hurdle has been crossed and the list is narrowed, use the Final Choices worksheet to write the final picks for first, middle and last names (you know—if you're going the hyphenated route), along with the final grades for your top name choices.

～ Mom's List ～

Name	Sex	Mom's Grade	Dad's Grade
		A B C D F	A B C D F
		A B C D F	A B C D F
		A B C D F	A B C D F
		A B C D F	A B C D F
		A B C D F	A B C D F
		A B C D F	A B C D F
		A B C D F	A B C D F
		A B C D F	A B C D F
		A B C D F	A B C D F
		A B C D F	A B C D F
		A B C D F	A B C D F
		A B C D F	A B C D F
		A B C D F	A B C D F
		A B C D F	A B C D F
		A B C D F	A B C D F
		A B C D F	A B C D F
		A B C D F	A B C D F
		A B C D F	A B C D F
		A B C D F	A B C D F
		A B C D F	A B C D F
		A B C D F	A B C D F

~ Dad's List ~

Name	Sex	Dad's Grade	Mom's Grade
		A B C D F	A B C D F
		A B C D F	A B C D F
		A B C D F	A B C D F
		A B C D F	A B C D F
		A B C D F	A B C D F
		A B C D F	A B C D F
		A B C D F	A B C D F
		A B C D F	A B C D F
		A B C D F	A B C D F
		A B C D F	A B C D F
		A B C D F	A B C D F
		A B C D F	A B C D F
		A B C D F	A B C D F
		A B C D F	A B C D F
		A B C D F	A B C D F
		A B C D F	A B C D F
		A B C D F	A B C D F
		A B C D F	A B C D F
		A B C D F	A B C D F
		A B C D F	A B C D F
		A B C D F	A B C D F

⌐∿ Final Choices ∿⌐

Girls

First	Middle	Last	Grade
			A B C D F
			A B C D F
			A B C D F
			A B C D F

Boys

First	Middle	Last	Grade
			A B C D F
			A B C D F
			A B C D F
			A B C D F

Resources

Resources

www.infoplease.com/spot/celebrity-baby-names.html

www.cracked.com/article_15765_p2.html

www.celebritybabynamesblog.com/

www.usmagazine.com/news/why-gwen-stefani-named-her-son-zuma-nesta-rock

www.nydailynews.com/gossip/2008/03/18/2008-03-18_miley_cyrushannah_montanas_new_name.html

www.babycenter.com/0_hottest-baby-name-trends-of-2007_3637583.bc?page=2

www.storknet.com/babynames/celebabynames.htm

www.ivillage.co.uk/newspol/celeb/cfeat/articles/0,,528719_705011,00.html

www.mollygood.com/celebrity-baby-names-literally-20080513/

www.usatoday.com/life/lifestyle/2005-09-25-babynames_x.htm

www.dailyrecord.co.uk/news/uk-world-news/2008/08/13/traditional-baby-names-on-the-way-out-as-parents-follow-celebrity-trends-86908-20695079/

www.etonline.com/news/2008/10/66847/

www.people.com/people/article/0,,20160298,00.html

www.yeahbaby.com/celebrity-baby-names/article.php?page=116

http://pregnancychildbirth.suite101.com/article.cfm/baby_names_of_the_1970s_and_1980s

www.babynames.com/Names/Television/soap-operas.php

www.bloomberg.com/apps/news?pid=20601079&refer=home&sid=aelBbtOdQVgI

http://gossip.about.com/od/pregnanciesbirths/a/Celeb_08_Baby.htm

www.whosdatedwho.com/when/?year=2008&type=26

www.babycenter.com/0_hottest-baby-name-trends-of-2008_10303191.bc?page=2

www.associatedcontent.com/article/1260577/top_10_craziest_
celebrity_baby_names.html?cat=7

www.babyhold.com/babynames/Discussions/Popular_Baby_
Names_and_Trends_for_2008/

http://parenting.ivillage.com/pregnancy/pbabynames/0,,babynam
ewizard_83c61xk7,00.html

www.associatedcontent.com/article/394502/top_baby_name_
trends_for_2008.html

http://jam.canoe.ca/Movies/2008/07/20/6212656-sun.html

http://query.nytimes.com/gst/fullpage.html?res=9F0CE6D6143A
F935A35754C0A9659C8B63&sec=&spon=&pagewanted=2

http://lifestyle.msn.com/your-life/family-parenting/articleab.
aspx?cp-documentid=11257635&page=2

www.baby2see.com/names/decades_trends.html

http://pregnancychildbirth.suite101.com/article.cfm/baby_
names_of_the_1990s_and_2000s

http://people.howstuffworks.com/baby-name-trends-ga3.htm

www.parents.com/pregnancy/baby-names/themes/top-baby-
name-trends-2008/?page=4

www.italyfromtheinside.com/2007/04/give-your-baby-italian-
name.html

http://pregnancychildbirth.suite101.com/article.cfm/international_
baby_names_for_boys

http://pregnancychildbirth.suite101.com/article.cfm/international_
baby_girl_names

www.guardian.co.uk/lifeandstyle/2008/apr/01/
familyandrelationships.timdowling

www.topbabynames.com/how_to_pick/detail/top_baby_name_
trends_for_2008/

www.babynamecentral.com/index.php/Baby-Name-Articles/
baby-naming-traditions-around-the-world.html

www.babycentre.co.uk/pregnancy/naming/
   top10namesaroundtheworld/

www.citynews.ca/news/news_25032.aspx

www.citynews.ca/news/news_28738.aspx

www.associatedcontent.com/article/1133186/baby_names_
   for_2009.html?cat=7

http://babyparenting.about.com/od/gettingready/a/choosinga-
   name_2.htm

http://pregnancyandbaby.com/pregnancy/baby/The-name-game--
   Baby-name-tips-74.htm

http://babynamesworld.parentsconnect.com/naming_tips/

www.yeahbaby.com/baby-naming-tips.php

www.healthatoz.com/healthatoz/Atoz/common/standard/transform.
   jsp?requestURI=/healthatoz/Atoz/hc/wom/preg/nametips.jsp

www.bestforbabynames.com/namingtips2.php

www.babyworld.co.uk/information/pregnancy/namecalling.asp

www.babynology.com/articles/baby_naming_ceremony_traditions_
   across_the_globe.html

www.rootsweb.ancestry.com/~genepool/naming.htm

www.babyzone.com/pregnancy/babynames/article/baby-naming-
   traditions

www.babycenter.ca/pregnancy/naming/namingaroundworld/

http://ukfamily.co.uk/ages-stages/pregnancy-birth/your-pregnancy/
   lifestyle/baby-names-country-rules.html

www.babynamefacts.com/namelists/list.php?id=18

http://en.wikipedia.org/wiki/Miss_Canada

www.associatedcontent.com/article/1023670/top_10_classic_
   rock_and_pop_songs_with.html?cat=33

www.popculturemadness.com/Music/Girls-Names-Songs.html

www.listology.com/content_show.cfm/content_id.10366/Music

CARLA MACKAY

Raised in Espanola, Ontario, Carla MacKay has always been a book lover, keeping track of every book she has read since she was 10 years old. So, when she recently moved to Edmonton from Toronto with her longtime beau, they started their own publishing and editorial services company. Wearing both writer's and editor's hats can sometimes be a challenge, but Carla is nothing if not adaptable. Carla is an avid runner and has completed two marathons.